BAC One-Eleven

BAC One-Eleven

Malcolm L. Hill

The Crowood Press

First published in 1999 by
The Crowood Press Ltd
Ramsbury, Marlborough
Wiltshire SN8 2HR

© Malcolm L. Hill 1999

British Library Cataloguing-in-Publication Data
A catalogue record for this book is available from
the British Library.

ISBN 1 86126 219 1

Photograph previous page: Swissair's leased 501EX
operated into Manchester in 1970. Brooklands
Museum

Typefaces used: Goudy (*text*),
Cheltenham (*headings*).

Typeset and designed by
D & N Publishing
Membury Business Park, Lambourn Woodlands
Hungerford, Berkshire.

Printed and bound by Bookcraft, Bath.

Acknowledgements

Grateful thanks are extended to all the following persons and organizations, whose co-operation, time and invaluable funds of information and memories made this book possible: Steve Bunting, Charles Burnett, Vikki Chatham, Martyn East, Phillip Eastwood, Steve Edmunds, Malcolm Ginsberg, Jennie Gradidge, Mary Kerby, Tim Kincaid, Julie King, Ben Kristy, Lyn Moreton, Larry Pettit, Brian Pickering, Janine Redmond, Frankie Scott, Graham M. Simons, Neil Smith, Homer Smith-Ward, Julian Temple, Tony Ward and Bryn Wayt; AB Airlines, *Aeroplane Monthly*, Air Malawi, Aloha Airlines, American Airlines' C.R. Smith Museum, American Airlines' Grey Eagles and Kiwis, Arkia, Aviation Hobby Shop, Brooklands Museum, Canadian Airlines International, Cyprus Airways, Dan-Air Services Staff Association, Maersk Air, Military Aircraft Photographs, Nationwide Air, Ryanair and TAROM.

Whilst every effort has been made to identify the source of all illustrations used in this publication, this has not been possible in all cases. Any persons claiming accreditation should contact the author via the publisher.

Contents

CHAPTER ONE

Tangled Roots

For an aircraft manufacturer to embark on any new project it takes a certain amount of courage. However detailed the initial market studies, however confident the company may be that it has the basis for a viable, profitable aircraft, there always has to be an element of risk-taking. When that manufacturer is entering a field where, however successful its past products have been, there is an element of uncertainty, it takes even more than courage – an overwhelming confidence in its own instincts.

In retrospect, the mid-1950s would have seemed an unlikely time for a relatively small company like Hunting Percival Aircraft Ltd to have embarked on a study for a short/medium-haul, jet-powered airliner. The only pure-jet airliner type to have seen service at the time, the pioneering De Havilland Comet 1, had experienced major problems. After an initially triumphant entry into service in 1952, Comets had started falling out of the sky for no apparent reason. Detailed investigations and a very public, Public Enquiry, would eventually find that metal fatigue leading to the explosive failure of the pressurised cabin was responsible. The Comet's operators, Britain's BOAC, The Royal Canadian Air Force and Paris-based Air France and UAT found their expensive new aircraft grounded in 1954. Airline customers for the more powerful and stretched Comet 2 and Comet 3 versions, of which several aircraft were already on the production line, had their orders cancelled before they could take delivery. It was hardly the atmosphere in which to propose a new jet airliner to the world's commercial aircraft operators.

Nonetheless, until the disasters, passenger reaction to the Comet had been phenomenal. Load factors were high even though only first class fares were on offer on the 36-seater jets. It was obvious that this was the style of transport the public would be expecting in the future and many aircraft manufacturers around the world were in a hurry to overtake De Havilland's initial lead. Even while the crashes were

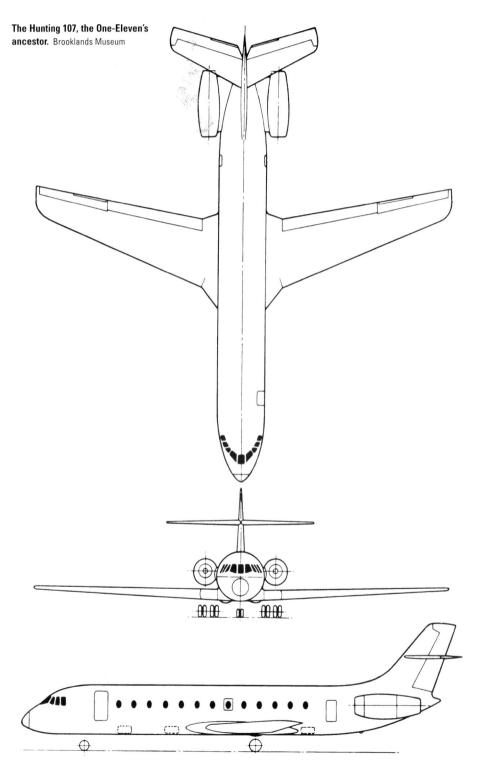

The Hunting 107, the One-Eleven's ancestor. Brooklands Museum

Specification – Comet 1

Powerplant:	4 × 4,450lb Rolls-Royce Ghost 5D Mk I	Max. Capacity:	36–44
Dimensions:	Span 35.05m (115ft); length 28.38m (93ft); height 8.98m (28ft 4in)	Performance:	Range 2,816km (1,750 miles) Cruising speed 788km/h (490mph)

The DH Comet 1, the world's first jetliner. BAe, via Author

still being investigated, the world's aircraft builders knew that lessons would be learnt once the causes of the losses were discovered. With the market for jet air travel having been proven to exist, they could press ahead with the design studies and be confident that they could incorporate any new knowledge into the final product.

Following behind the Comet's head start, rival jet airliners were already in various stages of development. America's Boeing 707 would make its maiden flight in 1954 and its compatriot, the Douglas DC-8 design would be on offer in 1955. Even Soviet Russia's Tupolev Tu-104 was barely two years away from stunning the West with its surprise entry into service in 1956. They were all to benefit from the hard lessons learnt from De Havilland's misfortunes. The Comet would return too. Strengthened and enlarged, it was to experience one more triumph by just beating the Boeing 707 to operate the first scheduled trans-Atlantic jet service, by BOAC, in 1958. Although subsequent sales were to suffer from the lead being lost by the grounding of the early aircraft, the Comet 4 series sold in respectable enough numbers to several airlines around the world.

The first of the new jet airliners to be designed specifically for short-haul services was also on the horizon. France's Sud-Aviation SE.210 Caravelle was to fly from

Specification – Caravelle 111

Powerplant:	2 × 11,400lb Rolls-Royce Avon 527	Max. Capacity:	80
Dimensions:	Span 34.3m (112ft 6in); length 32.01m (105ft); height 8.7m (28ft 6in)	Performance:	Range 1,740km (1,081 miles) Cruising speed 779km/h (484mph)

France's rear-engined Caravelle. Aviation Hobby Shop

The popular turbo-prop Viscount 700. Jennie Gradidge

Specification – Vickers Viscount 701

Powerplant:	4 × 1,540 ehp Rolls-Royce Dart 506
Dimensions:	Span 28.55m (93ft 8in); length 24.4m (81ft 2in); height 8.05m (26ft 9in)
Max. Capacity:	47
Performance:	Range 2,813km (1,748 miles); cruising speed 508km/h (316mph)

Toulouse in May 1955. The Caravelle benefited from the Comet design in an even more positive way, its nose section and flight deck being directly based on the Comet's. Significantly, Sud-Aviation chose to mount the engines, two Rolls-Royce Avons, on the rear fuselage. This particular innovation was initially treated with a great deal of scepticism by other aircraft manufacturers.

Almost contemporary with the Comet, another unique British airliner design had experienced much more success than the ill-fated jets. Vickers Armstrong had produced the Viscount turbo-prop in 1948. Although technically a jet engine, the Rolls-Royce Dart, four of which powered the Viscount, used their jet thrust to drive propellers. This gave a much more economical fuel consumption and offered similar comfort levels to the pure-jet alternative. The initial 47-seat, 700 series Viscounts had entered service on British European Airways continental and Mediterranean services in 1953.

Instantly popular with the public that appreciated the reduced noise and vibration levels compared to piston-engined predecessors and the jet-like speed, the Viscount started to build up an impressive

worldwide order book. Particularly satisfying for Vickers was the eventual sale to several North American customers, Trans Canada Airlines, Capital Airlines, Northeast Airlines and Continental Airlines.

As Viscount orders continued to flow in, Vickers opened a new production line at Hurn, near Bournemouth, to supplement their long-established Weybridge, Surrey, facility. The enlarged, 60–75-passenger, 800 and 810 series Viscounts replaced the 700s and Vickers' own sights as to an eventual Viscount replacement remained firmly set on turbo-prop power. The 100–130-seat Vanguard, powered by four Rolls-Royce Tynes, was seen by them as the economic way ahead for mainline short-haul services.

The company was far from averse to the trend towards pure-jet airliner design. However, Vickers pure-jet design options were all intended for long-haul service. Based on the Valiant jet bomber, the Vickers 1000 was being designed for the Royal Air Force as a long-range jet transport, with a civil version, the VC7 being developed for BOAC. Despite the prototype being in an advanced state of construction, the Gov-

ernment cancelled the RAF order, killing off the Vickers 1000, on economic grounds, in 1956. The limited airline interest for the VC7 from BOAC and Trans-Canada Air lines was not enough to save the aircraft. Experience gained on the project was not wasted though and was channelled into the later, much more successful VC-10 design.

Vickers' view that the only economic jets for short-haul work were turbo-props, was not an exclusive one. Even the Chairman of British European Airways, Lord Douglas, stated publicly in 1956, that the core of the airline's fleet would continue to be British-built turbo-props. Less than nine months later he had to concede that BEA would have to order jets in order to remain competitive against its rivals. Also, the Lockheed Company in the USA, having supplied many of the world's airlines with the popular Constellation series of piston-powered airliners, shared Vickers and Lord Douglas's initial opinion. Unlike their Boeing and Douglas rivals, Lockheed decided not to produce a pure-jet transport. Instead, they produced America's first turbo-prop airliner, the L188 Electra. Flying two years before the Vanguard, it did sell better than

Vickers' similarly sized aircraft. However, the initial popularity of both types was to suffer from the public's demand for more jets. After a few short years of front-line service, by the late 1960s they would be shunted to less competitive routes or sold off.

It was not only the major aircraft constructors that were deciding their policies, right or wrong, as to the future of jet transport operations. Many of the smaller companies were also setting up their own design and feasibility studies with a view to

capturing a slice of the new market. With the worldwide success of the Viscount fresh in their minds, a jet-powered replacement for the aircraft soon became a common goal and a number of companies took to their drawing boards to come up with a

Specification – Lockheed Electra

Powerplant:	4 × 3,750 shp Allison 501D	Max. Capacity:	98
Dimensions:	Span 30.18m (99ft); length 31.85m (104ft 6in); height 10.03m (32ft 10in)	Performance:	Range 4,458km (2,770 miles) Cruising speed 652km/h (405mph)

Aviation Hobby Shop

Specification – Vickers Vanguard 951

Powerplant:	4 × 4,985 ehp Rolls-Royce Tyne 506	Max. Capacity:	126
Dimensions:	Span 36.15m (118ft 7in); length 37.45m (122ft 10in); height 10.64m (34ft 11in)	Performance:	Range 2,945km (1,830 miles) Cruising speed 684km/h (425mph)

Aviation Hobby Shop

solution. One of these was Hunting Percival Aircraft Ltd, based at Luton Airport, in Bedfordshire.

Percival's Origins

Edgar W. Percival had founded the original company, Percival Aircraft Ltd in 1932 in a converted glider construction workshop in Maidstone, Kent. Percival was also the Chief Designer, supervised the construction of the first aircraft, the Percival Gull, test flew it and even piloted it in the round-Britain King's Cup Race of 8–9 July 1932.

The 1930s saw a phenomenal growth in the popularity of private and club flying, not only in Britain, but around the world. Designed to capitalize on this, the Percival Gull was a very modern-looking, three-seat, all-wood, low-wing monoplane with a folding wing for easy storage in limited hangar space. Powered by a single 130h.p. Cirrus Hermes IV engine, the prototype, G-ABUR, led to an eventual production run of 48. About half of these were initial-ly built under contract by George Parnall and Co. of Yate, in Gloucestershire, before Percival opened their own new factory, at Gravesend, back in Kent, in 1934. Customers for the production aircraft had a choice of either Cirrus Hermes, De Havilland Gipsy Major or Gipsy Six, or Napier Javelin engines.

Sales ranged far and wide, with aircraft being exported to Japan, South America and Australia, for both commercial, corporate and private operators. The aircraft was also used by several well-known pilots including Jean Batten, who flew Gull Six G-APDR on record-breaking flights to Brazil, Australia and New Zealand. Edgar Percival himself piloted Gull G-ADEP on a record-breaking trip between Gravesend and Oran and back in one day, in 1935.

Encouraged by the success of the Gull series, the company moved again, in 1936, to new premises at Luton Airport. The Gull series continued to be improved and modified until the last production aircraft, ZS-AKI, was delivered to the Shell Company of South Africa in October 1937.

A single-seat racer, the Mew Gull and the four-seat Vega Gull followed the original Gulls off the production line. These were then followed by an ambitious twin-engined design for up to six passengers, plus a pilot. Designated the Percival Q6, the attractive plywood and fabric-built

The prototype Percival Q6. MAP

A production Q6 in military garb. MAP

One of the many ex-military Proctors to be converted for civil use. MAP

(Below) The Jet Provost military trainer, Hunting's first jet. MAP

monoplane was powered by two De Havilland Gipsy Six engines. A retractable undercarriage, still a very innovative feature for the 1930s, was available as an option. However, only four aircraft were sold as such. The Q6 first flew in 1938 and less than 26 production aircraft were sold before the outbreak of war the following year.

Percival returned to the single-engined layout for their next aircraft, the Proctor. Developed from the Vega Gull, the Proctor was designed to Air Ministry specifications for a communications and training aircraft. The prototype, P5998, first flew on 8 October 1939, less than a month after the outbreak of war. Throughout the war years, the adaptable Proctor was improved and several special versions were produced for various tasks. Over 1,100 of the various types were built during the war, at Luton and under sub-contract at Manchester by F. Hills and Sons Ltd. With the return of peace, a purely civil version, the Proctor 5 was produced. Over 150 of these were built, soon to be joined on the civil scene by several hundred converted ex-RAF aircraft.

The RAF was to return to Percival for a replacement for the war-weary Proctors. The result was the P.40 Prentice, with deliveries starting in 1948. As with the previous Percival trainer types, the Prentice was designed as a single-engined 2–3-seat trainer. The Prentice was also ordered by several foreign air forces, notably Argentina, India, Italy and the Lebanon. Between 1955 and 1958 no less than 252 Prentices were sold by the RAF to Aviation Traders Ltd for civil conversion. However, in the event, only 28 of them were to find new civilian owners. The rest were consigned to scrap after all useful, resalable spares were stripped from the airframes.

The sale of the Prentices had been prompted by the arrival of yet another

Percival's Merganser with the long-awaited, borrowed engines. via Author

Percival training and communications design, the Provost. One hundred of the new aircraft were in service with the RAF by February 1954, by which time a pure-jet basic trainer, the Jet Provost was well under development. The Jet Provost was to be powered by an Armstrong Siddeley Viper turbo-jet. Later that year the company's title was changed to Hunting Percival Aircraft Ltd, to reflect the Hunting Group's financial interest in Percival.

While building on its established reputation as a supplier of military training and light communications aircraft, the company had also begun to look into more commercially oriented designs. As

early as 1946, the P.48 Merganser, a five-passenger, high-wing, stressed-metal-skin aircraft with a tricycle undercarriage, was built. Post-war supply difficulties led to a lack of suitable engines and this delayed the prototype's first flight from Luton until May 1947. It had finally been fitted with two Gypsy Queen 51s loaned by the Ministry of Supply. Following a busy summer of development flying, the sole Merganser, G-AHMH, was displayed at that year's S.B.A.C. Show at Radlett in September. Interest expressed in the design encouraged Percival to speed up the building of an enlarged version, the P.50 Prince.

The Prince prototype flew for the first time in 13 May 1948. Sold mostly to private and corporate owners, the Prince was offered in several different types for varying assignments and customer needs. One of these was an air survey version, with sales to Switzerland, the Tanganyika Government and the Thai Air Force, as well as to an associate company, Hunting Aerosurveys Ltd. Corporate customers included Shell, who obtained several aircraft for use in a number of locations around the world, the Standard Motor Company and Martin-Baker Aircraft Ltd. Three Prince 3Bs were utilized by the Ministry of Civil Aviation Flying Unit from Stansted on airfield calibration work around the UK.

Military versions of the Prince, the Sea Prince and Pembroke were supplied in large numbers to the Royal Navy and Royal Air Force, respectively, for a variety of duties including staff transport and navigational trainers. Military customers for transport versions of the Prince/Pembroke included the air forces of the Sudan, Rhodesia, Belgium, Australia, Sweden, Finland and West Germany. A civilianized version of the Pembroke, the President, was also offered.

Airline sales of the Prince were confined to an order from Aeronorte for three ten-passenger Prince 2s, to be based at Sao Luis in northeastern Brazil. An order for three Presidents for Bilbao-based T.A.E. was never finalized, despite two of the aircraft being completed and stored in full

Hunting Survey's camera-equipped Prince, G-ALRY. via Author

T.A.E. livery at Luton. Polynesian Airlines did, however, operate a number of second-hand Princes on their Pacific island network in the early 1960s.

Production of the Jet Provost and Prince/Pembroke aircraft kept Hunting Percival's Luton factory busy enough through the 1950s, but future projects were always under review. Their own answer to the Viscount replacement problem firmed up during 1956 into the Hunting Percival H-107 jet airliner design. Initially, the use of two Bristol Siddeley Orpheus turbojets was proposed, mounted on the rear fuselage of the 32-passenger aircraft. This once controversial Caravelle feature was now becoming recognized as a good idea, keeping engine noise in the cabin to a minimum, as well as keeping the engines clear of any runway debris thrown up in rough field operations. The low-wing, short field aircraft had its tailplane located in the mid-fin position, also as in the Caravelle.

Approaches to potential customers indicated that more economical turbo-fans would be preferred over the pure-jet Orpheus engines. Turbo-fan engines suitable for commercial applications were still in their experimental stages and the H-107 project was put to one side until suitable power plants were developed.

In 1959 the embryonic H-107 design was reviewed by Hunting Aircraft, the Percival name having been dropped in 1957. Using two Bristol Siddeley BS.75 turbo-fans as the basis of its power, the aircraft was enlarged with capacity increased to forty-eight passengers. However, early in the following year, two events were to have a major effect on the future of the H-107.

Big is Beautiful?

For many years, the British aircraft industry had been divided into numerous small companies, competing eagerly against one another as well as overseas rivals. Even the more successful concerns, such as Vickers, De Havilland and Bristol were smaller

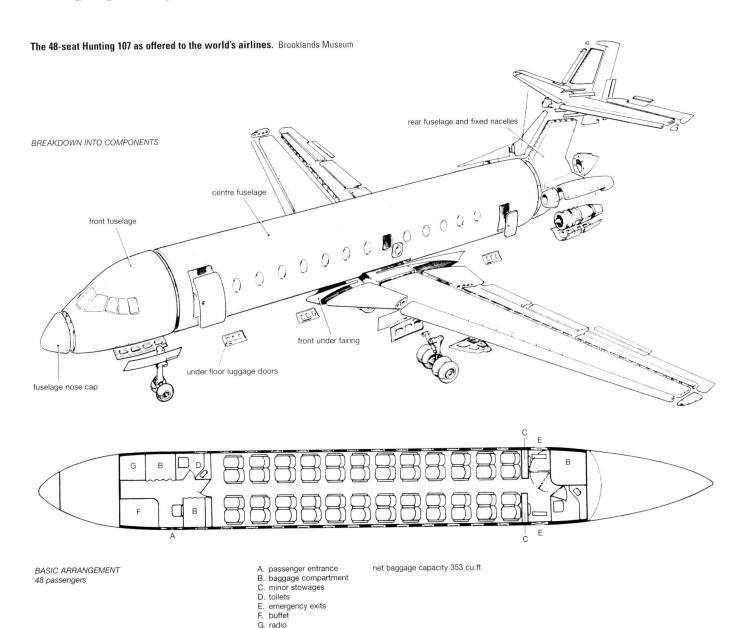

The 48-seat Hunting 107 as offered to the world's airlines. Brooklands Museum

BREAKDOWN INTO COMPONENTS

rear fuselage and fixed nacelles

centre fuselage

front fuselage

front under fairing

fuselage nose cap

under floor luggage doors

BASIC ARRANGEMENT
48 passengers

A. passenger entrance
B. baggage compartment
C. minor stowages
D. toilets
E. emergency exits
F. buffet
G. radio

net baggage capacity 353 cu.ft

The Hawker Siddeley Trident 1C entered service in 1964. MAP

Specification – Hawker Siddeley Trident 1C	
Powerplant:	3 × 9,850 Rolls-Royce Spey 505/EF
Dimensions:	Span 33m (89ft 10in); length 40.6m (114ft 9in); height 10.36m (27ft)
Max. Capacity:	101
Performance:	Range 5,004km (1,300 miles); cruising speed 917km/h (579mph)

than some of the sub-contractors that supplied giant trans-Atlantic rivals such as Douglas and Lockheed. Competitive duplication of projects and proposals, both civil and military, was rife between all the companies. Both industry and government circles were beginning to recognize that if the British aircraft industry was to have any chance of competing in the modern global aircraft market that was developing, there would have to be a degree of rationalization.

Thus, in early 1960, two large companies were formed by the merger of several of the competing manufacturers. Hawker Siddeley took over De Havillands and Blackburn Aircraft to form one, and in March, the British Aircraft Corporation was formed as the holding company for several others. BAC was to encompass the design and manufacturing divisions of Vickers-Armstrong (Aircraft), Bristol Aeroplane Co. Ltd and English Electric Aviation. Initially it could call on resources of £20m, with £4m each coming from Vickers and English Electric and £4m from Bristol. In May, the still barely formed corporation bought a controlling interest in Hunting Aircraft Ltd.

Not all the established British aircraft manufacturing concerns were to lose their independence. Short Brothers, at Belfast and the long-established Handley Page

were among the few that managed to avoid being swallowed up by either of the two new concerns. Avro and Armstrong Whitworth, in which Hawker Siddeley already had considerable influence, both survived briefly with a certain measure of independence, only to be completely absorbed into the parent company by 1965.

Once the dust stirred up by the mergers had settled, both new concerns started a thorough review of the designs they had on offer. Both were anxious to cut out competitive projects within their own organizations, one of the main reasons behind the mergers in the first place. Extensive market surveys were conducted throughout the world involving the leading airlines of the day, to gauge the market. From this data the new BAC and Hawker Siddeley decided which of their acquired designs stood any chance of becoming a commercially successful reality.

As far as Hawker Siddeley were concerned, their jet transport philosophy was summed up solely in the ex-De Havilland design, the DH-121 Trident. First proposed in 1957, the Trident had eventually been sold to British European Airways in 1958, but not until BEA had insisted on a scaling down of the aircraft. The reduction in size was later seen as a major reason for the Trident not selling as well as its main

rival, the similarly configured Boeing 727. Construction of the BEA ordered aircraft was already under way when De Havilland became absorbed by Hawker Siddeley and the first flew, as the HS-121 Trident 1, in January 1962.

BAC also wanted a slice of the second generation jet airliner market and had a number of options amongst the portfolio inherited from its constituent companies to choose from. As already mentioned, Vickers had eventually developed the VC-10 for BOAC after the Vickers 1000/VC-7 project was dropped. Vickers also offered the VC-11 to BEA, as a short-range version of the VC-10. Meant as a 136-seat replacement for the Vanguard, it was much bigger than the H-107 and would have been powered by four Rolls-Royce Speys, in place of the VC-10's four Rolls-Royce Conways.

Bristol Aircraft, ironically then in partnership with Hawker Siddeley, had offered its own short-medium jet airliner design, the Bristol 200, as far back as 1958. Directly competing with the then De Havilland Trident, the Bristol 200 was to have been powered by three Bristol Olympus engines and been capable of carrying up to 100 passengers over 1,000 miles at a cruising speed of 600mph. The two designs were far from dissimilar, both mounting their engines at the rear, with a T-tail configuration. Competition between Bristol/Hawker Siddeley and De Havilland for the BEA order was keen, with the airline's preference swinging between the two types almost by the week. Bristol offered a US-engined version to the American market in 1958, with Pan American being one of several carriers to look seriously at the proposed aircraft.

H-107 to consider. Retitled the BAC 107, several changes were made, with much of the new input inspired from the findings of the market surveys and proposed by the ex-Vickers design team now incorporated into BAC. The H-107's mid-fin-positioned tailplane was relocated to become a T-tail and the fuselage was enlarged again to accommodate up to 59 passengers. The

ing, increasing the capacity to 70–80. Features more in keeping with the high-utilization, multi-stop style of American domestic operations were also added. Integral airstairs at the front main entrance door and a ventral stair under the tail were offered, as well a the addition of an auxiliary power unit to aid start-up and run the aircraft's systems at transit stops. Maximum take-off

The definitive BAC One-Eleven design finally emerged in 1961. Brooklands Museum

Once BEA had made their final decision in De Havilland's favour, the Bristol 200 faded out of the picture. Not willing to give in totally, Bristol began promoting a 58-seat, four Rolls-Royce Orpheus-powered model, the Bristol 205, to BEA. Firmly aimed at the Viscount replacement market, the 205 found little support with the airline and was also eventually consigned to the filing cabinet.

When Hunting was absorbed into the BAC family, the corporation also had the

proposed engines remained two Bristol Siddeley BS.75s, rated at 7,350lb static thrust, which could give the new design a range of 500 miles with a full load. This new version of the original Hunting proposal soon found favour within BAC over the Vickers and Bristol-inspired options.

Anxious to repeat the export success of the Viscount, especially in the lucrative United States market, more changes were made to the BAC.107. The fuselage was enlarged to accommodate five-abreast seat-

and landing weights were increased to cut down on refuelling between sectors and help speed up turnrounds.

The increased weights led to the dropping of the Bristol Siddeley engine, in favour of the more powerful Rolls-Royce RB163 Spey, then under development for the Hawker Siddeley Trident. All these changes were sufficient to warrant the redesignating of the improved BAC 107 as the BAC.111, later to be marketed as the One-Eleven. In March 1961, the corporation finally authorized production of twenty of the finalized design, to include a flying prototype and two static test-frames. The aircraft were to be assembled at Hurn, from components built at Filton, the ex-Bristol factory (rear fuselage and tail section), Weybridge, ex-Vickers (centre section, wing skins and undercarriage) and Luton, ex-Hunting (wings, ailerons and flaps). Hurn, ex-Vickers, was also to build the forward and mid-fuselage sections.

The public launch of the new aircraft came on 9 May when an order for ten aircraft was announced from London-Gatwick-based British United Airways Ltd. BUA also took out an option on five additional aircraft.

More Merging

BUA was itself the result of a similar series of mergers and buy-outs, contemporary to those that had resulted in BAC. As in aircraft manufacturing, Britain's independent airlines of the late 1950s were made up of a collection of small operations, many specialized, most barely profitable. The major-ity of the survivors, those that made it through more than a couple of summer seasons, usually did so by lurching from crisis to crisis, surviving on *ad hoc* work, short-term charter contracts or barely profitable, usually highly seasonal, scheduled services.

The 'big is beautiful' philosophy started looking attractive to a number of the disparate independent airlines. They started to see it as a way of providing a stronger independent sector, better able to stand up to the state-owned BEA and BOAC. Some groupings of financial interests began in the late 1950s, with Airwork acquiring Transair, Air Charter and Bristow Helicopters, among others, although all the companies continued to operate independently for the time being.

The roots of BUA's constituent companies reached back to the beginnings of British commercial aviation. Airwork's operational history went back to 1928. The company had operated Heston Aerodrome in the 1930s, as well as several other flying centres around the country. Airwork had also been contracted to assist in the formation of Misrair, in Egypt, and Indian National Airways, whose descendants still continue to operate as national carriers. During the Second World War, Airwork contributed to the war effort by operating airfields and maintenance facilities for the military, as well as undertaking flying training and associated activities. A subsidiary company, Airwork General Trading, had manufactured wings for the Bristol Blenheim bomber under contract.

Post-war, Airwork entered the burgeoning air charter market, in 1946, with a fleet of De Havilland Rapides and Vickers Vikings flying from Blackbushe Airport, southwest of London. At about the same time, Hunting Air Travel was formed, also operating Vikings along with De Havilland Doves and other light twins, from Croydon Airport, later moving to less cramped facilities at Bovingdon. Air Charter also came into being in the late 1940s, but initially concentrated its activities on aircraft engineering and conversion work with only a handful of Rapides operating commercial charters from Croydon.

After peace returned to Europe, all scheduled service airlines in the UK were nationalized into the government-owned BEA, BOAC and BSAA. Any carrier

Hunting-Clan and Airwork's Vikings flew a leisurely 'Safari Service' to Africa. MAP

wishing to maintain its own identity was restricted to charter and contract work. It soon became clear though that there were a number of potentially profitable routes and markets that the large public corporations would be unwilling or unable to pursue profitably. Licences began to be issued to the independent airlines for scheduled operations under 'Associate Agreements'. The corporations though, reserved the right to take back the agreement and operate such services themselves if they saw fit.

For instance, BEA decided to take over a number of routes to the Isle of Man after enterprising independent carriers had shown them to be profitable. This sort of practice led to a number of operators going out of business and the survivors were becoming more and more reluctant to apply for the agreements. What was the point in investing in expensive aircraft and developing a market, if it was to be taken from you as soon as it was proved to be a profitable venture? However, after a change of government in 1951, independent carriers were again allowed to operate licensed scheduled services on their own account.

Throughout the 1950s the three airlines destined to comprise British United, then still great rivals for what work there was, carved out their shares of the independent market. The smaller aircraft were eventually joined by longer ranging, and larger, Avro Yorks, Avro Tudors and Handley Page Hermes. Airwork and Air Charter, especially, relied heavily on government trooping work to supplement their *ad hoc* and contract civil flights. With a large British military presence still in operation around the world, despite the conversion of the old British Empire into the Commonwealth, there was a large requirement for transport of military personnel, their families and equipment. Post-war, the RAF had reduced its transport capability and readily turned to the independent airlines to provide the required capacity. That the airlines were competing for the work also helped to keep the costs down as proposed rates were slashed in order to win the contracts.

Hunting also held several trooping contracts, once described by one of their stewardesses as 'all big boots and tattoos'. However, Hunting also made a brave attempt to take advantage of the scheduled service restrictions being lifted and established a new northern outstation at Newcastle-upon-Tyne with DC-3 services to Europe

and, domestically, to Scotland. In 1952 though, Airwork and Hunting were to begin a co-operative venture that started them down the road to eventual merger and the arrival of BUA.

Both Airwork and Hunting were frequent operators on charter services between the UK and Africa. The remaining vestiges of the British Empire and the established government and commercial links with the new Commonwealth nations ensured a ready market in expatriate workers, government officials and their families requiring transport to and from 'home'. With the change in air transport policy the two companies, previously deadly rivals for any charter contract, negotiated an agreement to co-operate in operating a joint scheduled service from London to Nairobi, to be aimed at the low-cost traveller but with a high standard of personal service.

Their well-proven fleets of Vickers Vikings would operate weekly, alternately from either Blackbushe, for Airwork, or Bovingdon, for Hunting. The flights were routed via Malta and the Sudan, where night stops would be made and the 27 passengers' hotel accommodation and meals would be included in the price. The fares were very competitively set at £98, one way, £180, return and were a substantial saving over the £140 and £252 equivalent first-class fares charged by BOAC. Tickets were interchangeable between both companies, providing a comprehensive weekly service.

The first flights left the UK on 14 June 1952 and, not surprisingly, the 'Safari Service' was a great success from the start. Load factors were up to more than 90 per cent before the first six months of operations were complete. On 18 February 1958, the frequency was doubled to two services a week, one operated by each company. Spurred on by their success in East Africa, plans were soon in hand to open similar services to West Africa. On 10 May 1954 the London–Freetown 'Safari Service' that also served Accra and Bathurst was opened. Just as successful as the East African routes both Airwork and Hunting-Clan, as the latter company had become in late 1953 following investment by the Clan Line shipping company, were well satisfied with their co-operative venture.

The customers for the 'Safari Service' enjoyed a leisurely journey. As well as the night stops, at least one refuelling stop had to be made en route each day. The Vikings were unpressurized, so the flights were at

low, potentially rough, altitudes and the on-board service provided by the sole stewardess on the small Vikings was of necessity rudimentary, although certainly personalized and friendly. However, the night stops were made at good quality hotels and most welcomed the chance to rest in exotic surroundings for a few hours. Many were commuting back and forth a couple of times a year, to enjoy leave periods at home and came to regard the Viking flight as part of the holiday. In many cases the companies and government agencies that employed them would have readily paid for them to use direct flights by BOAC or other 'major' carriers. Nonetheless, the expatriate passengers on leave found that they could more easily afford to bring extra family members with them by using the cheaper 'Safari' service. Before, in order to take family members, they would have had to endure long sea journeys, which took too large a bite out of their precious home leave.

Hunting-Clan Air Transport moved its base from Bovingdon to Heathrow in October 1954 and, in 1955, opened an all-cargo service to East Africa. This was to utilize Avro York freighters, supplemented by the occasional Viking. The 'Africargo' flight carried more than a million pounds of freight in the first eighteen months of operations and soon became legendary in its own right. Airwork entered the scheduled cargo market too, with Viking flights to Europe and a trans-Atlantic service provided under contract by Transocean Air Lines using the American carrier's DC-4s. However, Airwork's cargo network was much less successful than Hunting-Clan's and was closed down by the end of 1955.

Hunting-Clan had wanted to introduce Viscounts onto the 'Safari' routes in 1955, but objections from BOAC prevented this. BOAC regarded the Viscounts as capable of providing a service too close to its own standards and not in keeping with the cheap-rate 'third-class', as it regarded the 'Safari' flights. The fleet of three Viscount 700s was delivered, but Hunting-Clan had to be content with utilizing them on trooping flights to Gibraltar and Malta. The Viscounts also made an appearance on the northern network, on scheduled services between Newcastle, London, Oslo and Stavanger. This was far from a profitable operation though and, at the end of the trooping contracts in September 1955, the Viscounts were leased to Middle East Airlines in Beirut. Sadly, the decision was then

*Fly with pleasure
and nightstop leisure*
NOW with Viscount s-p-e-e-d

VISCOUNT **Safari** U.K.-AFRICA-U.K.

80A   UNITED KINGDOM — EAST AFRICA   80A

AIRWORK (AW)
HUNTING-CLAN (HC) } — Vickers Viscount

"The Viscount Safari Service" ☐   20 kg.   provided

mls.	AW 001	HC 103				AW 002	HC 104
0	19 30 ②	17 00 ④	dep	LONDON (England), London Airport Central...... arr		18 05 ③	10 40 ⑦
955	23 X 15 ②	20 X 45 ④	arr dep	ROME (Italy), Ciampino		14 X 10 ③	06 X 45 ⑦
	23 X 45 ②	21 X 15 ④				13 X 40 ③	06 X 15 ⑦
1790	04 X 00 ③	01 X 30 ⑤	arr dep	BENGHAZI (Libya), Benina		11 X 25 ③	04 X 00 ⑦
	04 X 30 ③	02 X 00 ⑤				10 X 55 ③	03 X 30 ⑦
2782	08 X 15 ③	05 X 45 ⑤	arr dep	WADI HALFA (Sudan)		07 X 00 ③	23 X 15 ⑥
	08 X 45 ③	06 X 15 ⑤				18 X 10 ④	23 05 ⑥
3210	10 X 40 ③	08 X 10 ⑤	arr dep	KHARTOUM (Sudan), Civil		16 X 15 ④	21 X 10 ⑥
	11 X 10 ③	09 X 10 ⑤				15 X 45 ④	20 X 10 ⑥
4300	16 20 ③	14 20 ⑤	arr dep	ENTEBBE (Uganda) ...... ◆		12 35 ④	17 00 ⑥
	16 50 ③	14 50 ⑤				12 05 ④	16 30 ⑥
4620	18 20 ③	16 20 ⑤	arr	NAIROBI (Kenya), Embakasi ...... ◆	dep	10 35 ④	15 00 ⑥

London, Brompton Air Station, opposite Brompton Oratory, 105 mins. (⟶ 5/0)

80B   UNITED KINGDOM — NORTHERN & SOUTHERN RHODESIA   80B

AIRWORK (AW)
HUNTING-CLAN (HC) } — Vickers Viscount

"The Viscount Safari Service" ☐   20 kg.   provided

mls.	HC 303	AW 003				HC 304	AW 004
0	11 00 Alt. ⑥-A	19 30 Alt. ⑥-B	dep	LONDON (England), London Airport Central...... arr		10 25 Alt. ⑫	18 05 Alt. ④
958	14 X 45 ,, ⑥	23 X 15 ,, ⑥	arr dep	ROME (Italy), Ciampino		06 X 30 ,, ⑪	14 X 10 ,, ④
	15 X 15 ,, ⑥	23 X 45 ,, ⑥				06 X 00 ,, ⑫	13 X 40 ,, ④
1790	19 X 30 ,, ⑥	04 X 00 Alt. ⑦	arr dep	BENGHAZI (Libya), Benina		03 X 45 ,, ⑫	11 X 25 ,, ④
	20 X 00 ,, ⑥	04 X 30 ,, ⑦				03 X 15 Alt. ⑫	10 X 55 ,, ④
2782	23 X 15 ,, ⑥	08 X 15 ,, ⑦	arr dep	WADI HALFA (Sudan)		23 X 20 ,, ⑪	07 X 00 Alt. ④
	00 X 15 Alt. ⑦	08 X 45 ,, ⑦				22 X 50 ,, ⑪	18 X 10 ,, ③
3210	02 X 10 ,, ⑦	10 X 40 ,, ⑦	arr dep	KHARTOUM (Sudan), Civil		20 X 55 ,, ⑪	16 X 15 ,, ③
	02 X 40 ,, ⑦	11 X 10 ,, ⑦				19 X 55 ,, ⑪	15 X 45 ,, ③
4300	07 X 50 ,, ⑦	16 X 20 ,, ⑦	arr dep	ENTEBBE (Uganda)		16 X 45 ,, ⑪	12 X 35 Alt. ③
	08 X 50 ,, ⑦	09 X 00 Alt. ⑪				16 X 15 ,, ⑪	16 X 15 ,, ②
5250	11 30 ,, ⑦	11 40 ,, ⑪	arr dep	NDOLA (N. Rhodesia) ...... ◆		11 35 ,, ⑪	11 35 ,, ②
	12 30 ,, ⑦	12 40 ,, ⑪				11 05 ,, ⑪	11 05 ,, ②
5400	13 25 ,, ⑦	13 35 ,, ⑪	arr dep	LUSAKA (N. Rhodesia) ...... ◆		10 10 ,, ⑪	10 10 ,, ②
	13 55 ,, ⑦	14 05 ,, ⑪				09 40 ,, ⑪	09 40 ,, ②
5660	15 15 Alt. ⑦	15 25 Alt. ⑪	arr	SALISBURY (S. Rhodesia), Salisbury Airport ...... ◆	dep	08 20 Alt. ⑪-C	08 20 Alt. ②-D

A—Dep London May 10th, 24th, June 7th, etc.   B—Dep London May 3rd, 17th, 31st, etc.   C—Dep Salisbury 12th, 26th, June 9th, etc.   D—Dep Salisbury May 6th, 20th, June 3rd, etc.

London, Brompton Air Station, opposite Brompton Oratory, 105 mins. (⟶ 5/0)

80C   UNITED KINGDOM — GAMBIA — SIERRA LEONE — GHANA   80C

AIRWORK (AW)
HUNTING-CLAN (HC) } — Vickers Viscount

"The Viscount Safari Service"   20 kg.   provided

mls.	AW 005 or HC 403				AW 006 or HC 404
0	08 45 ① -A	dep	LONDON (England), London Airport Central...... ◆ arr		17 35 ④
1030	12 40 ①	arr dep	LISBON (Portugal), Portela ...... ◆		13 45 ④
	13 10 ①				13 15 ④
1850	15 25 ①	arr dep	LAS PALMAS (Canary Is.), Gando		09 00 ④
	07 00 ②				17 15 ③
2885	10 50 ②	arr dep	BATHURST (Gambia), Yundum		13 25 ③
	11 20 ②				12 55 ③
3300	13 10 ②	arr dep	FREETOWN (Sierra Leone), Lungi		11 05 ③
	13 40 ②				10 35 ③
4300	17 20 ②	arr	ACCRA (Ghana)	dep	07 00 ③ -B

A—Airwork service operates May 12th, 26th, June 9th, etc. and Hunting-Clan service May 5th, 19th, June 2nd, etc.   B—Airwork service operates May 14th, 28th, June 11th, etc. and Hunting-Clan service May 7th, 21st, June 4th, etc.   C—Traffic rights at Las Palmas subject to Government approval.

London, Brompton Air Station, opposite Brompton Oratory, 105 mins. (⟶ 5/0)

Other Services of HUNTING-CLAN AIR TRANSPORT—see Tables 44B (Cargo) and 190

Daytime flying — nightstop leisure

Operated jointly by :
HUNTING-CLAN, SKYport 4111 and WELbeck 7799
AIRWORK LTD., REGent 8494 and KNIghtsbridge 4371

taken to completely close down the northern network as unprofitable.

By late 1957 and early 1958, both Airwork and Hunting-Clan were finally permitted to introduce Viscounts onto the 'Safari' routes. Night stops were now cut out, except on the West African route where overnight stop was still made at Las Palmas. The much more modern comfort level of the Viscounts was a great improvement over the ageing Vikings and was much appreciated by passengers. Airwork now moved their London departure point for the flights to Heathrow, allowing even closer co-operation with Hunting-Clan. There were two weekly departures to Nairobi, via Rome, Benghazi, Wadi Halfa, Khartoum, Entebbe, Ndola and Lusaka and one a week to Accra, via Lisbon, Las Palmas, Bathurst and Freetown.

During 1959, Airwork ran down many of its trooping contracts, selling off the ageing Vikings and Hermes used on them, and came to rely more on the 'Safari' services.

Airwork's Viscount 831s operated from both Heathrow and Gatwick. MAP

Hunting-Clan's Viscounts flew numerous charters as well as schedules. MAP

In 1958 it had taken control of Gatwick-based Transair that operated a fleet of Viscounts and DC-3s on scheduled, trooping and charter flights. In early 1959 Airwork took control of Air Charter, by then operating a fleet of DC-4s, Britannias and a dwindling number of Tudors. Transair and Airwork Viscounts soon began to be operated more and more on each other's services, especially when Airwork became responsible for operating one of its aircraft on behalf of Sudan Airways between Gatwick and Khartoum.

Mr Laker's Air Charter

More significantly, Airwork gained the services of Air Charter's founder and Managing Director, Freddie Laker. Although Air Charter had started to operate a small fleet of aircraft from Croydon,

selves. Air Charter's Croydon operations were closed down and Aviation Traders concentrated its efforts on scrapping, spares provision and maintenance work.

A return to commercial flying was made in May 1951, when the assets of another charter company, Surrey Flying Services, were acquired by Aviation Traders. A single Avro York was used initially, for both freight and passenger work. A second York soon followed, as did a single Avro Tudor. Another struggling charter airline, Fairflight Ltd, was taken over in November and both Surrey and Fairflight merged their operations under the Air Charter name in July 1952. Fairflight had brought another Tudor into the operation, as well as a valuable contract for cargo flights from Hamburg to Berlin.

Although based at Stansted, much of Air Charter's work was to be centred on the German market. West Berlin found

Laker had an eye on the profitable trooping and government agency contracts that were available and was determined that Air Charter should have a fleet that would win them.

The Tudors that Air Charter had inherited from Surrey and Fairflight had enjoyed a chequered history. Originally hailed as the new standard for postwar airliner design, the Avro Tudor was nothing if not consistent in its failure to live up to its own publicity. At first large numbers of the aircraft were ordered by BOAC and other Commonwealth airlines. When testing of the prototypes began, major handling and performance problems arose. One by one, the initial orders were cancelled as the airlines grew more disillusioned with the Tudor. Following trials with the prototypes, BOAC insisted on dozens of new modifications and performance requirements that would have to be

Air Charter's original Tudors came to the carrier via mergers. via Author

in 1947, Laker's main aviation interests had remained in engineering and maintenance, through a sister company, Aviation Traders. When the Berlin Airlift began, Laker specialized in providing spares support and leasing aircraft to other British carriers involved in the operation.

He had acquired no less than 99 ex-RAF Halifax bombers, at £1,000 each, which were promptly sent straight to the scrapyard and broken up. The mountain of spare parts that this created became an invaluable source of spares for the numerous carriers operating converted wartime bombers on the Airlift. When the Airlift ended, the resultant slump in the air charter market saw many of the aircraft that Aviation Traders had supported being scrapped them-

itself being repeatedly harassed by Soviet-controlled East Germany throughout the 1950s and once again turned to air transport to keep it alive with essential goods and supplies. Although on a much smaller scale than the original Airlift, the second operation was just as vital. Air Charter's Yorks, later joined by a Bristol Freighter, flew several sorties a day, carrying both cargo and passengers, from Hamburg into Berlin, as well as flying similar services from Hanover.

Back in the UK, Laker was soon looking for replacements for the Yorks. Although reliable and sturdy, the Yorks had a rather limited capacity and were slow, their shortcomings becoming especially evident when long-haul operations were attempted.

incorporated before they would agree to take delivery of any more aircraft. Most of these were impossible to manage without expensive rebuilding and redesign and Avro had to accept that most of the Tudors already coming off the production line would never be delivered to the airlines that ordered them.

Only one customer stayed faithful to Avro and took delivery of their ordered Tudors. The British South American Airways Corporation was state-owned, as was BEA and BOAC, being nationalized before it could start postwar operations in its original form of British Latin American Airways Ltd. Led by the fiercely patriotic Air Vice-Marshal A.C.T. Bennett, BSAA operated Avro Lancastrians, basically converted from the wartime Lancaster bomber design, and Avro Yorks from London to the Caribbean and South America. Totally unsuitable against more modern types, BSAA desperately needed to update its fleet. Bennett insisted on a British type and the only viable long-range airliner then being designed for trans-Atlantic work was the Tudor.

Several of the Type Four version of the aircraft were put into service in 1947, with plans for larger Type Fives to follow. However, the mysterious disappearance of two of the aircraft over the following months led to the withdrawal of the passenger fleet. The new Type Fives were diverted to work on the Berlin Airlift, soon to be joined by a number of the surviving ex-passenger fleet.

around Britain. The Surrey and Fairflight aircraft managed to continue flying in Air Charter colours, initially limited to cargo flights only, later recertified for passenger services. Laker had been impressed by their load-carrying capabilities and started to look at the stored aircraft as possible York replacements. With his usual businessman's flair, in late 1953 he negotiated a deal to buy all the scattered aircraft at a bargain price. Aviation Traders then set about converting a number of the airframes into airworthy aircraft using components from other stored Tudors, many scrapped where they had stood for several years.

The result was the Avro Supertrader. With the pressurization system removed and new large freight doors installed, the

Air Charter continued to go from strength to strength under Laker's leadership. The long-range Tudor and DC-4 aircraft were joined by an enlarged Bristol Freighter fleet operating a successful cross-Channel ferry service that was to lead to the establishment of a new subsidiary, Channel Air Bridge. A pair of Bristol Britannias were bought in 1958 to operate the long-haul trooping and charter flights, leading to the 1959 retirement of the Tudors, which had more than repaid Laker's faith in them. Within days of delivery, Laker had sent the Britannias off on long-range charters to the Pacific. The Britannias also became familiar sights at airports around the world, including the USA, Canada and the Far East.

The 'Supertrader' conversions of Tudor IVs served Air Charter well. MAP

Bennett had left BSAA shortly after the first disappearance, to form his own company, Airflight, later renamed Fairflight. He had left BSAA after strongly defending the Tudor against a hostile board of directors and it was no surprise that he chose to buy surplus Tudors from Avro to start his new airline. Following the removal of the Tudor from the scheduled network, BSAA found itself hopelessly uncompetitive and all operations were merged into BOAC by 1949.

On their return from the Airlift, the ex-BSAA Tudors joined several unsold aircraft in storage at various airfields

revamped Tudors entered service in 1954. As well as the established German services, the Supertraders also flew European and long-range charters from Stansted on both civil and government contracts. Numerous flights were made by the Tudors as far distant as Australia and the Pacific, as well as *ad hoc* work to Africa and the Middle East. A small fleet of DC-4s joined the Tudors in 1955, initially operating from Hamburg. The newly arrived DC-4s were also chartered by BEA for use on their Berlin-based scheduled German domestic network.

Laker kept Aviation Traders busy too, with two of his own aircraft designs being produced by the company. The Aviation Traders Accountant was designed as either an inter-city scheduled airliner, or an executive aircraft. The latter was still a relatively new concept, especially in Europe. Powered by two Rolls-Royce Darts, the Accountant first flew in 1957. Although technically a success, the Accountant failed to attract any orders. Much more successful though was the project to produce a large-capacity aircraft for the Channel Air Bridge car ferry operations.

Produced by taking a standard Douglas DC-4 airliner, installing a taller tail unit and extending the nose to include a forward opening door, by moving the cockpit to a new upper deck, the Aviation Traders Carvair entered Channel Air Bridge service in 1962. The Carvair could carry five cars as opposed to three in the Bristol Freighter and there was more provision for extra passenger capacity as well. Several Carvairs went on to serve the Channel Air Bridge's successors, British United Air Ferries and British Air Ferries, for many years as both a car ferry and general freighter. A number of other DC-4s were converted by Aviation Traders for other airline customers and served as far afield as Australia, Canada, South America and the USA.

Strength through Unity?

Newspaper speculation began about the possibility of a full merger of Airwork, its associates, and Hunting-Clan in early 1960. The Daily Express reported that talks were nearing settlement in February but none of the parties concerned would comment. Finally, on 1 March it was officially announced that Airwork Ltd, Hunting-Clan Air Transport Ltd and the British and Commonwealth Group would merge their air transport interests. The new airline, with Freddie Laker appointed as its Managing Director, officially came into being on 1 July 1960, operating a varied fleet of Vickers Viscounts, Douglas DC-3s, DC-4s, DC-6s and Bristol Britannias.

DC-4s on long-range trooping and charters, Viscounts of various marks on a mixture of scheduled long- and short-haul services and inclusive tour charters within Europe. The DC-3s on contract, inclusive tour and scheduled services and the DC-6As which had replaced the Yorks, on the 'Africargo' freighting services, supplemented by inclusive tour passenger flights at busy periods. A period of consolidation was called for, to pull the disparate operation together into a more cohesive unit.

Most of the Heathrow-based operations were progressively moved to Gatwick during the summer of 1960. Gatwick was chosen as the new main base as it offered better prospects for expansion over the increasingly crowded ramps and terminals of Heathrow. In 1958 Gatwick had reopened

Britannias joined Air Charter's worldwide charter service in 1959. MAP

As the Britannias were going into service, Airwork entered into negotiations with Laker to buy Air Charter. These were completed by January 1959 although the two companies continued separate operations. Nonetheless, a certain amount of rationalization took place with crews and other staff within Airwork and Air Charter.

Hunting-Clan also put a pair of Britannias into service in 1959, operating them on long-range trooping, ships' crew and *ad hoc* charters from Heathrow. Both aircraft were flown with the titles of the British and Commonwealth Group that now owned 50 per cent of Hunting-Clan.

In addition, a large fleet of helicopters, inherited from Airwork subsidiary Fison-Airwork, was flown on worldwide support contracts and a number of Bristol Freighters were operated by Channel Air Bridge, now owned by BUA but continuing to operate under its own name in its specialized niche. Morton Air Services, also owned by Airwork, operated its scheduled and charter network, based at Gatwick, separately for several years after BUA came into being.

The newly merged fleets of British United initially continued their varied duties as before – that is, Britannias and

after a total rebuild, with a modern terminal complex and new runway. It was also beginning to be recognized that Gatwick was able to serve a whole new catchment area, south of London. The direct rail connection to London's Victoria Station was also a great improvement over the interminable traffic jams on the road routes to Heathrow.

Scheduled services to Africa continued, with Britannias supplementing the established Viscounts on the busier services. In addition to their own 'Safari' flights, BUA also operated UK–Africa services on behalf of both the East African, and Central African, Airways Corporations. 'Skycoach'

British United inherited a large fleet of Viscounts. Aviation Hobby Shop

services were flown on an irregular basis from Heathrow to East and South Africa, in association with BOAC and the 'Africargo' services continued to operate from there. The European network was consolidated, with scheduled flights operating from Gatwick to Gibraltar, Guernsey, Jersey, Le Touquet and Rotterdam.

BUA was anxious to expand their European schedules, as well as strengthen their position on the long-range services. It was their intention to become the strongest of the independents, finally able to hold its own with the state-owned corporations, in both licence applications and its public reputation. A new 1960 Act of Parliament had effectively ended BOAC's and BEA's

preferential position with the licensing authorities. At last the independents could see a chance to build up viable scheduled networks. In 1961 BUA made several applications for new scheduled services from Gatwick. Although a number were refused after objections from BEA, British United was given permission to start scheduled services from Gatwick to Barcelona, Genoa, Lourdes, Malaga and Palma.

With a stronger European presence in mind, BUA started to look about for new aircraft to replace their current short and medium-range fleet, in particular, the Viscounts. On its formation, BUA was operating a single Viscount 736 and three 804s taken over from Transair, two 831s from

Airwork and two 833s from Hunting-Clan. A major European trooping contract was awarded to BUA in October 1961. This led to the withdrawal of the Viscounts from African services to operate the new contract, except on flights to Accra, where they continued to operate for a few more years. They were replaced on the African routes by larger Britannias.

The initial eight Viscounts would soon be joined by three more, ex-Air France and Maitland Drewery Aviation type 708s. These joined the Gatwick-based fleet when the British Aviation Services Group and its regional scheduled network, operated by subsidiary Silver City Airways, was acquired by British United in January

Britannias took over a number of the African routes from Viscounts. MAP

1962. Silver City also operated a cross-Channel car ferry service, in fact, it had been the first to do so, from Lydd in Kent. This was merged with the Channel Air Bridge to form British United Air Ferries. A short-haul jet was the obvious choice for a long-term Viscount replacement. If BUA was to establish itself as Britain's leading independent carrier, it had to present a totally modern image. Jets were the way ahead in the public's mind and British United had to have them.

Not long after BUA's formation, Freddie Laker, now confirmed as Managing Direc-

tor, approached BAC, among others, with the airline's requirements for a new aircraft. He was presented with the ongoing BAC One-Eleven project as one possible solution. Following a great deal of input from Laker and his BUA colleagues, the design was further refined and eventually finalized with many of the airline's suggestions incorporated. When British United, and Laker, were satisfied, BAC finally had an airline customer for the One-Eleven. The contract for ten aircraft, and five options, was signed and sealed on 9 May 1961. This was only a few months over a year after the

British Aircraft Corporation had been formed and less than a year since the arrival on the scene of British United Airways.

With the first sales contract under its belt and the first aircraft components taking shape on the production lines, BAC began to start looking for signatures on the next one. Work on developing the initial type, now designated the Series 200, was stepped up. BAC was not about to rest on its laurels. The corporation was confident it had a winning design on its hands and was finally ready to tell potential customers, and the rest of the world, all about it.

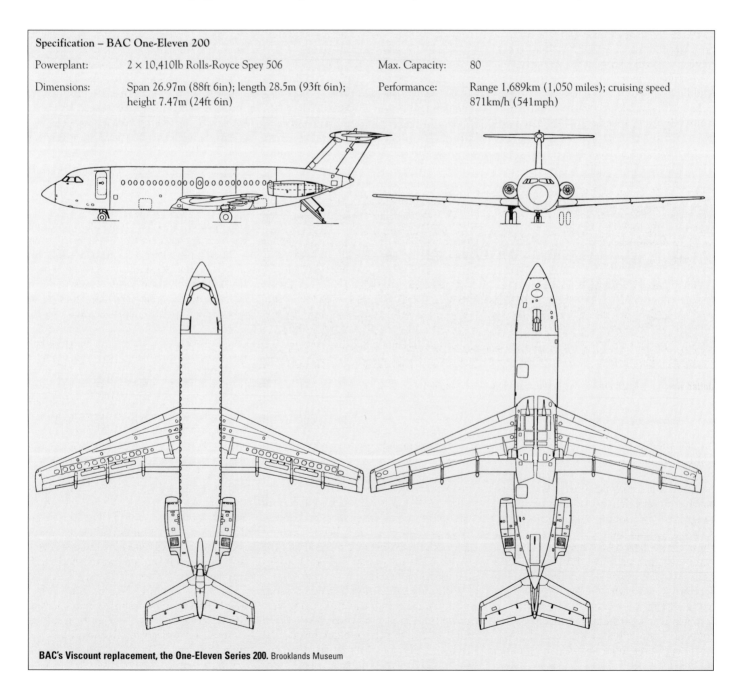

Specification – BAC One-Eleven 200

| Powerplant: | 2 × 10,410lb Rolls-Royce Spey 506 | Max. Capacity: | 80 |
| Dimensions: | Span 26.97m (88ft 6in); length 28.5m (93ft 6in); height 7.47m (24ft 6in) | Performance: | Range 1,689km (1,050 miles); cruising speed 871km/h (541mph) |

BAC's Viscount replacement, the One-Eleven Series 200. Brooklands Museum

CHAPTER TWO

Gestation

Even before its launch, the One-Eleven was certainly not the sole option for the world's airlines looking for a short-haul jet. The French-designed Caravelle had entered service with Air France and the Scandinavian Airlines System as early as 1959. Both airlines operated the aircraft on a mixture of short and medium-range routes, on both European inter-city services and to more distant points in the Middle East and North Africa.

Ironically, while Air France and SAS's Caravelles were speeding their passengers around Europe, customers on their high-profile, long-range trunk routes were still

The Caravelle's makers, Sud-Aviation, formed an alliance with the USA's Douglas Aircraft in an attempt to enter the vast American domestic airline market. Projects were pursued by both companies with a view to Douglas producing the Caravelle in the US, but nothing was to come of these. The Caravelles ordered by the type's only United States customer, United Airlines, were all still built in France. Instead, Douglas developed their own short-haul jet proposal. Initially these had centred around a reduced size DC-8, still with four wing-mounted engines. After consultation with the airlines it was aimed

Atlantic export orders for the One-Eleven. However, certain parties were less than enthusiastic that the British-built jet might emulate its prop-jet predecessor.

Shortly after the official One-Eleven launch, options or letters of intent had been received from American local service carriers, Ozark Airlines and Frontier Airlines, for five and six aircraft respectively. Unfortunately, intervention of the US Civil Aeronautics Board led to both these deals falling through. Responsible for regulating route licensing, and also administering generous government subsidies, the Civil Aeronautics Board wielded considerable power over the smaller carriers that depended on their financial support for their otherwise uneconomic local services. The CAB was not convinced that the small carriers would be able to operate jets economically without requesting considerable increases in their local service route subsidies. The threat to withdraw the subsidies altogether, which would probably have led to the close down of the airlines concerned was enough to ensure that no actual orders were placed.

Later, in November 1962, Arizona-based Bonanza Air Lines also signed a letter of intent for three Series 200s. The CAB refuse to guarantee the loan for their purchase and the order had to be cancelled. That Bonanza, and other local service carriers, later went on to operate American-built jets with little or no interference from the CAB, led to vitriolic accusations from the British press of veiled protectionism towards the US aircraft industry.

Less concerned with CAB subsidy threats though was the major American carrier, Braniff Airways, based at Dallas, Texas. On 23 October 1961, Braniff had placed a firm order for six BAC One-Eleven Series 200s, with options taken on a further six. Braniff was operating a fleet of Boeing 707s and 720s on their prestige North, Central and South American routes that stretched from Minneapolis and New York in the north, as far south as Santiago and Buenos Aires. The then President of Braniff, Charles E. Beard, was a pioneer of the concept of American

United was the only US airline to order the Caravelle. Aviation Hobby Shop

having their ear drums assaulted by 'old-fashioned' piston-engined types such as the Douglas DC-7C, Lockheed Super Constellation and Starliner. Air France was not to take delivery of their first long-range jet, the Boeing 707, until late in 1959. This was about six months after their Caravelles. SAS's passengers had to wait even longer, until 1960, when the carrier's first Douglas DC-8s were placed in service. One early Caravelle operator, Varig, of Brazil, even flew their aircraft in a major intercontinental route, from Rio to New York, albeit with several stops, while awaiting more suitable long-range jet aircraft.

at, this eventually gelled into a twin-engined design, the DC-9, of a similar size and identical rear engine/T-tail configuration as the BAC One-Eleven.

The DC-9 was finally launched in April 1963, nearly a year after the One-Eleven. Although there had been interest expressed, there were no firm orders for the type until the next month when Delta Air Lines ordered fifteen.

With the competition, both established and up and coming, the BAC sales team lost no time in placing their new product firmly in the airliner market place. The Viscount's previous success in the USA spurred them on to seek new trans-

BAC hoped to repeat the Viscount's export success. Aviation Hobby Shop

carriers operating jets on short-haul services. The One-Elevens would replace ageing Convair and Douglas piston-engined aircraft on the domestic services, as well as supplementing their fleet of jet-prop Electras. By being able to dispose of the piston types, Beard planned that Braniff would be one of the first US carriers operating an all-jet-powered fleet.

BAC's sales team scored another hit in the US in July 1962 when Mohawk Airlines of Utica, New York, signed up for an initial order of four Series 200s. One of the most respected Local Services Carriers, Mohawk's history was typical of many of its contemporaries. Beginning commuter operations in New York State, as Robinson Airlines, shortly after the end of the Second World War, the company changed its name to Mohawk Airlines in August 1952. Initially Robinson had operated single-engined Fairchild F-24s, replaced by six-passenger Beech 18s and, as Mohawk, later operating DC-3s, Convair 240 and 440s and Martin 404s. A short-lived experimental helicopter service was also operated during 1954, from Newark Airport to resorts in

the Catskill Mountains. By 1960, the company was operating 1,600 miles of routes throughout New England, New Jersey, New York, Michigan and Pennsylvania.

Once again the CAB attempted to intervene. The CAB stated their serious doubts as to the ability of the One-Eleven to attract sufficient traffic to avoid increased subsidy on Mohawk routes. Mohawk's then current fleet, mostly comprising Convair twin-piston-engined airliners, averaged 20 passengers per flight. The CAB calculated that at least 30–35 would be required for the One-Eleven to operate without an increased subsidy.

Nonetheless, Mohawk's President, Robert Peach, persisted. The CAB had just awarded the airline important route extensions as well as new non-stop authority between some major cities in the populous US northeast. This brought Mohawk into direct competition with trunk carriers, mostly in the form of American Airlines, on routes such as Syracuse–New York. Peach argued that they had to have modern equipment, of a high enough standard, to have any chance of competing effectively.

Peach sent a detailed letter to the CAB outlining Mohawk's reasoning behind the One-Eleven purchase:

The current and guaranteed operating specifications of the One-Eleven indicate seat-mile costs substantially below those of the most efficient short-haul transport now operational over the actual flight stage length proposed by Mohawk. Our planned operation of the four One-Elevens on 200-mile stage lengths shows a break-even load factor of 46.5 per cent which has historically been achieved by Mohawk. Mohawk is not, therefore, purchasing the BAC One-Eleven just for the sake of becoming a jet operator. It is purchasing it to meet economic and customer demand for the replacement of obsolescent equipment in orderly and well timed fashion.

For once the mighty Civil Aeronautics Board had to concede, albeit reluctantly, their chairman, Alan S. Boyd replying to Peach:

To the extent that your (jet) programme would not increase but rather contribute to a reduction of subsidy (as you have indicated it will), while at the same time improving services to the travelling public, such a programme would be viewed favourably by the Board.

Taking Shape

Meanwhile, at BAC, the first One-Eleven was nearing completion at Hurn. As well as the flying prototype, due to be joined on the flight test and development programme by the first production aircraft, two static test airframes were completed. One was used for a variety of wing and fuselage strength tests, the other for pressure tests in a water tank at Filton.

In addition, several components were rigged for separate testing. The test rig for the hydraulics and flying controls was based on a design that had given excellent results in Vickers' development of the VC-10. For instance, the flap drive system, comprising a control unit, transmission system and screw jacks was to operate 240,000 simulated 'flights' from March 1963. Variables such as different flight loads, environmental conditions, vibration, general faults and fluid contamination were all introduced, in varying combinations, throughout the test programme.

Full-scale cabin and flight deck mock-ups were used to test the flow and effectiveness of the planned air-conditioning systems. The engine fire-extinguisher system, designed by Graviner, was originally tested on a rig with a dummy engine. The system was then test flown in both a BEA and BOAC Comet, with false damage and contamination introduced. In 7,000 hours of operations, no false warnings occurred. The system was later flown in five other aircraft and achieved a clean record of 122,654 trouble-free hours.

Some components had slightly less intensive testing, as it was BAC policy to use well-proven materials whenever practicable. The fuel system was, basically, a scaled-down version of the VC-10's. The 30kVA One-Eleven generators, supplied by Plessey, were derated from the 40kVA units used on the BOAC Boeing 707s and VC-10s.

BAC's long-range, second generation, jet design, the VC-10, was an ex-Vickers project. Well under development before

Both Braniff *(top)* **and Mohawk** *(above)* **flew large fleets of Convairs on local routes.** Aviation Hobby Shop

A One-Eleven fuselage was used for water tank tests at Filton. Brooklands Museum

the formation of BAC, and also with a T-tail configuration, the VC-10 made its maiden flight on 29 June 1962. Originally ordered in substantial numbers by BOAC, the original Standard and stretched Super versions of the VC-10 were intended to replace the Comet 4 and so-called 'interim' Boeing 707s on BOAC routes. However, BOAC's historic, if controversial, preference for American airliners surfaced and the numbers of VC-10s on order were significantly reduced in favour of more 707s.

Nonetheless, the newly formed BUA saw the VC-10 as an ideal Britannia replacement for the African services. BUA also received authority to replace BOAC on South American routes and chose the VC-10 as their equipment for the new services. An order was placed for two VC-10s in 1961, later increased to three, all to be fitted with freight doors in the forward fuselage to allow combined passenger/cargo loads to be carried as required. With both the VC-10 and One-Eleven deliveries scheduled for late 1964,

BUA was expecting to be able to offer a modern, British-built and -powered jet fleet to the travelling public within five years of its formation.

Many of the One-Eleven test rig and fatigue programmes were scheduled to be still operating for a number of years after the aircraft entered service. In that way, any problems that arose could be identified long before they were likely to affect safe commercial operations. The entire ground test programme was planned around 45-minute 'flights' designed to reflect what was expected to be the aircraft's day-to-day, short-haul orientated, utilization. While testing of the individual components and systems continued, the first aircraft started taking shape at the Hurn production facility.

The BAC Sales Office continued to sign up new One-Eleven customers throughout 1962 and 1963. Kuwait Airways ordered three, with an option on another, in August 1962. The Central African Airways Corporation followed with an order

for two in September, followed by the later cancelled order from Bonanza in November. Happily, Braniff converted their six options into firm orders in March 1963 and the outlook became even brighter in May when Eire's Aer Lingus placed an order for four Series 200s.

A Letter Of Intent had also been signed by Western Airways for eight Series 200 aircraft. The order, later increased to ten, for Western was actually placed by East & West Steamship Co. (1961), of Karachi on behalf of Western Airways. However, in May 1963, Western advised BAC that they wished to dispose of four aircraft via a third party, Atomic Agencies (Aviation) Ltd and also wished BAC themselves to dispose of another four. In the event, no aircraft were delivered to Western or East & West.

Of greater significance had been the announcement of an order for fifteen of the more powerful Series 400 aircraft, by American Airlines. The order was announced on 17 July 1963 and was worth over £14 million. As well as being a milestone in break-

The hydraulics and controls rig made many simulated 'flights'. Brooklands Museum

Specification – Vickers VC-10

| Powerplant: | 4 × 21lb Rolls-Royce Conway Rco 42 | Max. Capacity: | 135 |
| Dimensions: | Span 44.55m (146ft 2in); length 48.36m (158ft 8in); height 12.04m (39ft 6in) | Performance: | Range 8,850km (5,500 miles); cruising speed 928km/h (580mph) |

The VC-10 fuel system was scaled down for the One-Eleven. MAP

ing even further into the US market, it was, significantly, the first time that American Airlines had ordered a foreign aircraft type.

The President of American Airlines at the time was C.R. Smith, a Texas-born businessman of extraordinary ability who had, literally, become a legend in his own lifetime. Trained as an accountant, Smith was employed in the 1920s by an accountancy firm that had a Texas utility as a client which held shares in a small airline. Texas Air Transport had gained valuable mail contracts from the US Post Office and had asked Smith to take over the administration of the airline. Eventually Texas Air Transport was merged with Southern Air Transport and Smith ran the new operation and moved on to St Louis when Southern became a part of the new American Airlines. At that time, American was comprised of a collection of merged carriers with a rather rambling route structure. Some routes in the system did not even link up with the rest of the network. The company's sales slogan of 'Coast to Coast and from Canada to Mexico!' was soon reworked by critics as 'Coast to Coast VIA Canada and Mexico!'. As the airline's trans-Continental New York–Los Angeles service called for such distant stops as Buffalo and New Mexico it was not too far from the truth.

C.R. Smith quickly rose through the executive ranks and was eventually appointed President of the airline. Under his leadership, the American Airlines system was reworked into a much more coherent unit, with the routes cleaned up and the fleet standardized. Following the introduction of Douglas DC-2s, Smith approached Douglas to build a wider fuselage version, capable of being used as a sleeper plane. American already operated Curtis Condor biplanes on trans-Continental sleeper flights, in which passengers dozed away the miles of America's longer routes in bunks. The Douglas Sleeper Transport was built, with Smith committing American to buying twenty, sight unseen, off the drawing board. It was, though, as its 21-passenger day-plane version, the Douglas DC-3, that it caught the imagination of the world's airlines.

Smith had continued to guide American Airlines both through the war years and the exciting post-war booms and slumps. His choice of the UK-built One-Eleven came as a shock to the US aircraft industry, which had expected the airline to stick to Boeing, from whom it had

Capital Airlines had been a major Viscount customer in the US. via Author

purchased the majority of its jets, or go back to Douglas which had supplied most of its pre-jet age fleet.

The Series 300 and 400 One-Eleven would be powered by Spey 25 Mk.511–14 engines, as opposed to the Series 200's RB163 Spey 2 Mk.506–14s. Otherwise, the external dimensions of the Series 200, 300 and 400 were identical, bar a 5in extension to the engine nacelles of the higher powered models. The Series 200 maximum take-off weight was 73,500lb, the Series 300 MTOW was 82,000lb. The Series 400 was designed specifically with US regulations over the maximum weight

of an aircraft operated by only two pilots in mind, and had an MTOW of 78,500lb. The Series 300 and 400 were also capable of carrying more fuel, 3,050 Imperial Gallons, as opposed to the Series 200's 2,200. The greater fuel capacity was achieved by installing centre-section wing tanks.

Offering an 'Americanized' version of the One-Eleven, the Series 400, was a tactic that had reaped significant rewards with the Viscount. Initially developed for Trans-Canada Air Lines, the upgraded version of the Series 700 Viscount was offered with a large amount of US-built or compatible equipment, with increased

The first One-Eleven, G-ASHG, was rolled out on 28 July 1963. Brooklands Museum

weights and many systems redesigned to fit in more with the US style of airline operation. As well as Trans-Canada, Capital Airlines eventually ordered a large fleet of the improved series 700s and Continental Airlines also operated a number of Series 810s with similar modifications. Several non-US carriers also placed large orders for the 'improved' aircraft, a trend that BAC hoped would continue with the One-Eleven.

Roll Out and First Flight

At the time of the prototype's roll-out at Hurn, on 28 July 1963, the One-Eleven boasted a very healthy order book for no less than 60 aircraft. With the Douglas DC-9 still only recently launched, BAC were confident that the One-Eleven would be able to keep up its lead in both the technical field and commercial sales.

Painted in BUA's rather staid black and white livery, with the airline's title in red, the One-Eleven prototype, G-ASHG, was introduced to the press and public amidst much publicity fanfare. It was unusual for a new British airliner to be presented not wearing the colours of either BEA or BOAC. For once, one of the independent airlines was benefitting from the limelight of being a pioneer. BUA's management could possibly be optimistic that the independents might start to be regarded as respectable commercial concerns rather than a collection of aerial pirates with dubious safety standards.

State-owned BEA was certainly offered the initial One-Eleven design. In 1960, BEA was still operating nearly 100 Viscounts of various marks. As the major operator of the type that the One-Eleven had been designed to replace, a BEA order would have been a distinct feather in BAC's cap. Unfortunately, BEA was not impressed with the early proposals. Citing passenger capacity, about the same as the Viscount's, as the prime reason for rejecting the aircraft, BEA wanted to see the chance of an economic gain over the operation of the popular, established turbo-props. With Comet and Trident jets, and the large-capacity turbo-prop Vanguard all scheduled to enter service between 1960 and 1964, BEA saw little advantage in trying to cope with yet another new type that it was not convinced it needed in the first place. BEA's comments regarding the One-Eleven's initial size were not lost on

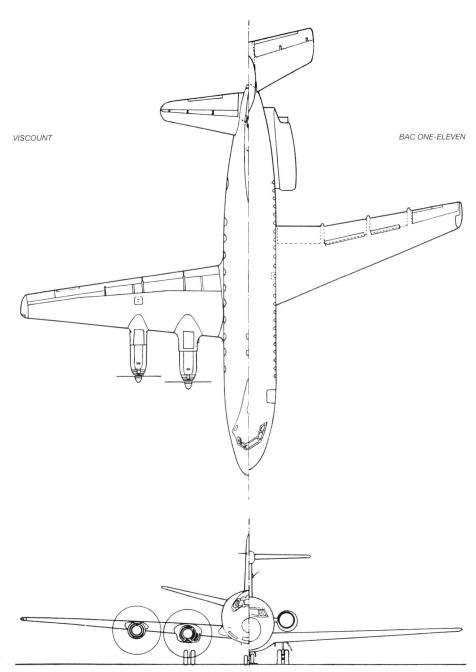

VISCOUNT

BAC ONE-ELEVEN

Comparisons between Viscount and One-Eleven were encouraged. Brooklands Museum

BAC though. The design team were sent off to ponder the problem and see how capacity could be increased, with a minimal increase to operating costs.

The prototype's first flight finally took place on 20 August 1963. In command was BAC's Chief Test Pilot, G.R. (Jock) Bryce. Bryce had participated in the development flying for a number of Vickers aircraft over the post-war years. As well as all the various versions of the pioneering Viscount and

later Vanguard turbo-props, he had flown experimental pure-jet-powered versions of both the Viking and the Viscount and had flown the VC-10 on its first flight in 1962.

A nice touch was the presence at Hurn of Viscount 843, G-ASDS. One of the last Viscounts to be built, G-ASDS was shortly to be delivered to Communist China's state airline, CAAC. On that day though, it ferried Hunting executives from Luton to Hurn to witness the first One-Eleven

On 22 October the aircraft was to operate a routine test flight to assess its stability and handling characteristics in stall conditions, as well as measurements of the wing-lift coefficients. Assigned to the flight were test pilots Lt-Cdr M.J. Lithgow and Capt R. Rymer. In the cabin, operating the test and recording equipment, were Ben Prior, Vickers' Assistant Chief Aerodynamicist, C.J. Webb, Hunting's Assistant Chief Designer, R.A.F. Wright, the Senior Flight Test Observer, One-Eleven, G.R. Poulter, a Vickers Flight Test Observer and D.J. Clark, a Hunting Flight Test Observer.

Over Wiltshire, after stall tests at various other flap settings had been satisfactorily completed, a stall was approached with an 8 degree flap setting. The previous flap settings had gradually moved the centre of gravity from a forward one to towards the rear. With the 8 degree setting the CofG was at its extreme rear and an abrupt stall condition was entered, causing a rapid acceleration downward. The elevators trailed up with the downward acceleration and an increasingly rapid rise in the aircraft's incidence. Despite attempts by the crew to get the aircraft out of this fatal configuration, the aircraft plummeted to the ground and crashed near Chicklade. All on board perished.

The loss of G-ASHG, the only complete One-Eleven, as well as the tragic loss of valuable, experienced personnel, was a severe blow to the programme. The swift recognition that the deep stall, under extreme conditions, was the cause of the accident led to equally swift alterations of the wing leading edge and modifications to the elevator linkage. The latter allowed a more direct mechanical connection between the elevators and the pilot's controls.

While the static test rigs continued their monotonous work, Hurn was, by now, close to turning out the first production aircraft. The flight test programme was finally able to recommence on 19 December 1963, when G-ASJA, BUA's first aircraft, made a 25-minute maiden flight on a sunny, cloudless winter's day. The flight had followed one low-speed and one high-speed return taxi run. No refuelling was required before the flight and the take-off weight had been 60,000lb. Again, Jock Bryce was at the controls, with D. Glaser acting as co-pilot.

Moving over to Wisley on 14 January 1964, to begin its working life, G-ASJA was provided with research equipment for

aircraft systems development. The next three BUA aircraft, G-ASJB, G-ASJC and G-ASJD were also fitted out with instrumentation and were to take part in flight trials, their delivery to BUA being delayed in an effort to catch up on some of the time lost when there was no flying aircraft available.

G-ASJB arrived at Wisley exactly a month later, on 14 February. 'JB was the first One-Eleven to be fitted with a modified leading edge that increased the wing chord and changed the profile. G-ASJC, also modified, left the production line on 15 March and flew for the first time on 1

flight, the culmination of what had once been solely their own project.

Following the first flight, operations moved to BAC's flight test centre, at Wisley. From there, the G-ASHG began a series of general handling flights, helping to refine the production aircraft still further and proving the design to be a viable one. By mid-October the aircraft had flown over 70 hours.

April. All following aircraft had the new leading edge fitted on the production line.

Between 'JC's rollout and first flight though, G-ASJB was damaged beyond repair when it made a heavy landing at Wisley on 18 March. Although the undercarriage collapsed, neither of the BAC test pilots, S. Harris and C. Moore, who was being checked out on the aircraft, were injured. Initially, 'JB was declared reparable but eventually the aircraft was broken up and all the salvageable components returned to the production line.

G-ASJD flew for the first time on 5 May. This was the first aircraft to be fully furnished, equipped with Aviation Traders seats and galley. The next aircraft off the production line, G-ASJE was also furnished and visited BUA's main base at Gatwick on 28 May. The visit was to undertake some night flying trials but also gave many BUA staff their first glimpse of the aircraft their employers were placing so much faith in.

The first flights outside the United Kingdom were operated by G-ASJA on 2 March to Zurich, and 18/19 March to Rome. By April nineteen pilots from eleven airlines, both actual and potential customers, had flown the aircraft from the left-hand seat, in addition to the nine BAC pilots assigned to the aircraft development and testing programme. Up to 16 April a total of 236 hours had been flown by the type, in 140 flights.

The flight testing continued to be concerned with preliminary assessment of all aspects of the aircraft, intended to identify any basic problems as soon as possible. The accident to the first prototype was an extreme result of this policy, designed to safeguard the future passengers and crews against such an incident happening in operational conditions. Items to be investigated during the programme were preliminary handling and calibrations; assessment of control forces and characteristics; feel unit adjustments; structural load measurement; single engine handling; flapless take-off and landing; autopilot and electronic equipment performance; engine and APU performance including relighting and systems development. Test flying for the Series 200 was planned to be over 1,600 flying hours, with an average of more than one landing per hour.

As well as the redesigned leading edge and elevator systems, a more streamlined nose cone was introduced. A stick shaker/pusher system was also installed to prevent

G-ASJA restarted the flight test programme in January 1964. via Author

the fatal deep stall configuration being entered in airline service. Interestingly, the Douglas-built rival design, the DC-9 was also modified in the light of the loss of G-ASHG. The DC-9 tailplane area was increased by 20 per cent and vortilons, to change the airflow, added beneath the wing. Running nearly two years behind the One-Eleven, these changes could be made by Douglas to the DC-9 during the initial design stages and no delay to their programme resulted.

More Sales

One-Eleven orders continued to come through, with American increasing their order for Series 400s by ten, then another five more. This doubled the initial American Airlines order from fifteen to thirty. C.R. Smith had already written to Sir George Edwards of BAC following the prototype and testing accidents, reassuring him of American's continued confidence in the design:

> Accidents in aviation are always regrettable and the accident to the One-Eleven especially so because you lost some brave and valued associates. But the problems that brought about the accident can and will be removed and the airplane will be a welcome addition to our fleet as soon as you can make it available. It is encouraging to learn that delays in deliveries to American may be quite modest.

Mohawk converted options to firm orders and took out more options for their Series 200 fleet and Helmut Horten Gmbh, a West German chain store, ordered the first executive One-Eleven, also a Series 200, in June

1964, with a £900,000 price tag. The 34-seat Helmut Horten aircraft was intended to transport executives between the company's 46 stores in Germany, replacing a Fokker F.27. Page Airways International was appointed US sales agent for executive versions of the One-Eleven, and promptly ordered two, in November.

In July, BAC was able to announce a number of improvements in the predicted performance of the aircraft, directly as a result of the data gathered in both ground rig and flight test programmes. The Series 200 maximum take-off weight was increased by 500lb, the maximum landing weight by 1,000lb and the maximum zero fuel weight was increased to 59,000lb. Similar improved weights were also offered on the Series 300 and 400.

Unfortunately, yet another setback occurred to the flying programme on 28 August when G-ASJD force landed on Salisbury Plain. Purely as a precautionary measure, the BAC pilot had deployed a tail parachute during stall trials. Parachutes had been fitted to the trials aircraft as a precaution, designed to raise the tail during a deep stall and permit a recovery. None of the occupants were injured during the forced landing and the aircraft was only slightly damaged. As it happened, analysis of flight data recordings showed that the streaming of the parachute had been unnecessary. The aircraft was dismantled at the landing site and repaired at Hurn, eventually being delivered to BUA as planned.

More aircraft were rolling off the production line, including the first for Braniff Airways on 24 May. Initially placed on the UK register as G-ASUF, this first Braniff destined aircraft was also the first of the type to visit London Heathrow Airport, on 6 July. Early production airframes for both BUA and Braniff were used for flight trials in an attempt to get the test and certification programme, now well behind schedule following the accidents and incidents, back on track. This was in addition to the crew training and customer acceptance work planned for them before delivery. As a result, the airline delivery dates were slipping further and further back. BUA found it had to charter in a great deal of extra capacity from both fellow UK and foreign operators, in order to cover the shortfall.

performance. 'JA was also used for more hot and high trials at Johannesburg in January 1965.

As a result of the improved performance gained during the flight trials Kuwait Airways decided to upgrade their order from Series 200s to Series 300s, although they were never to take delivery. As part of a modernization plan, the One-Elevens had been ordered to replace Viscounts on regional services and Hawker-Siddeley Trident 1Es were ordered to replace Comet 4Cs on routes to Europe. As it transpired, Kuwait Airways experienced financial dif-

The One-Eleven was operated six days a week, using a two-day routine, providing twenty-four hours of route proving, twelve hours of demonstration flying to at least two destinations and a twelve-hour maintenance break. Overall, 8.7 hours of flying was achieved per day and the aircraft proved very reliable. The proving services operated included a flight over the West African route, to Accra. G-ASJF made the first of a series of proving flights into Manchester on 17 March. The type was awarded its full United Kingdom Certificate of Airworthiness on 19 April. On that day,

BUA and Braniff's aircraft on the Wisley flight test line. Brooklands Museum

G-ASJA took part in tropical trials in October/November. On 16 October the aircraft left for Dakar, Senegal, via Madrid and Las Palmas. Nine days of trials in West Africa's humid climate followed before the aircraft flew to Madrid where two more weeks of tests and demonstration flights followed. Several teams of engineers and technicians from both BAC and various component suppliers accompanied the aircraft throughout this tour and pronounced themselves well satisfied with G-ASJA's

ficulties in late 1965 and were unable to justify the introduction of two expensive new types simultaneously. Initially the One-Eleven deliveries were only deferred and the Trident order went ahead on schedule, the first of two being handed over by Hawker-Siddeley in March 1966.

BUA took delivery of their first aircraft, G-ASJI, on 22 January 1965 and entered into an intensive period of training and route proving. The route proving involved 226 flying hours, resulting in 108 landings.

G-ASJJ flew the first revenue service, carrying BUA passengers on a scheduled service from Gatwick to Genoa, Italy.

The BUA's One-Elevens were soon also demonstrating their ultra short-haul capabilities when they were introduced on the Gatwick–Rotterdam and Gatwick–Le Touquet routes, the latter taking barely 35 minutes, block to block. In contrast, the One-Elevens were also used to replace the Viscounts on West African services to Lagos, via Lisbon, Las Palmas (where an

(Above) **G-ASJJ opened the first One-Eleven scheduled service from Gatwick to Genoa.** Brooklands Museum

BUA's One-Elevens joined VC-10s to offer a modern jet fleet. via Author

Braniff took delivery of their first One-Eleven in March 1965. Brooklands Museum

overnight stop was made), Bathurst, Freetown and Accra.

The portion of the One-Eleven's West African services between Freetown and Lagos was operated under joint British United/Sierra Leone Airways flight numbers. BUA was providing technical assistance to Sierra Leone at the time and the airline's Britannias and VC-10s also operated a joint service to London. The One-Elevens were also introduced onto BUA's inclusive tour charter services, carrying holidaymakers to numerous continental and North African resorts, mostly from Gatwick.

BUA had already introduced the VC-10 on their longer routes, with a trooping charter on 1 October 1964. They had also opened BUA service on the new twice-weekly scheduled routes to South America, taken over from BOAC, and were later to replace Britannias on the east and central African schedules. With One-Elevens joining the VC-10s on the Gatwick ramp, BUA had certainly managed an image-changing triumph over their more humble beginnings. Determined to take full advantage of their new status, the airline began to bombard the authorities for new route licences for both long and short-haul services, most

of them specifying the use of their new British-built and British-powered jets.

First US Services

Braniff was able to inaugurate their One-Eleven services on 25 April, after American FAA certification for the Series 200 had been granted on the 16th. A month earlier, on 11 March, the first Series 200 for Braniff left the UK for the USA, flying via Prestwick, Keflavik, Sondestrom Fjord, Goose Bay, Montreal and Newark, where the aircraft was officially handed over from BAC to Braniff officials, and on to Dallas's Love Field, arriving on the 13th. Unlike the BUA aircraft, which were fitted with an all economy class configuration, the Braniff fleet was operated with a two-class style of passenger accommodation. Twenty-four first-class and thirty-nine coach class seats were fitted in the Braniff aircraft that the airline had also elected not to be fitted with the optional rear ventral stairs. Instead, also in contrast to BUA's aircraft, the Braniff Series 200s were fitted with retractable airstairs at the forward passenger entry door.

The first Braniff scheduled service was a multi-stop service from Corpus Christi, in Texas, to Minneapolis-St Paul, in Minnesota. This long, multi-stop, inter-city route was to typify Braniff's use of the One-Eleven throughout their association with the type. The longest sector regularly flown by Braniff's One-Elevens was Dallas–Washington DC, the shortest being the 67-mile hop from San Antonio to Austin, both in Texas. A typical daily programme for one aircraft would see it scheduled to operate Dallas–Lubbock–Amarillo–Lubbock–Dallas–Houston–Dallas–Lubbock–Dallas, between 08.25 and 17.25, with flights varying between 112 to 300 miles. Turn-rounds averaged 35 minutes and some other daily One-Eleven schedules were even more intensive. All fourteen Braniff aircraft were delivered during 1965, as were BUA's ten.

The first aircraft of the Braniff order were all delivered in the airline's established red white and blue colour scheme. However, by the end of 1965, Braniff had embarked on a major new marketing strategy, the central theme of this being a startling new livery policy for all members of the aircraft fleet. Billed as 'the end of the

The Braniff One-Elevens entered service on 25 April 1965. Brooklands Museum

One-Elevens soon took on Braniff's new image. Brooklands Museum

plain plane', each aircraft was painted in a solid colour livery of one of several shade options ranging from lemon yellow, orange, ochre, dark or light blues or greens or even beige. A One-Eleven was painted in a representative version of the livery, using a strip-off paint finish, in order to obtain final Board approval for the new

scheme. Once this was forthcoming, the aircraft was stripped of its temporary bright colours and returned to service in its old livery, at least for a while.

The new look was designed by the New Mexico-based architect, Alexander Girard, the New 'BI' logo and new 'Braniff International' titles being created by the

Jack Tinker & Partners Agency. It certainly earned Braniff a great deal of media attention. Even ramp vehicles, airport ticketing areas and uniform for passenger contact staff were revamped in the new style. The female uniforms, designed by Italian *couturier* Emilio Pucci, featured a curious plastic 'bubble' style of headgear,

Aer Lingus's One-Elevens were shown off with a European tour. Brooklands Museum

The One-Elevens augmented Aer Lingus's Viscount fleet. Aviation Hobby Shop

over a velveteen hat, as well as reversible coats and a raspberry-coloured suit with purple culottes as another 'sartorial' option. Updated over the years, the multi-hued fleet was instantly recognized at any airport ramp. A number of the later built One-Elevens were delivered from Hurn in the new colours, the others being repainted by Braniff.

Aer Lingus was the next carrier to inaugurate One-Eleven service on 6 June with a Dublin–Cork–Paris flight. The inaugural revenue flight followed a six-day promotional tour of Europe, undertaken between 27 May and 1 June for Aer Lingus to show off their new airliner. The Irish carrier had actually originally favoured a fleet of Caravelles, announcing its intention to place an order for three Series IVRs in 1962. Unfortunately for the French manufacturers, the Irish Government refused to finance the order and Aer Lingus had to withdraw from negotiations for 1963 Caravelle delivery positions.

The main Government objections to the Caravelles had been on financial grounds. Their acquisition would have called for a £5m loan. Upgrading Aer Lingus's trans-Atlantic routes to a jet service

had recently cost £7m and the Minister for Finance could not be convinced that a similar amount would be well spent on European routes when the airline was already barely making a profit with their turbo-prop and piston fleets. They could be said to have had a point, with the continental routes bringing in only £850,000 in revenues for 1960/61. The airline industry, as a whole, had also been suffering from over-capacity and a certain amount of disquiet was expressed by the Minister at the thought of half-empty 86-seat Caravelles leading to substantial losses for the airline.

Although it was too late to save the Caravelle order, Aer Lingus eventually managed to refute many of the Ministry's more pessimistic predictions. Success by other carriers with short-haul jets and the obvious need for the national airline to remain competitive finally swung the argument in Aer Lingus's favour. The refusal to finance the Caravelles had, with hindsight, worked in the airline's favour. By the time it had persuaded the Government financiers that it was optimistic jets could profitably operate on the continental services, the next, improved, generation of short-haul jet

transports, in the shape of the BAC One-Eleven, was available.

Even before they entered service, the four 74-seat One-Eleven Series 200s delivered to Aer Lingus were already regarded as too small for the major trunk services between Eire and the United Kingdom. One hundred and fifteen-seat Boeing 720s, initially operated on trans-Atlantic jet routes, were already being scheduled on flights from Dublin to London, and other major European routes, to help deal with blossoming load factors. The One-Elevens were still used to good effect though, operating on many of the thinner European routes and short-haul flights across the Irish Sea to regional UK points such as Liverpool and Manchester. Charter flights also featured heavily in Aer Lingus's One-Eleven programme, with *ad hoc* and inclusive tour services operating from both Eire and the UK. A Glasgow–Tbilisi charter was flown in January 1966, utilizing EI-ANE 'St Mel', carrying the Glasgow Celtic soccer team.

Mohawk Airlines were to operate their first One-Eleven scheduled service from Utica, NY, on 15 July 1965, introducing the jets on to the busier commuter routes to New York. The first aircraft had arrived at

Mohawk's One-Elevens began operations in July 1965. Aviation Hobby Shop

The smart Mohawk Airlines' 'lounge' effect One-Eleven cabin. Brooklands Museum

(Below) **The One-Eleven's Rolls-Royce Spey.**
Brooklands Museum

Utica on 17 May, the 300 Mohawk staff and spectators that gathered to greet the new jet being treated to a ten-minute, impromptu flying display by the proud Mohawk Chief Test Pilot at the controls. A few weeks later, a Mohawk One-Eleven was exhibited at the nearby Rome, New York, Griffis Air Force Base open-house day. As well as seeing the One-Eleven displayed alongside the USAF military hardware, a few lucky visitors were able to purchase tickets for short demonstration flights.

Jet services spread over the network throughout the Northeastern United States as more and more aircraft were delivered, five being in service by the end of the year. Mohawk's initial seating arrangement for their One-Elevens was unusual in that the rows alternated between four and five seats per row, with facing rows over the wing. This was designed to give a comfortable 'lounge' effect and was certainly an improvement over the rather basic accommodations offered by the noisy, piston-engined Convairs that the jets were replacing on the busier flights.

The cabin furnishings were fitted by Mohawk at Utica, their main operational and engineering base, following delivery of the One-Elevens from the UK. It was, and still is, common practice for the £875,000 price-tag per aircraft not to cover the passenger comforts. On arrival at Utica, usually via Prestwick, Keflavik and Gander, the aircraft would be taken into the Mohawk hangar, where the seats, in their respective rows, were laid out ready for installation. Some Mohawk One-Elevens

were fitted out and placed into revenue service within three hours of delivery.

Despite the certification and production delays during 1964–65, BAC had continued to receive orders. Mohawk had converted options to firm orders for two and took out new options on three extra Series 200s in February 1965. In March, a new US customer, Aloha Airlines of Hawaii, ordered two Series 200s, taking an option on a third. The aircraft made its first entry into what was to become a healthy market for the type, when TACA International Airlines, of El Salvador, in Central America, ordered two Series 400s and took options on two more.

In Europe, British Midland Airways and British Eagle International Airlines both ordered two Series 300s, with British Eagle taking an option on a third. Philippine Airlines had ordered two Series 400s in November 1964 and increased the order to three in December 1965. Two VIP configured Series 200s were also ordered in December, by the Royal Australian Air Force, to be operated by 34 (ST) Squadron, based at Fairbairn, Canberra. The RAAF aircraft were to be powered by uprated Spey Mk.511–14s, as opposed to the 506–14s on earlier Series 200s, to further improve airfield performance.

UK Domestic Jets

With their fleet increasing steadily as their ordered aircraft were gradually released from test flying and finally delivered to Gatwick for revenue service, British United was able to embark on a new venture. In January 1966, the airline opened its new 'Interjet' service, linking Gatwick with Belfast, Edinburgh and Glasgow. The schedules were initially designed to act as feeder services to BUA's network from Gatwick. It soon became clear though that business commuters would become an important source of income for the routes and the international schedules were modified to allow the domestic services to take advantage of this.

The first 'Interjet' service was operated by G-ASJJ on 4 January on the Gatwick–Belfast route, following a Gatwick–Edinburgh press flight by G-ASJI on 13 December. At the time of their inauguration, the Glasgow flights used the long-established airport at Renfrew. Runway restrictions led to the revenue loads on the One-Elevens being limited to 58 passengers in the 74-seaters. A new airport for Glasgow, at nearby Abbotsinch, was due to open in May 1966, the use of which would eliminate the load restriction.

As introduced, the winter schedule called for the use of two of the One-Eleven fleet, one operating Gatwick–Glasgow–Gatwick–Edinburgh–Gatwick–Belfast–Gatwick between 0840 and 1940 daily. The second aircraft then operated the evening Gatwick–Glasgow–Gatwick service. From April, the Edinburgh service became twice daily, with the aircraft operating the morning Gatwick–Glasgow service, flying a return service from Gatwick to Genoa before operating the evening Gatwick–Glasgow–Gatwick flight. Eventually, twice-daily services were offered on all 'Interjet' routes.

BUA's expanding One-Eleven fleet was based at Gatwick. Aviation Hobby Shop

From the beginning, load factors were encouraging, even with the Renfrew restrictions. The first Glasgow–Gatwick flight carried 40 passengers, out of the 58 available for sale. Interestingly, 23 of these were taken by stand-by passengers who had been unsuccessful in getting seats on an earlier BEA Vanguard flight. The inaugural Belfast–Gatwick flight had produced the best inaugural load factor, carrying 53 passengers out of a possible 74.

The distance travelled to Gatwick from these domestic points was further than BEA had to fly, with the BUA aircraft having to route round London to reach Gatwick, to the south. Northbound flights had initially to route eastwards to Sevenoaks and then around London to Brookmans Park. Southbound services normally routed west of London, to Dunsfold and down on to Gatwick. With BEA still operating turbo-prop aircraft on the services though, gate to gate times were similar and BUA also exploited the advantage of the direct Gatwick–Victoria Station rail link in their sales campaign.

Despite a number of headlines at the time to the contrary, the 'Interjet' network was not the first UK domestic jet service. For some time, it had been possible for enterprising passengers to travel to or from Heathrow by BOAC Comet 4 or 707 to Glasgow-Prestwick, or Manchester on aircraft calling in en route to or from trans-Atlantic flights.

British United were not the first independent airline to offer competition to BEA on trunk domestic services. British Eagle International Airlines had opened their own services from Heathrow to Belfast, Edinburgh and Glasgow in 1963, using Britannia and Viscount turbo-props. It also operated the London–Liverpool trunk route from Heathrow, in competition with Cambrian Airways, in whom BEA had a substantial shareholding.

British Eagle was led by a dedicated founder, Harold Bamberg, who had formed the company as Eagle Aviation in April 1948. Much like the founders of the BUA companies, Eagle grew steadily over the years, operating on the Berlin Airlift, trooping services to the Far East and Africa and pioneering scheduled and inclusive tour routes all over Europe.

British Eagle operated a large fleet of Britannias from Heathrow. MAP

Eagle's attempts to expand the scheduled service side of their business led to a series of battles with licensing authorities and the national corporations. Nonetheless, a small scheduled European network was eventually established, based at both London and Manchester.

Local subsidiaries were set up on the British island of Bermuda and in the Bahamas and operated successful scheduled services, using Viscounts and DC-6s to the USA. The success of these operations was all the more notable for being in direct competition with major US carriers, such as Eastern Airlines and Pan American World Airways. The Cunard Steamship Company had invested heavily in the company in 1960, leading to the establishment of a trans-Atlantic scheduled network from London to Bermuda and the Caribbean, linking the two halves of the rapidly expanding Eagle empire.

Cunard Eagle Airways, as the company had become, took delivery of the first of an order for two Boeing 707s, in 1962, the first independent UK company to operate a pure-jet. The jet was put into service on the Caribbean routes, replacing Britannias. The company also had ambitions to operate a scheduled London–New York jet service, but the licence, although awarded, was revoked after intervention by BOAC. Before the second 707 was delivered, Cunard came to an agreement with BOAC, merging the Atlantic routes into

the BOAC network and selling the 707s to the corporation. From then on, BOAC operated a number of its routes under the banner of BOAC-Cunard.

Furious that his trans-Atlantic ambitions had been thwarted by Cunard's apparent lack of nerve, Bamberg bought back their 60 per cent holding in February 1963. In August the company name was changed to British Eagle International Airlines and Bamberg set about rebuilding the company from the handful of DC-6s, Britannias and Viscounts that the Cunard/BOAC merger left him with.

As well as opening the trunk domestic routes in 1963, the Liverpool-based carrier, Starways, was taken over in early 1964. This brought British Eagle more valuable domestic routes from the northwest, based on Liverpool and the southwest, with a seasonal network to the Cornish commercial and tourist centre at Newquay. New European expansion, fed by the domestic network, took the company to Stuttgart, from London, as well as the established scheduled services to Dinard, Innsbruck, Jersey, La Baule, Luxembourg, Palma, Perpignan, Pisa and Rimini.

British Eagle's domestic ambitions were hampered by heavy frequency restrictions imposed by the licensing authorities. Frustrated at the lack of progress in increasing their domestic frequencies, following spirited opposition from BEA, British Eagle eventually ceased operations on the

Belfast and Edinburgh routes. Fortunately, the company had been more successful with other applications and was operating a total of seventeen scheduled routes out of London and a further fifteen routes from sixteen other UK cities. It also operated a large inclusive tour network both from London and the provincial airports. Bamberg had already ordered Series 300 One-Elevens, but, for once, politics intervened in British Eagle's favour and the opportunity arose for the airline to re-enter the jet age even earlier.

The two Series 200s ordered by the Central African Airways Corporation had been completed but their delivery had been delayed by Rhodesia's unilateral declaration of independence on 11 November 1965. CAA served the needs of Rhodesia, Zambia and Malawi, operating regional and domestic services within and from the three African states. The decision of the white-led government of Rhodesia caused turmoil in the region, international trading sanctions were imposed and the export licences were refused for the two One-Elevens. Central African Airways itself was soon split into three, bringing about the formation of Air Malawi, Air Rhodesia and Zambia Airways. The government of Zambia eventually accepted responsibility for the One-Elevens, but the country's political and financial circumstances were such that they were unable to accept delivery.

CAA's One-Elevens remained undelivered. Peter Vine
via Jennie Gradidge

(Below) **British Eagles leased G-ATTP, 'Swift', at Heathrow.** via Author

Instead, an eighteen-month lease was arranged with British Eagle. The agreement with Zambia included the setting up of maintenance facilities and assistance in training Zambian personnel. The first aircraft, now bearing the Zambian registration 9J-RCH, was delivered to British Eagle at Heathrow on 18 April 1966. There it was painted in British Eagle's One-Eleven livery, re-registered G-ATTP and named 'Swift'. On 2 May the aircraft operated a proving flight to Glasgow's new airport at Abbotsinch that opened that day, becoming the first jet to land there. Revenue One-Eleven services

began on the Heathrow–Glasgow route, replacing Britannias, on 9 May.

The ex-CAA aircraft were actually equipped with the Spey 25 Mk.511–14 engines of the Series 300, as were the RAAF aircraft. The CAA pair, though, also had a water-injection system to improve take-off performance. British United's Series 200s also had a water-injection system fitted to their Spey 2 Mk.506–14 powered One-Elevens, specifically to improve performance on the West African routes. Helmut Horten also took up the water-injection option offered for their Series 200. However, all the Spey 2

engined aircraft were later demodified and the system was made inoperable as it became surplus to requirements in the aircraft's day-to-day use.

The second ex-CAA aircraft, 9J-RCI, was also delivered to Heathrow, on 25 April, but instead of British Eagle's red and black colours, it was painted in a temporary Zambia Airways livery. After participating in British Eagle's crew training programme, 'CI was flown to Lusaka and demonstrated to its new owners. On 21 May the aircraft was back at Heathrow to begin its lease to British Eagle, who named it 'Serene' and placed it into revenue service on 27 May.

9J-RCI in temporary Zambia colours. Brian Stainer via Jennie Gradidge

On 28 May, the type had been operated on a new route to Tunis and Djerba and the next day it was introduced on flights to Luxembourg and Stuttgart. The 30th saw a One-Eleven used on the London–Dinard–La Baule route and by July the aircraft were also operating on flights to Liverpool, Newquay, Palma, Perpignan, Pisa and Rimini from London.

The three Series 300s whose delivery had been deferred, and finally cancelled by Kuwait Airways, also found a home with British Eagle in June and July. The aircraft were soon operating alongside the Series 200s on both scheduled and inclusive tour services. Both types flew in a 79-passenger configuration.

The reaction of BEA to the two independent upstarts introducing jets onto trunk routes was swift. Up until then, the limited incursion by British Eagle with their Britannias and Viscounts was not regarded as too much of a threat. BEA continued to operate turbo-prop Vanguards, on the trunk domestic services, supplemented by Viscounts at off-peak times. The arrival of the rival One-Elevens though, especially on British Eagle's head-to-head competition from Heathrow to Glasgow, led directly to a change in policy. On the day of Glasgow-Abbotsinch opening, 2 May 1966, BEA inaugurated DH Comet 4B jet services from Heathrow on morning and evening peak-time flights. The corporation claimed that it was doing so reluctantly, citing that it made little, if any profit with the Vanguard services to Glasgow and would lose more money with

Comets. BEA even claimed to have offered to ban jets on domestic services, in the cause of noise reduction, if the independent airlines did the same.

However, since March 1966 BEA had been actively studying the DC-9 Series 40 and Boeing 727 for the West Berlin-based Internal German Service, operated since 1946. It seemed, despite any BEA public relations protests to the contrary, that the short-haul, inter-city jet was recognized as being here to stay, with the BAC One-Eleven doing its very best to prove it. BAC's problem now was to keep the momentum going and make sure it had the product that the airlines were starting to clamour for – that is, a jet that could live up to its marketing claims and actually make money.

On return from Africa, 9J-RCI became G-ATVH, 'Serene'. Jennie Gradidge

CHAPTER THREE

Dispersion

The One-Eleven's main US rival, the Douglas DC-9, had made its maiden flight on 25 February 1965. Inevitable comparisons were being made between the two types. The One-Eleven at least had the advantage of being the first of the two into revenue service. The DC-9, though, was also able to exploit its huge home market, with both the large nationwide and small regional carriers being on the lookout for short-haul jets to replace their ageing piston and turbo-prop-powered fleets. Since Mohawk had successfully set the precedent for local service jet operations, the CAB was hardly in a position to continue voicing their objections to jets on economic grounds. Douglas had also made a wise decision in offering several versions and sizes of aircraft from the beginning. Although the three different types of One-Eleven then on offer were designed for different uses in different operational spheres, all three had identical capacity.

A stretched version of the DC-9, the Series 30, was available within a year of the initial, 90-seat, Series 10. Many carriers appreciated the flexibility, switching to the larger aircraft once the smaller type had established the profit potential of jets on the more local routes. Although offering the

American's series 401AKs moving down the Hurn production line. Brooklands Museum

range of types of DC-9 available increased Douglas's costs a great deal, it certainly helped sell aircraft and gave the company an eventual, substantial edge over BAC's offerings. The DC-9 was also designed with a larger freight hold and scheduled carriers in particular often regarded this as an advantage to the American aircraft, and a vital revenue-earning opportunity for them.

The Caravelle, the 'first generation' short-haul jet continued to sell throughout the 1960s and 70s, although in steadily decreasing numbers. Various modernized, stretched and re-engined versions were successfully produced. The arrival of the One-Eleven, the DC-9, and, later, more modern aircraft on the scene saw the demise of the design and the type was no longer being built by the early 1970s.

Europe's presence in the jet airliner market increased when the long-established and respected Dutch company, Fokker, revealed their option. The F.28 Fellowship was first announced in 1962, as a jet successor to the best-selling Fokker F.27 turbo-prop. Powered by Rolls-Royce Spey Mk.55-15 turbofans, development of the design was protracted though and the prototype did not fly until May 1967. The Fellowship was an early example of European multinational co-operation, with Fokker sub-contracting much of the aircraft's component construction to Shorts, in the UK, and Germany's MBB.

What was to become a more serious rival to both the One-Eleven and the DC-9 began to be on offer to airlines, just as the two pioneering types were starting to spread their wings over the world's commercial air routes. Despite the growing interest in the short-haul jet market, the Seattle-based Boeing Airplane Company had continued to concentrate on large-capacity and long-haul aircraft. Eventually bowing to commercial pressure, the Boeing 707 was redesigned as a medium-haul aircraft, the Boeing 720. The three-engined Boeing 727 soon followed, which snatched the initial advantage away from the pioneering Hawker-Siddeley Trident by offering more capacity and range and running off with most of the available market.

Boeing announced their entry into the short-haul market with the unveiling of the Boeing 737 design in February 1965. Unlike the BAC and Douglas rivals, the Boeing aircraft favoured wing-mounted engines. Despite the positioning of the engines, the 737 wing was still based largely on the T-tail, clean-winged 727. Linked with a triple-slotted flap/Krueger flap system, the aircraft was able to offer an excellent short-field performance.

Initially a 60-seater, the original concept grew to an aircraft capable of carrying 75–103 passengers. The 737 effectively completed the Boeing 'family' of jetliners, with the company able to offer aircraft ranging from intercontinental 707s, to the 737 for inter-city services. The commonality of components within the different Boeing types was certainly played upon by the marketing department, although in practice it was rather more limited. One major advantage that was inherited from the larger aircraft though was the fuselage cross-section. On the 737, this permitted six-abreast seating and gave a much roomier feel to the cabin than on either the One-Eleven or the DC-9.

The original Boeing 737, the Series 100, was to be delivered to West Germany's Lufthansa, Columbia's Avianca and to Malaysia-Singapore Airlines. Pacific Air Lines of San Francisco also ordered, but then cancelled, four Series 100s. An opportune six-foot stretch had brought forth the 115–130 passenger Series 200, to which the majority of airline interest immediately switched. This opened the floodgates for sales, with over a hundred Boeing 737-200s on order over two years before the first flight of the prototype was scheduled.

The One-Eleven's first developed version, the Series 300, had first taken to the air on 19 April 1966. There was no specific prototype, the first purely Series 300 aircraft being one of the three production aircraft originally intended for Kuwait Airways. The main difference over the Series 200 was the uprated engines and provision for extra fuel, permitting greater operating range. British Eagle, who had leased the trio of Kuwaiti aircraft, as well as taking delivery of two others in their own right, found this especially useful for new scheduled and charter services to North Africa and the Canaries.

Freddie Laker was the only other customer for the Series 300, although this time not on British United Airways' behalf. Laker had resigned from BUA in late 1965, already stating that he intended to start another airline 'one day'. That day came as soon as 8 February 1966 when he announced the formation of Laker Airways Ltd, to be based at Gatwick. Initially operations were intended to commence on 1 April 1967, utilizing three BAC One-Eleven 300s at a cost, with spares, of £4 million.

Laker Moves On

For a new independent British airline, especially one intending to specialize in the charter market, to consider acquiring brand-new aircraft to begin operations was unprecedented at that time. It spoke well of the financial institutions' faith in Freddie Laker that he was able to raise backing for such a venture so comparatively quickly. The faith extended to potential crews and staff. At one point, up to 100 letters a day were arriving from highly experienced applicants, many of them from both the State-owned corporations. One evening, Laker was telephoned at home from the captain of a night-stopping BEA crew in Zurich, applying for positions on behalf of the entire crew.

In fact, Laker had also considered operating Comets, several of which were available on the second-hand market, as well as investigating the possibility of ordering new Boeing 737s or DC-9s. However, the Comet, in Laker's opinion, had only five years' competitive life left and was too expensive to operate. The 737 was dismissed after comparing acquisition and operational costs with the home-grown One-Eleven. The DC-9 was actually discounted after comparisons showed no economic advantage over the British jet. Laker's involvement with the One-Eleven from its early days probably swayed his decision as well. He had worked with the British Aircraft Corporation and its predecessors for many years and undoubtedly had built up many useful working relationships with its staff and management.

However, Laker's name was to actually appear on an aircraft a year earlier than originally intended, in March 1966, when the first of a pair of ex-BOAC Britannia 102 turbo-props was delivered. The Britannias entered service in July, mainly operating *ad hoc* and sub-charters on behalf of other carriers. Air France leased one of the aircraft from July to September 1966 for use on its scheduled services, based at Paris-Orly.

Lord Brothers, a major inclusive tour holiday operator, signed Laker Airways' first contract for the supply of air transport for their 1967 programme. Worth in excess of £500,000, the contract guaranteed a minimum utilization of 1,700 hours for one One-Eleven for a year. The contract was the first of a new style of 'time charters' whereby the tour operator had exclusive use of an aircraft and the crews to fly it.

G-AVBW was Laker Airways' first One-Eleven. Brooklands Museum

Air Congo leased in One-Elevens from Laker Airways. Brooklands Museum

Lord Brothers were given guidelines for schedule planning, turnround times, overhaul and maintenance checks and so on, but were otherwise free to arrange an aircraft's flying hours to their requirements.

The 84-seat aircraft were nominally owned by Laker Airways (Leasing) Ltd, the parent company, with Laker Airways being the operating company. The three One-Elevens had been delivered in February, April and May 1967, with commercial jet operations beginning in March. One of the Laker One-Elevens was leased out to Air Congo for use on their regional scheduled network to neighbouring African states, as well as a domestic service from Kinshasa to Lubumbashi. The original aircraft entered service in May 1967 and was returned to the UK in February 1968. Another Laker One-Eleven took over the lease until May 1968.

Laker's One-Elevens were soon busy on IT charters. Aviation Hobby Shop

Back in the UK, Laker's other two One-Elevens were operating from the main base at Gatwick, as well as flying services from Manchester. The Britannias continued in service, with one being leased out briefly to a new operator, Treffield International Airways. When Treffield ceased operations suddenly in June 1967, Laker took over many of the company's inclusive tour contracts from Gatwick and East Midlands Airport. Laker also bought Arrowsmith Holidays during 1967, resulting in the One-Elevens and Britannias operating a series of tour flights from Liverpool.

During 1967, Laker Airways' first full year of operations, the Britannias and One-Elevens had flown 2,614,000 miles on 2,611 sectors totalling over 7,000 hours of flying. A fourth Series 300 was delivered in April 1968 and a Series 400 was leased from BAC during August and September 1968. This aircraft was operated in Bahamas Airways' colourful pastel livery, with temporary Laker Airways titles. Another Series 300 was acquired second-hand by Laker in 1969, followed by another in 1971.

Only nine of the Series 300s were to be built. In 1966 the upper weight limit for two-crew operation in the USA was lifted and all Series 400 aircraft could be certificated at the higher Series 300 weights. The first of two Series 300/400 development aircraft, G-ASYD, first flew on 13 July 1965, nine months before the first 'proper' series 300, followed by the second, G-ASYE, on 16 September. In practice both were Series 400s, with 'YD intended as a technical development airframe, undertaking tropical trials at Madrid from September. 'YE, on the other hand, was flown to Marshalls of Cambridge (Engineering), and fitted with an executive interior in the forward cabin and a representative airline configuration in the rear cabin. Page Airways International, the agent and distributor for any US sales, had commissioned the design of the executive fittings from Charles Butler Associates of New York.

G-ASYD was one of two Series 300/400 development aircraft. Jennie Gradidge

World Tours

Once this work was completed, between 5 and 12 November, the aircraft departed on the first of a series of marathon demonstration and sales tours. 'YE left Wisley on 17 November, bound for the USA, Mexico, Guatemala, Honduras, Nicaragua and El Salvador. Early in the tour, during December, 'YE was leased to American Airlines and used by them for crew training, prior to the delivery of their own first Series 400 on 23 December. The American FAA had granted a type certificate to the Series 400 on 22 November. Continuing on to Mexico and other Central American countries, 'YE was to fly a total of 50,000 miles before returning to the UK on 8 January 1966.

To help deal with demand, BAC set up a secondary production facility for the One-Eleven at Weybridge. In early 1966, six aircraft were completed there, alongside the VC-10 production lines.

There was only a brief respite before 'YE was off on its travels again, departing Wisley on 21 January. This time it was headed for New Zealand, visiting Italy, Syria, Bahrein, India, Thailand, Singapore, Indonesia and Australia en route. Once in New Zealand, the aircraft flew over 700

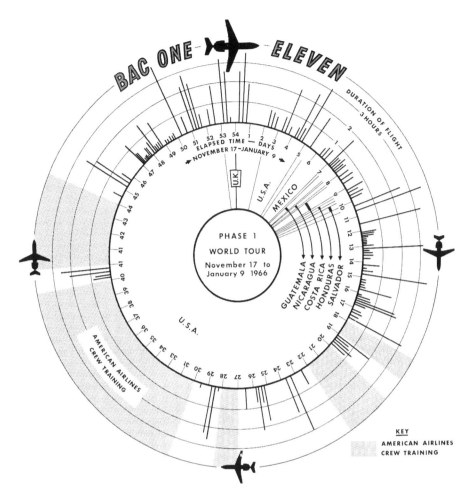

(Above) **The first phase of G-ASYE's world tour.** Brooklands Museum

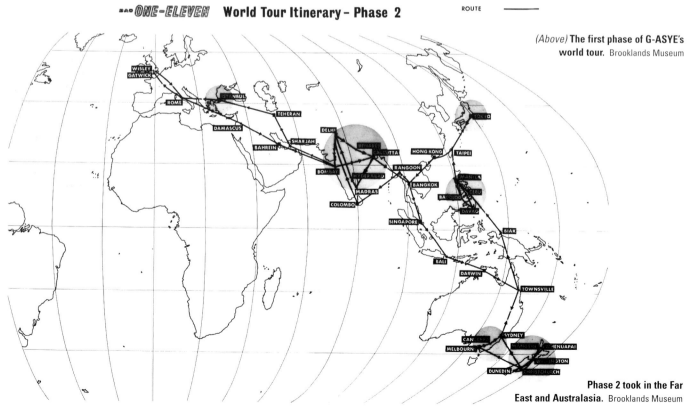

Phase 2 took in the Far East and Australasia. Brooklands Museum

passengers, including the Prime Minister and Governor General, on demonstration flights, including an appearance at an airshow at Mangere, where a 'Farnborough-type' flying display was given.

The corporation personnel had been joined by several UK government officials who hoped to be able to persuade the New Zealand government to order up to six One-Elevens to replace the National Airways Corporation's fleet of Viscounts. Unfortunately, their strategy backfired in the local press. The presence of the UK ministry officials, including Mr John Stonehouse, then Parliamentary Secretary to the Minister of Civil Aviation, was misconstrued as an attempt to blackmail the New Zealanders into ordering the British jet in return for more favourable trading terms.

Australia was visited next, with a week's worth of demonstrations taking in Canberra, Melbourne and Sydney. Although two aircraft had already been ordered for Royal Australian Air Force VIP work, no airline orders were to be forthcoming from Australia. 'YE then moved on to the Philippines and operated several passenger flights over the routes of Philippine Air Lines, who had already placed an order for Series 400s. The PAL demonstrations took in the regional airports at Bacolod, Cebu and Davau as well as the main base at Manila.

The tour then continued to Japan, with more demonstrations at Taipei en route. After three days base at Tokyo, the aircraft then flew to Hong Kong, again via Taipei, where both 'YE and the crew and personnel took a well-earned three-day break. The

(Above) **G-ASYE was demonstrated to a number of Japanese carriers at Tokyo.** Brooklands Museum

G-ASYE called at Gatwick en route home to Wisley.
Brooklands Museum

return leg of the marathon trip took the One-Eleven to Colombo, via Bangkok and Rangoon, with demonstrations all along the way. Four days were then spent flying around India, visiting Benares, Bombay, Calcutta, Delhi, Hyderabad and Madras. Sharjah, Teheran, Istanbul and Rome were all called into after leaving India and 'YE finally landed at Gatwick on 8 March within minutes of the scheduled arrival time.

The One-Eleven had been away from the UK for 47 days, during which 125 flights had been made over 70,000 miles, carrying over 2,700 passengers. 'YE had never once dropped behind schedule and the Spey engines had been free from any mechanical problems throughout the tour. Thirty pilots from different airlines, most of them with little or no jet experience, had taken the controls of 'YE on demonstrations to their employers.

Barely a month passed before 'YE left on the last of the three trips that were to make up the One-Eleven's world tour. The aircraft left Wisley on 5 April and headed west to Keflavik, Gander, Bermuda and Nassau in the Bahamas. The first demonstration flights took place around the Bahamas and to Florida. The tour then continued southwards to Port of Spain and Brazil, where the aircraft took up temporary residence at Rio's Galeao Airport. From there demonstrations were made to the Brazilian domestic airlines, taking in Belem, Brasilia, Sao Paulo, Urububunga, Londrina, Porto Alegre and Curitiba. Ascunsion in Paraguay, Montevideo in Uruguay, Argentina's Buenos Aires, Chile's Santiago, and Lima in Peru were visited next, providing a wide range of airport standards and operational difficulties to be successfully overcome. The Peruvian President, Fernando Belaunde, was taken on one flight, after which, at his own instigation, the President gave a broadcast talk on his impressions.

The Peruvian regional airports at Cuzco and Arequipa were called into en route to Quito in Ecuador. At Cuzco, 10,500 feet above sea level, one-engine touch-and-goes were demonstrated. Then it was on to Bogota in Columbia and Caracas in Venezuela. A domestic Venezuelan flight was then operated from Caracas to Barquisimeto before 'YE returned to Port of Spain. The eventual return to Wisley, on 1 May, was made via Nassau, New York, Chicago, Montreal, Goose Bay and Keflavik. As well as rarified Andean elevations, temperatures varying from tropical jungle heat and stifling humidity, to

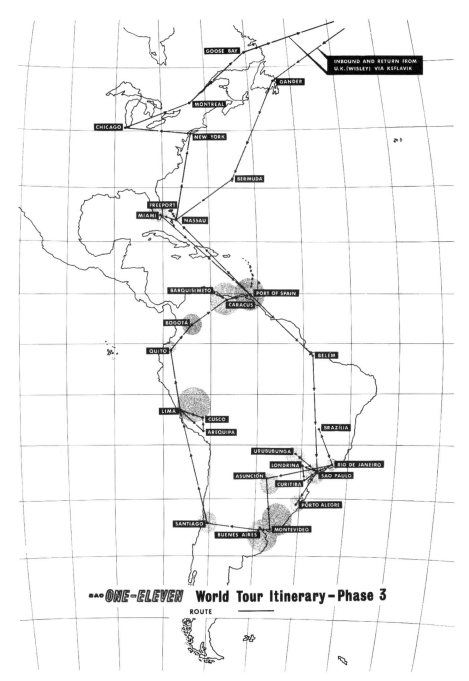

The final phase, including South America and the Caribbean. Brooklands Museum

bitter Arctic cold were among the various extremes encountered by 'YE on this tour.

While 'YE had been busy notching up over 160,000 miles on its three-part world tour, sister ship 'YD had been far from idle. A great deal of development flying for the Series 400 certification had been completed and on 7 July flight trials were begun for Category 2 clearance for low-visibility landings.

Astrojets Enter Service

Following the lease of 'YE for training, American Airlines had started to take delivery of their Series 400s from December 1965. Training of American's flight crews had begun with an initial course for nine pilots in October 1965 at Wisley. Ground school training for the majority of the American crews to be transferred to the

American Airlines began to take delivery in December 1966. Brooklands Museum

The cabin of the '400 Astrojet' felt spacious. American Airlines CR Smith Museum

One-Eleven opened at New York (Kennedy) a month later. The three-and-a-half week lease of G-ASYE saw the first flight training in December. Over 200 pilots needed to be trained to operate the thirty aircraft ordered, and most checked out in a maximum of 10–12 hours actual flying, following ground school. A digital simulator was scheduled for delivery in July 1966 to supplement the training programme.

Between 22 February and 1 March 1966, a familiarization programme took in thirteen American Airlines destinations, visiting Baltimore, Boston, Buffalo, Chicago, Cleveland, Detroit, Hartford, Newark, Philadelphia, Rochester, Syracuse, Toronto and Washington (National). The first scheduled service opened on 6 March over the New York–Toronto route, followed by New York–Syracuse, in direct competition with the Mohawk One-Eleven Series 200s, on the 28th.

The American Airlines aircraft, designated '400 Astrojets', were to be true short-haulers, with the longest sector planned being the 500-mile Boston–Detroit route. Eleven daily round trips were scheduled to operate between New York and Buffalo from April and the Boston–New York–Washington corridor was to be a major market for the American's One-Elevens.

American's loads on the Boston–New York route, in particular, had been suffering from the competition of Eastern Airlines' legendary no-reservation 'Shuttle' service that had been in operation between New York, Washington and Boston since 1961. Eastern took advantage of their owning a large fleet of fully paid for Lockheed Super Constellations to have a cheap back-up aircraft available to carry any extra passengers that turned up once the first aircraft was full. Lockheed Electras had replaced the Constellations on the Shuttle and had almost wiped out the competition from American with their more conventional style of service. However, electing to fight back rather than drop the service, from 12 February 1967, American promoted the routes as the 'Jet Express'. The One-Elevens offered hourly service with confirmed reservations and the option of a first-class fare, with the forward four rows on the One-Eleven being reserved for 16 higher paying passengers.

Never let it be said that US carriers would let a publicity opportunity slip away and American, not surprisingly, laid on a media presence for the first flight. However, as the first flight was to be on a Sunday morning, the revenue load booked was not a high one. The media reports of an empty aircraft would not have given a good impression, so a couple of dozen off-duty American Airlines employees were recruited to make up the numbers of the first 'Jet Express' load of passengers. American need not have worried too much though, as load factors for the first few weeks were in the 70 per cent range, which remained the norm for the rest of the life of the 'Jet Express' service.

Although on such routes, the time saving of the jet One-Elevens over the turboprop Electras was minimal, American managed to make their presence felt. Until the introduction of 'Jet Express', American had been struggling to carry about 9,000 passengers per month between New York and Boston. By 1969 this figure had grown to 50,000 a month.

Washington (National), with its downtown location and restricted runways, only allowed jets to use it from 24 April 1966, and on that day American opened six nonstop flights from Boston. The lifting of the jet ban also allowed Braniff to open their

La Guardia Airport was America's main One-Eleven base. Brooklands Museum

One-Eleven service to National from Dallas and Mohawk also routed more of their Series 200s on flights through National as more aircraft were delivered.

Although the One-Eleven was their first twin jet, American was certainly no stranger to pure-jet operations. As one of the biggest and longest established members of the US airline industry, four-engined Boeing 707s, 720s and Convair 990A jets had been operating on American's trans-continental services for several years. The airline had been a launch customer for the three-engined Boeing 727 jet and had been flying them on medium-haul and busy inter-city routes since 1964.

The One-Elevens, along with more 727s on order, were mostly to be used to replace the remaining piston-engined aircraft still in American's fleet. Over forty piston-engined DC-6s and DC-7s were still in use in 1966. The One-Elevens were also used to supplement or replace larger jets or turboprop Lockheed Electras on some routes. Although the Electras were undoubtedly

economic aircraft, they suffered from the increasing passenger prejudice against any type that was powered by propellers. Some of American's Electras had been sold on after as little as three or four years' frontline service, as the earlier jets had been delivered.

Since first taking an interest in the BAC 107 concept at the 1960 SBAC Farnborough Show, American Airlines had a great influence over the final Series 400 design, much as Freddie Laker's BUA had done for the Series 200. From mid-1961 onwards, American's engineers were able to evaluate the developing detail design and projected maintenance costs and reliability. An American Airlines engineering team took up residence in the UK and, like similar teams from Mohawk and Braniff, were able to instigate several improvements and refinements, favouring American's operational needs that were often incorporated by BAC into the One-Eleven both as standard and customer options. As the first modern foreign-built aircraft operated by

American, the engineering team emphasized particularly high standards on delivery. This resulted in a high-quality product and generally benefited the One-Eleven programme as a whole.

Detail structural innovations that came about included an improvement in the appearance of both the forward and ventral airstairs. The ventral airstairs were now also fitted with spring assistance for emergency operation. Stainless steel scuff plates were fitted around the sills of all loading doors and screw-on panels were fitted on the inboard flap sections to allow easy replacement in the event of damage from stones thrown up by the undercarriage. A centre fuel tank took advantage of the Series 400's higher weight limits. As well as allowing longer range and less refuelling required on transit stops, the extra tankage also allowed for longer holding times over congested or weather-affected airports, both common occurrences on American's east-coast network.

In the 69-seat cabin, a Dreyfus-designed interior was fitted, coloured mainly in beige, dull gold and red and the sidewall panels were attractively styled with an alternate diagonal 'straw' pattern. If required, by removing some of the forward galley units, an extra seating row could be installed and an extra passenger window fitted in that area. Public address speakers were fitted into the overhead racks, instead of the headline position used on earlier One-Elevens. Drop-out oxygen systems and a double capacity domestic water system were also fitted first in the American Airlines '400 Astrojets'.

In the cause of commonality with other aircraft in its fleet, the One-Elevens were equipped with a great deal of US-built systems. Hydro-Air Hytrol Mk 2 anti-skid units, as originally used on American's Convair 990As and Boeing 727s, were used, with Bendix wheels and thickened brake pads.

The flight certification programme for the Series 400 had involved not only the Series 300/400 development aircraft, G-ASYD and 'YE, but also American's first aircraft off the production line, N5015, that had first flown on 4 November 1965. Over 400 hours were flown during the development programme, a quarter of which, much of the performance-related work, was carried out at Madrid. Over 100 of American's training, production, maintenance and flight personnel passed through BAC's service schools at Weybridge and

American's One-Elevens were in competition with TWA's DC-9s. Brooklands Museum

Hurn during 1965. BAC instructors also monitored the first courses run by the American Airlines personnel once they had returned to the US to train their colleagues. American's One-Eleven operations was to be centred at New York's La Guardia Airport. A One-Eleven steering committee had begun preparation for the '400 Astrojets' as early as 1963, at the carrier's maintenance centre at Tulsa, later transferring to La Guardia before operations began. A progressive maintenance programme, similar to one already in operation for the Boeing 727, was designed for the One-Eleven by BAC and the other US One-Eleven operators and had been approved by the FAA in 1964.

After a month of One-Eleven operations, with the first fifteen of the thirty ordered aircraft already in service, American's operations staff were able to report a remarkable technical delay rate of nil. The airline's maintenance organization generously attributed this to BAC's *'excellent support'* and there had also been much favourable passenger reaction to the new British jet.

In light of the success of the Vickers Viscount in the US earlier, BAC already had a well-established product support programme in place. An after-sales service facility had been established at Arlington, Virginia, alongside Washington (National) Airport in the 1950s. Fully adapted to cater for the One-Eleven, the facility employed over 70 staff and had 48,000 sq ft of warehouse space available.

Another tradition inherited from the Viscount saw the convening of the first One-Eleven operators meeting, at the East Cliff Hotel, Bournemouth on 14–15 March, 1966. This followed a similar meeting arranged by Rolls-Royce at Derby on 10–11 March, concerned with Spey maintenance and overhaul. Thirty senior engineering representatives of thirteen One-Eleven customers attended the intensive symposium at Bournemouth. They met with thirty BAC senior design and servicing personnel and representatives of fifteen British and US equipment vendors.

The One-Eleven featured strongly in a tour of North America by HRH Prince Philip, the Duke of Edinburgh, also in

Patty Poulsen was appointed 'Miss 400 Astrojet'. American Airlines CR Smith Museum

Aloha welcomed their first One-Eleven in April 1966. Aloha Airlines

March. The Committee for Exports to the USA was able to arrange for the Duke to meet the president of Braniff and lunch with him and top executives of the airline during his stay in Dallas. During the tour, the Duke and his party flew by Braniff One-Eleven between Houston and Dallas and then from Dallas to Tucson, Mohawk One-Eleven between Toronto and Ottawa and by American One-Eleven from Chicago to New York-Kennedy. The royal sampling of the One-Eleven services of all the US operators gave the programme a much appreciated publicity boost.

Yet another US carrier joined the ranks of One-Eleven operators a month later, with Aloha Airlines, of Honolulu, Hawaii, taking delivery of the first of an eventual fleet of three Series 200s on 15 April. Aloha was engaged on a never-ending equipment war with its main rival, Hawaiian Airlines and saw the One-Eleven as a chance to keep up.

Until the arrival of the One-Eleven, Aloha had pitched Fairchild F-27s, and a few second-hand Series 700 Viscounts against Hawaiian's piston-engined DC-3s, a mixture of piston and turbo-prop-powered Convairliners and their own small fleet of Viscounts. A DC-6C was also used by Hawaiian, supplementing the smaller aircraft on the inter-island network and also operating longer ranging charters, usually carrying Hawaiian-based military personnel. The two carriers had been bitter rivals since Aloha had been formed, initially operating as Trans Pacific Airlines, in 1946.

The name Trans Pacific had reflected the company's early, unfulfilled ambitions to operate across the Pacific to Asia. Nonetheless TPA eventually began operations as an inter-island operator and it was in this field that the company was destined to make its name. Previously enjoying a monopoly, Hawaiian had fought every attempt by TPA to gain scheduled certification and the new carrier was restricted to operating only charter flights for several years. However, TPA gained popular support through a ready flair for publicity and a staff recruiting policy that went against the then established practice of a racially based bias. Up until then, and probably for many years afterwards, most of the plum jobs on the islands were traditionally, though for the most part unspokenly, reserved for Caucasians. TPA's founders came from the oriental and native population and went out of their way to give employment opportunities to the undervalued ethnic groups.

In their supporters' minds, the initials 'TPA' soon came to stand for 'The People's Airline' and certification for scheduled flights was finally granted after many lengthy and protracted court actions both for and against the company. At one point,

cabin service as was possible on the short inter-island flights.

Aloha's early use of the popular F-27, built by Fairchild under licence from Fokker, against the Convairs of Hawaiian, gave the airline a new competitive edge. The acquisition of the Viscounts had been intended to offer a higher capacity while

own. However, Hawaiian eventually introduced DC-9s shortly before the Aloha One-Elevens entered service, and all their Convairs were eventually upgraded to jet-prop power by having their piston engines replaced by Rolls-Royce Darts.

Aloha's first two 79-seat Series 200s were delivered in April and June 1966, the first one opening the airline's first pure-jet service in April. Despite encountering weight restrictions that limited revenue loads on flights into some airports on their network, Aloha was impressed enough with their One-Elevens to convert an option for a third to a firm order that was delivered in May, 1967. Further options were also taken out for two more. The third Aloha One-Eleven was exhibited by BAC at the Paris Air Show in May 1967 before the long delivery flight to Honolulu.

While only operating their first One-Eleven, Aloha was operating an average of twenty sectors a day, many of them lasting less than 25 minutes. On the mainland, Braniff's fleet was averaging 14 sectors per aircraft per day, with no back-up aircraft rostered. Mohawk's five delivered aircraft were also averaging up to 14 sectors a day each, with five- to ten-minute turnrounds commonplace throughout the system. To aid quick turnrounds, Mohawk's aircraft were fitted with brake-cooling fans. Mohawk also reported a 27 per cent increase in passenger traffic in the first three months of 1966 and mainly attributed this to the One-Eleven operation.

On 31 March, Mohawk had taken the next step in its modernization plan by taking delivery of the first of a fleet of Fairchild FH-227s. A stretched version of the licence-built F-27, the new 52-passenger prop-jets complemented Mohawk's One-Elevens on local service routes, feeding passengers into the denser jet routes. Powered by Darts, the FH-227s hastened the replacement of the remaining piston-engined Convairs and offered the prospect of Mohawk eventually operating an all Rolls-Royce powered fleet. In May, Mohawk took the important step of becoming an active member of the International Air Transport Association (IATA).

Helmut Horten had taken delivery of the first executive configured One-Eleven in January 1966. This was followed by delivery of another Series 200 executive aircraft to Tenneco, previously the Tennessee Gas Transmission Company, in April. After its work for BAC was over, the much travelled Series 300/400 development aircraft,

Aloha's One-Elevens specialized in ultra-short flights. Brooklands Museum

Hawaiian was even driven to make an abortive attempt to buy out their upstart rival. The certification began a fierce head-to-head commercial rivalry between the two airlines operating on almost identical route networks. TPA was eventually renamed Aloha Airlines, derived from a long-established marketing slogan. Both carriers upgraded their DC-3 fleets, fitting large panoramic windows to allow better views of the lush Hawaiian scenery for tourists and offering as high a standard of

retaining the jet-prop advantage. Unfortunately, they turned out not to be too popular with either crews or passengers. The pilots complained that the Viscounts flew 'like a truck' and the passengers were less than impressed with the high capacity, and therefore rather cramped, seating. Hawaiian also introduced Viscounts, as an interim measure, in an effort to update their image against Aloha. At one point Hawaiian had entered into negotiations with BAC for a fleet of One-Elevens of their

Mohawk's home base was Utica, New York State. Brooklands Museum

Helmut Hortens D-ABHH was the first executive One-Eleven. Brooklands Museum

G-ASYE, still in its half executive, half airline style configuration, was delivered to Victor Comptometer, also of the USA. Both Tenneco and Victor Comptometer were previous Viscount customers.

Tragic Days

Sadly, the pioneering US carriers were to experience the first fatal accidents to commercially operated One-Elevens. On 6 August 1966, Braniff's N1553 was operating a typical day's work for the carrier's One-Eleven fleet. Operating a New Orleans–Shreveport–Fort Smith–Tulsa–Kansas City–Omaha–Minneapolis multi-stop service, the aircraft exploded in the air and crashed near Falls City, Nebraska, during the Kansas City–Omaha sector, after being seen to fly into a cloud bank. All on board perished.

Ten months later, on 23 June 1967, Mohawk's N1116J, 'Discover America', suffered an in-flight fire in the tail section and crashed at Blossburg, Pennsylvania, killing the four crew and thirty passengers. A malfunctioning non-return valve, near the air inlet area in front of the APU, had allowed engine bleed air to flow through an open air delivery valve. The hot air had ignited sound-proofing material, which in turn melted hydraulic lines. The fire had burned away the spars holding the empennage and caused the break-up of

D-ABHH boasted an exceptionally comfortable cabin. Brooklands Museum

the aircraft. In view of the cause of this accident, all the eighty One-Elevens then in service were examined, and the wear and damage was found to be common on many of the non-return valves; swift corrective action was taken to prevent another occurrence.

The first eastern hemisphere operation of the One-Eleven, with Philippine Airlines, had opened on 1 May 1966. The first of an order for three Series 400s had been handed over at Wisley on 12 April. As well as busier domestic flights from Manila to Bacolod, Cebu and Davao, the

Braniff's N1553 crashed in 1966. Peter Vine via Jennie Gradidge

aircraft also flew internationally to Hong Kong and Taipei. PAL's 72-seater One-Elevens supplemented established Viscount 700s, in service since 1957, and Fokker F.27s. Fares on the three types were set at a slightly higher 'Rolls-Royce' rate and tickets on the One-Elevens' jet services carried a fixed surcharge over that.

Philippines Airlines was facing an ongoing struggle with numerous independent carriers, especially on domestic flights. Most of the rival companies had doubtful operating standards and questionable safety records. Nonetheless, the travelling public appreciated the low fares and although PAL was operating more modern equipment, they flocked to the new independents' ticket desks. Internationally too, PAL was facing increasingly stiff competition from major operators. The company's initial trans-Pacific service to San Francisco had only recently been reopened after PAL was forced off the route several years earlier by mounting losses. PAL looked upon the introduction of the One-Eleven, with the use of new DC-8s on long-range services and Fokker F.27s on local routes, as the start of a 'new era' and new beginning in the commercial fight against its rivals.

The last month of 1966 saw the One-Eleven entering scheduled service in Central America, with TACA International Airways of El Salvador taking delivery of the first of a pair of Series 400s. The 74-seaters opened jet services on routes from San Salvador to other regional capitals, the Caribbean and as far as Miami and New Orleans. Both LACSA (Lineas Aereas Costaricenses), of Costa Rica, and

PAL's One-Elevens entered service on busy local routes. Brooklands Museum

TACA International and LANICA both introduced One-Elevens. Brooklands Museum

LACSA One-Eleven 409AY, TI-1056C, in a typical Central American setting. Brooklands Museum

LANICA (Lineas Aereas de Nicaragua) of Nicaragua, both took delivery of Series 400s in April 1967. LANICA had actually leased an Aer Lingus Series 200 from October 1966 to April 1967, conveniently coinciding with the European carrier's low traffic season. Delivered in basic Aer Lingus livery with LANICA titles, the aircraft was placed on the Nicaraguan register and entered revenue service on the Miami–Managua route on 1 November. The operation of LANICA's leased Series 200 and, later, the 400 was shared with TAN (Transportes Aereos Nacionales SA), of Honduras. On the joint services to Miami, both companies were responsible for selling 50 per cent of the capacity. TAN also flew the aircraft to Belize and

Mexico City from the Honduran capital, Tegucigalpa.

The Central American carriers were replacing a variety of older types with the One-Elevens. As well as the ubiquitous Viscounts and Convairs, large piston-powered airliners such as DC-6s and DC-7s were completely replaced or sidelined to less important routes by the new jets. Up until then, the image of the airlines in Central America had suffered from a reputation for operating old-fashioned aircraft, usually having been handed down after heavy use by one or more previous owners. The arrival of the One-Elevens meant that the cash-strapped governments could finally boast a national carrier able to attract the prestige brought about by modern jet operations.

South American Debut

Argentina became the first South American home for One-Elevens, when the independent airline, Austral, placed their first of four Series 400s into service in October 1967. Competing against state-owned Aerolineas Argentinas, the One-Elevens replaced or supplemented Austral's C-46 and DC6 piston-engined aircraft on trunk services to South and West Argentina. The use of the British jets led to great increases in the company's traffic share.

Austral was associated with another Argentinian airline, ALA (Aerotransportes Litoral Argentina), which placed its own One-Eleven 400s in service on routes north of Buenos Aires from December

Austral's One-Elevens competed against the national carrier. Brooklands Museum

PP-SRT was the first VASP One-Eleven. Brooklands Museum

1968. For the most part, Aerolineas had previously operated turbo-prop Avro/HS 748s and the occasional Caravelle jet where it competed against Austral or ALA, and was forced to investigate the possibility of obtaining more short-haul jets of their own.

Brazil followed closely on Argentina's heels, with VASP (Viacao Aerea Sao Paulo) having taken delivery of the first of a pair of Series 400s in December 1967. VASP was an established BAC customer, having operated a large fleet of Viscounts, of both the 700 and 810 series, for several years. The Sao Paulo-based airline had been planning on operating a fleet of ten Handley Page Dart Heralds, having placed an order in April 1965. With the acquisi-

sonal services to the Channel Islands, Belgium, the Netherlands and France. These continued to be operated by the established turbo-prop fleet of Viscounts and HS-748s, although the One-Eleven was regularly seen on some busier schedules when additional capacity was required. An experimental 'bus stop' service from Southend to Scotland was proposed. Approval for the service had already been approved by the ATLB back in May 1967, but it was not until October that a proving flight was made over the route.

Curiously, the One-Eleven was used on the proving flight, routing Southend–Luton–East Midlands–Leeds–Teesside–Newcastle–Edinburgh–Aberdeen, carry-

traffic. Although planned to be mostly used on longer ranging inclusive tour work, the One-Eleven followed Channel's high-density tradition, with no less than 99 seats being fitted in the second aircraft to be delivered. To allow this exceptionally high-capacity seating, the highest in any short body One-Eleven, an extra emergency exit was fitted each side of the fuselage.

For the second season of Channel's jet operations, the One-Eleven was to be joined by the first of a fleet of Trident 1Es. The third Channel One-Eleven arrived in June 1968, bringing the operational fleet up to two. Noise complaints and runway restrictions at Southend had led to the move of the jet fleet to Stansted. More

Channel's second One-Eleven featured extra over-wing emergency exits. MAP

tion of the One-Elevens though, the order was cancelled, with displaced Viscounts moving to the regional routes that the Heralds had been intended for.

Back in Europe, Channel Airways, based at Southend, had introduced a single Series 400 onto inclusive tour work on 16 June 1967 with a night-time Southend–Palma charter. The One-Eleven, G-AVGP, operated charters from Southend to Ibiza, Malaga, Palma and Tangier. Initially ordering four One-Elevens, with an option on a further two, Channel actually took delivery of the second aircraft after it had returned the original to BAC in May 1968.

As well as charters, Channel operated a scheduled network, mostly with highly sea-

ing press and council officials. The actual scheduled service was to be operated by the Viscounts and 748s, although financial considerations led to the inauguration being further delayed until January 1969. Even then the route only lasted until November when Channel finally called a halt, the by then renamed 'Scottish Flyer' having amassed losses of over £160,000.

Channel Airways had been a pioneer in inclusive tour charter work and had previously operated large fleets of DC-3s, Vikings, HS-748s and Viscounts of various marks, as well as a single DC-4. The company had pioneered the use of very high-density configurations on their passenger fleet, somewhat justified by the ultra short-haul nature of much of their cross-Channel

destinations were served, with Athens, Barcelona, Djerba, Faro, Gerona, Ibiza, Jerez, Lisbon, Las Palmas, Mahon, Malaga, Malta, Naples, Palma, Pula, Rimini, Rome, Split, Titograd, Tunis, and Venice featuring in the 1968 jet programme. The One-Elevens and Tridents also flew services from Bristol, Cardiff, East Midlands, Manchester and Teesside, as well as Stansted.

German charter carrier, Bavaria Fluggesellschaft, leased a Philippine Airlines Series 400, via BAC, prior to delivery of their own ordered aircraft. Delivered in March 1967, the leased One-Eleven was operated on inclusive tour charters until October, supplementing the airline's established fleet of Dart Heralds. Bavaria's first owned One-Eleven was delivered to their Munich base in late December. This was joined by a second leased aircraft from mid-May 1968 until it was replaced by yet another leased aircraft, originally intended to be Channel Airways' fourth before the order was cancelled, which was operated from June to November.

An important order, whose significance would become more apparent in later years, was signed on 26 February 1967. The Romanian state carrier, TAROM (Transporturile Aeriene Romane), placed an order for six Series 400s. The first aircraft was delivered in June 1968 and TAROM, the first European customer for the One-Eleven, began services on 20 June with a Bucharest–Frankfurt service. Two days later, the new Bucharest–London Gatwick route was opened with the One-Elevens.

The ex-Central African Airways aircraft came to the end of their lease to British Eagle at the end of 1967. After their long-awaited delivery to Lusaka, the pair of Series 200s were placed into Zambia

Airways service on scheduled flights to Dar-es-Salaam, Nairobi and Lubumbashi from 1 January 1968. British Eagle had actually leased out one of the Series 200s to Swissair from April to November 1967, replacing it with a Series 300 until the end of April 1968. In August 1967, another British Eagle Series 300 had been leased to Scandinavian Airlines System, in full SAS livery, again to be replaced by another identical aircraft in December, until March 1968. KLM, Royal Dutch Airlines, followed the

TAROM's 424EU, YR-BCA opened the Bucharest–Gatwick route. Brooklands Museum

Swissair leased G-ATVH from British Eagle. Brooklands Museum

example of their Swiss and Scandinavian colleagues, by leasing yet another British Eagle Series 300, in full KLM colours, from March to October 1968. Probably much to BAC's quiet satisfaction, the leases of the One-Elevens had been brought about by the late delivery of DC-9-30s. Swissair flew their aircraft from Zurich to Dusseldorf, Nice and Prague, SAS used theirs mostly between Copenhagen and Zurich

were handed over in January 1968. As well as their domestic transport duties, the aircraft took part in extensive diplomatic tours of the Far East. Initially the aircraft were configured with two separate cabins, seating 26 and 30 respectively. This was later changed to a VVIP layout, with the cabin being modified so that the aircraft could only seat 28. Another private aircraft was completed in late 1967, with a

in an executive layout, the other with 24 first-class-style seats. The cabins had been fitted out by Marshalls of Cambridge. The aircraft operated on Government and military VIP work, flying their pampered passengers around the vast country of Brazil and to neighbouring nations.

Another UK operator introduced the One-Eleven into charter service in time for the 1968 summer season. Three Series 400s

RAAF and FAB VIP One-Elevens. N. Parnell via Jennie Gradidge/Brooklands Museum

and the KLM One-Eleven specialized in the Rotterdam–Heathrow service.

Military Deliveries

As the increasingly busy production line at Hurn rolled on, the end of 1967 saw the first flights of the two Series 200s for the Royal Australian Air Force. Both aircraft

Series 400 being delivered to Engelhard Industries Inc. via US agent, Page Airways. This corporate aircraft was delivered with a standard 74-passenger, airline-style configuration, although this was later changed to a VIP interior.

The Brazilian Forca Aerea Brasiliera, placed the first of their two VIP One-Eleven Series 400s in service in late 1968. Both aircraft had two separate cabins, one

were delivered to Autair International Airways of Luton in February, March, and May. Founded as a helicopter charter company in 1955, Autair had started fixed-wing operations from Luton in 1960, with a single DC-3. Swift expansions over the following years saw Autair International Airways establish itself as a major operator in the inclusive tour market. Over 70 per cent of Autair's 1968 capacity was sold to

Clarksons Holidays, both companies now being owned by the shipping company, Court Line. Autair had previously operated Vikings, Airspeed Ambassadors and HS-748s on the charter services, as well as opening scheduled services from Luton Airport to various points in the North of England and Scotland, and from the North to Amsterdam and the Channel Islands. A second-hand fleet of Dart Heralds had started to replace the 748s on these routes during 1967.

Although investing a great deal of time and money into the scheduled network, charters remained Autair's bread-and-butter work. Although never seriously intended to operate on Autair's schedules, BAC actually demonstrated a One-Eleven over the Luton–Teesside route. Suitable jets had been sought since early 1967, with Boeing making a serious presentation of their 737 twin-jet to Autair at one point. However, BAC were able to propose some very favourable lease-financing terms, greatly influencing Autair's final choice and the £3 million contracts were signed on 25 February 1967.

Ground and flying training for Autair's pilots on the One-Eleven was carried out for Autair by British United at Gatwick. Once they had gained certification on the jets, the Autair crews built up their One-Eleven experience and hours, while waiting for their own fleet to be delivered, by operating on BUA's scheduled and charter network on their Series 200s.

The delivery of the first Autair One-Eleven was planned with a military-style precision. G-AVOF, 'Halcyon Dawn', was scheduled to arrive at Luton Airport at midday on 8 February. For several days before, a careful check was made on actual and forecast weather conditions. Being February, it was feared that low cloud, fog, snow, or crosswinds – none of these conditions being strangers to the hilltop Luton Airport – would cause disruption. However, in the end, the delivery from Hurn, via Wisley, passed off without incident and well on schedule.

Operated in an 89-passenger configuration, the Autair One-Elevens were mostly responsible for the company carrying a total of over 270,000 inclusive tour passengers in 1968. For 1969, four of their own One-Eleven Series 400s were in operation, plus a fifth leased from BAC. This aircraft was the ex-Channel Airways aircraft, G-AVGP, now in full Autair colours. 'GP only operated commercially

for Autair International over the busy weekend periods, spending the rest of the week with BAC at Wisley, busily training pilots for new One-Eleven customers.

During August 1969, one of Autair's One-Elevens set a utilization record, flying 402 hours, 36 minutes. This averaged 13 hours' flying per day, exceptional even in the busiest holiday month of the year. It

East and Australia came to an end in March, but the summer inclusive tour season was ahead and looked to keep the company profitable. Unfortunately, severe currency restrictions on foreign travel deterred many potential passengers from taking holidays abroad and the company suffered over a million pounds worth of inclusive tour cancellations.

Autair's staff visited their new aircraft at Hurn. via Janine Redmond

also served as a remarkable testament to the reliability of the One-Eleven in the high-pressure environment of short-haul operations.

Eagle Grounded

One established One-Eleven operator was fated to fall by the wayside though. British Eagle entered 1968 with an optimistic outlook. Two Boeing 707s had been acquired second-hand from QANTAS with a brand-new aircraft on order. The company had reopened services to the Caribbean, albeit charters, and applications were on file for new trans-Atlantic scheduled services. Large government contracts for trooping and immigrant flights to the Far

However, the scheduled and charter flying programmes continued, with the One-Elevens operating on both networks. Despite the cancellations, the fleet was still operating schedules and charters from Heathrow to Alghero, Dinard, Djerba, Ibiza, Istanbul, Gerona, Glasgow, La Baule, Liverpool, Luxembourg, Mahon, Newquay, Palma, Pisa, Rimini, Stuttgart and Tunis. The One-Elevens also operated from Liverpool to Ibiza, Palma and Rimini, Birmingham to Ibiza and Palma and from Manchester to Alicante, Gerona, Ibiza, Malaga, Palma, Tenerife and Venice.

Delays in granting British Eagle authority for the scheduled trans-Atlantic service led to the new Boeing 707 being leased out to Middle East Airlines after its delivery was initially deferred. The rest of the fleet though, the two ex-QANTAS 707s, the five One-Eleven Series 300s, now all returned from their European leases, three Viscounts and no less than fourteen Britannias were kept busy enough.

Behind the scenes though, all was not well. Following the losses made over the 1968 summer season, the Liverpool base was closed down in October, throwing 400 staff out of work. On 30 October, the airline's financial backers, Hambros and Kleinwort Benson had approved arrangements to support the carrier through the rest of 1968 and into 1969. However, two days later, British Eagle's licences for the Caribbean charter services were revoked. Alarmed at this, and with little sign of the North Atlantic licences being granted, the bankers suddenly withdrew their support. Despite the Caribbean programme only accounting for 3 per cent of the proposed 1969 flying programme, and a licence for new scheduled services from the Bahamas to New York and Canada having been approved, the banks refused to put the financial package back into place. Eventually, the British Eagle Board had to admit defeat and all operations ceased as of midnight on 6 November. All the aircraft returned to Heathrow or Liverpool after their last flights. The very last British Eagle International Airlines service was operated by a Britannia freighter, landing

Autair's fleet soon set new utilization records. Aviation Hobby Shop

back at Heathrow on 7 November carrying a cargo of oranges from Tel Aviv. A number of 'rescue' plans were put forward, most of them involving the continued operation of a smaller fleet of Britannias and One-Elevens, but none of them were to come to anything. The British Eagle One-Elevens were eventually flown to Weybridge for storage and later repositioned to Wisley.

Despite the dramatic loss of British Eagle, the One-Eleven was now firmly established as a popular and successful commercial airliner. With the arrival, hard on its heels, of the DC-9 and the Boeing 737, the One-Eleven no longer had the field to itself. BAC was having to look at ways of keeping the design on the options lists of the airline executives. The obvious answer was a stretched aircraft, carrying more passengers for the same, or similar costs. By early 1968, a larger One-Eleven was well on its way, but would it be to little too late?

G-ATPK was with British Eagle when the company folded. Jennie Gradidge

CHAPTER FOUR

The Stretch – and the Shrinking

BAC had proposed a stretched version of the One-Eleven as early as 1963. Although some interest had been shown by the airlines, BAC was reluctant to continue with the project without a decent-sized order book for the new variant. In retrospect this can be seen as a major error of judgement. The main rivals for the One-Eleven, the DC-9 and Boeing 737 both made a feature of offering a variety of stretched options. This may have added to the Douglas and Boeing's development costs and made for a much more complicated production schedule, but it had led a number of potential One-Eleven customers to switch to the American types. More importantly, some early One-Eleven customers were forced to switch their allegiance when larger jet aircraft were needed to exploit the smaller British jet's success with their passengers.

One established One-Eleven operator, Aer Lingus, was especially frustrated by BAC's apparent indecision over increasing the One-Eleven's capacity. Their four Series 200s had been operating successfully, but more jet capacity was badly needed on the trunk services to London. Eventually, Aer Lingus ordered a pair of Boeing 737-200s specifically for the UK services and went on to operate a large fleet of the Boeing twin-jets on their European routes. Originally announcing that the One-Elevens would be sold off once the 737 fleet had increased enough to cover them, the four Series 200s were actually retained and managed to chalk up over 25 years of service with Aer Lingus before being retired and sold off in 1991.

Aloha Airlines also changed their allegiance to Boeing. Following the weight restrictions to a number of their island airports, especially the short runway at Kona, Aloha introduced their first 737 in 1969 and the One-Elevens were disposed of. The change over to Boeings was an expensive exercise for Aloha, linked with a delay in the start-up of new services from the mainland by a number of major carriers whose connecting passengers Aloha had been

Aer Lingus One-Elevens frequently visited Liverpool. Aviation Hobby Shop

relying on to fill the 737s. Over the next year, things got so bad that main rival Hawaiian again looked into the possibility of merging the two operations. Negotiations were advanced enough for Aloha to cancel orders for extra 737s and begin reducing services in preparation for a Hawaiian take-over. Hawaiian Airline's management then broke off talks in 1971, reasoning that there was little point in going to the expense of taking over an operation that was about to go bankrupt anyway. Fortunately, by a series of leasing deals and selling off the remaining Viscounts, Aloha not only survived, it turned a corner to become profitable with an all-737 fleet.

British European Airways had been approached very early in the design stages of the One-Eleven. However, the corporation was not interested in the initial variant, regarding it as too small for their needs. BEA's' attitude changed when it became clear that they were to face head-on competition from Pan American on the German Internal Service, based at

West Berlin. The airlines of the occupying forces had been obliged to offer air services to West Berlin, following the division of pre-war Germany into its democratic western and communist-controlled eastern halves at the end of the Second World War. Berlin, itself divided into two halves, was stranded in the middle of East Germany and the East German authorities refused to allow a West German carrier to fly through their airspace.

BEA, Air France and American Overseas Airlines began internal services from several West German points to Berlin's downtown Tempelhof Airport in the late 1940s. American Overseas was taken over by Pan American in 1950 and from then on BEA and Pan American were keen rivals out of Berlin's downtown Tempelhof Airport. Initially, BEA flew DC-3s and Vikings against Pan American's larger DC-4s. BEA Airspeed Ambassadors made a limited appearance on the Berlin-based routes, but in the late 1950s much of the service was operated on BEA's behalf by

The Series 500 finally met BEA's Viscount replacement criteria. Brooklands Museum

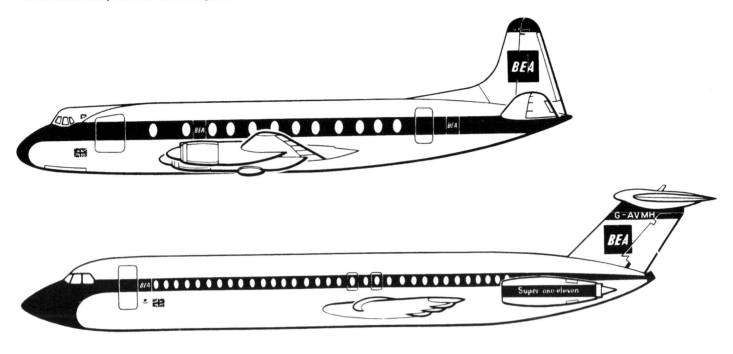

BAC eventually, belatedly, finalized the stretched One-Eleven. Brooklands Museum

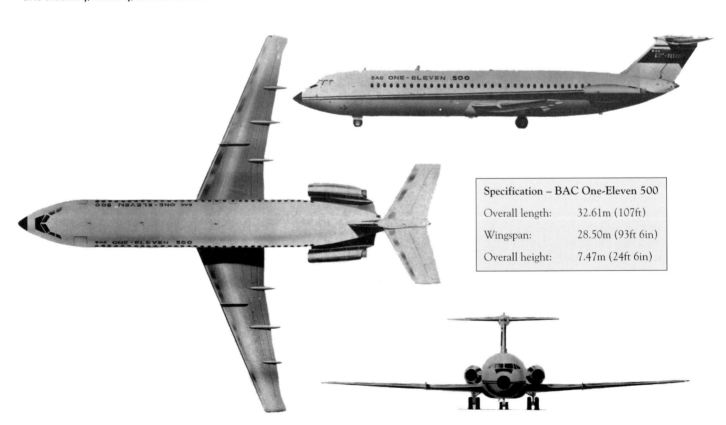

Specification – BAC One-Eleven 500	
Overall length:	32.61m (107ft)
Wingspan:	28.50m (93ft 6in)
Overall height:	7.47m (24ft 6in)

Freddie Laker's company, Air Charter Ltd, using their DC-4s. BEA returned on their own behalf with Viscounts as Pan American upgraded their services with DC-6Bs.

Jets had arrived on the Berlin services with Air France's Caravelles, whose lack of reverse thrust forced them to operate into Tegel Airport, outside the city, and Pan American's Boeing 727-100s managing to squeeze themselves into Tempelhof via the notoriously interesting approaches in between apartment blocks. BEA's reaction was to upgrade the cabins of their Viscounts to offer 'Silver Star' class service, with only 53, first-class-style seats in the cabin, giving greatly increased leg room and better catering facilities. However, this did little to stop a slide in BEA's passenger boarding figures as Berliners overwhelmingly voted with their feet and chose the rival jets. By 1967 BEA's share of traffic on the total West German Internal Service had dropped from 40 per cent to 30 per cent.

BEA's Contract

BEA had wanted to order a mixed fleet of Boeing 727s and 737s, but the government, controlling the nationalized carrier's pursestrings, ordered the airline to look for British-built alternatives. As a result, BEA reluctantly ordered an enlarged HS Trident 3B, ironically now close to the original-sized Trident, before BEA had insisted on the design being reduced in size. For the long-awaited 'Viscount replacement', for lower capacity routes, BEA was able to offer BAC the large order that the manufacturer felt it needed to begin developing the stretched version of the One-Eleven. Initial studies for BEA's version of the One-Eleven began early in 1966, with the specifications being finalized by September. The contract for eighteen Series 500s, with an option for a further six, was signed on 27 January 1967. The development cost of the new aircraft, some £9 million, was to be paid for by the government, to be recouped from a levy on each aircraft sold. Curiously, BEA elected to decline the option of forward airstairs, as BUA had also done on their Series 200s. No other Series 500 customer was to follow their example, all preferring the benefit of less ground equipment being needed on turn-rounds, as opposed to the comparatively small weight-saving of doing without them. The contract brought the total of Weybridge-designed aircraft, including the Vickers-designed Vikings, Viscounts and

Vanguards, bought by BEA since 1946 when it began operations, to 161. This comprised 53 Vikings, 70 Viscounts, 20 Vanguards and the 18 One-Elevens. The total BEA investment in the One-Eleven order was £32 million.

To act as a Series 500 prototype, the Series 400 development aircraft, G-ASYD, was returned to Hurn for conversion, the work beginning on 4 February 1967. Up until then, in its original configuration, the aircraft had logged 770 flying hours in 476 flights. Two fuselage plugs, one forward of the wing of 8ft 4in (2.54m) and another to the rear of 5ft 2in (1.57m) were inserted. Overwing exits were doubled to two per side and under-floor hold capacity was increased from 534 sqft (15.12 sqm), to 687 sqft (19.45 sqm). Most importantly, passenger capacity in scheduled configuration

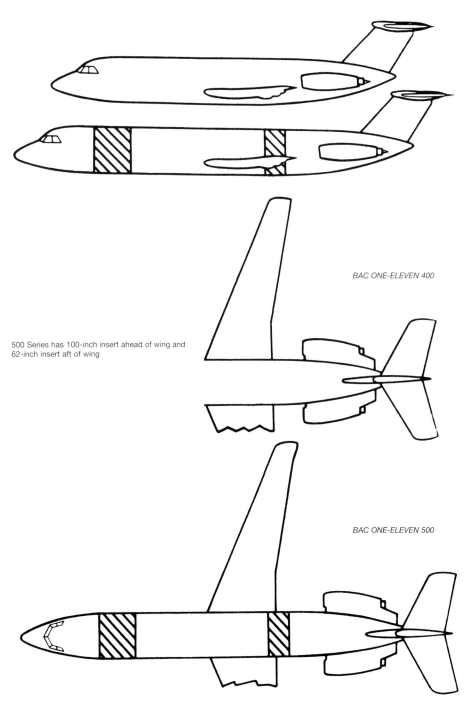

BAC ONE-ELEVEN 400

500 Series has 100-inch insert ahead of wing and 62-inch insert aft of wing

BAC ONE-ELEVEN 500

The stretch was achieved with fuselage plugs and a new wing. Brooklands Museum at 34in seat pitch, was increased to 97. The wingspan was increased by 5ft (1.52m) by inserting wing-tip extensions and other modifications included a beefed-up undercarriage and higher capacity APU and cabin air-conditioning systems. The uprated engines were to be Rolls-Royce Spey Mk.512-14Es with 12,000lb static thrust.

'YD's first post-conversion flight was made on 30 June 1967, six weeks ahead of schedule, after the aircraft had been rolled out on the 22nd. It was captained by Brian Trubshaw, then Manager, Flight Operations for BAC, with Roy Radford, Assistant Chief Test Pilot for BAC Weybridge. 'YD was instrumented to record 800 parameters. The test gear included automatic cameras, 50-channel trace recorders and three magnetic tape recorders, each with 13 channels. Being a conversion, rather than a 'proper' Series 500, 'YD had lower operating weights than were planned for the production aircraft and still had the Series 400 Rolls-Royce Spey Mk.511-14s fitted for the first few weeks of flight testing. From 3 July 'YD was transferred to Wisley, where it was based for the remainder of the test programme. A certain amount of the certification flying was carried out at Torrejon, near Madrid.

The BEA order was followed on 4 March by one from British United for five Series 500s. Ten days later, on 14 March Caledonian Airways placed an order for three. Powered by higher-rated Rolls-Royce Spey 25 Mk.512DW engines, with water-injection systems for improved performance, the two airlines specified one-class seating for 109 passengers. Both carriers were planning to use their Series 500s for inclusive tour work, BUA using a mixed fleet of rapidly ageing Britannias and Viscounts, as well as the original One-Eleven Series 200s, for this work up until then.

The order from Caledonian Airways (Prestwick) Ltd for One-Elevens was quite a change in their equipment policy. Formed in 1961, Caledonian Airways was operated under the leadership of Glasgow-born Adam Thomson. An ex-Fleet Air Arm pilot, Thomson had started his civil flying career in the late 1940s with a small charter company operating pleasure flights from the Isle of Wight. As his career progressed, Thomson found himself commanding Handley-Page Hermes aircraft with Silver City Airways, carrying pioneering inclusive tour passengers around Europe. Frustrated at Silver City's owners' lack of foresight in exploiting this new market, Thomson determined to found his own charter airline. While still flying the Hermes, although this time as a freelance captain with Air Safaris, Silver City having ceased to operate as an independent airline, Thomson and several colleagues were busy gaining the financial backing and operating licences to found Caledonian Airways (Prestwick) Ltd. Initially the fledgling airline's offices were established over an estate agent's premises in Horley, near Gatwick.

The company finally began operations with a single DC-7C, leased from Sabena, in November 1961. Caledonian originally specialized in long-haul charter work, with charter services to South Africa, the Far East and across the Atlantic, for a variety of civilian and military clients. Caledonian's fleet grew steadily over the next few years, still with the majority of its fleet of DC-7Cs being leased from Sabena. Despite the Scottish flavour of the airline's full title, heraldic livery, styling itself as 'The Scottish International Airline', not to mention the famous tartan-clad stewardesses, Caledonian Airways was firmly based at London-Gatwick. However, a large number of charter flights were operated through Prestwick every year.

Like most charter operators, Caledonian had to take work where it could find it and eventually more European inclusive tour work began to feature in the flying programme. As well as their world-wide services, the DC-7s were just as likely to spend their time flying shorter flights from Gatwick, Prestwick or Manchester to Mediterranean holiday resorts. A pair of DC-6Bs were leased, as usual, from Sabena, in 1964, primarily for European inclusive tour charters. In addition, the DC-6Bs also operated on a series of trooping flights to Singapore.

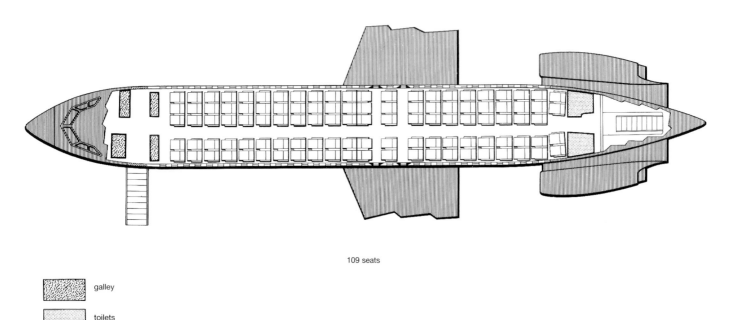

109 seats

galley

toilets

Initial high-density layouts carried 109 passengers. Brooklands Museum

Bristol Britannia turbo-props were to start replacing the leased Douglas aircraft from 1965. At first the Britannias concentrated on the long-haul flights and the remaining DC-7Cs flew the European network. However, more Britannias were acquired, leading to their introduction on to the inclusive tour services and the leased DC-7Cs were returned to their owners.

Plans to operate a Boeing 707 were delayed by wrangles over customs duty and the first aircraft remained temporarily in the USA, on lease to the Flying Tiger Line. Caledonian finally placed Boeing 707s in service in January 1968. The new jets also flew from Gatwick to the Far East and Australia, as well as the established trans-Atlantic charters from Gatwick, Prestwick and Manchester.

The Britannias were shifted to European charters, but the increase in pure-jet

delivered, but the Board made it clear that no such concessions would be forthcoming for the 737s. It was also implied that the charges may be reinstated for the 707s had the 737 order gone ahead. Faced with the sort of financial burden that could have ruined Caledonian, Adam Thomson and the board of directors were forced to think again and the One-Eleven order was signed, albeit reluctantly.

The first production Series 500, BEA's G-AVMH, joined 'YD on the Wisley-based flight development programme from 7 February 1968. This was ten weeks ahead of schedule. Fitted with similar test equipment as 'YD, the aircraft was used for confirmatory checks. Being a production version, 'MH was able to be used to confirm the strength and performance at specific maximum design weights, which had not been fully possible on the development

The Series 500 received its full and unrestricted passenger transport ARB certificate on 15 August. Over 800 hours had been logged in the pursuit of the certificate, 387 of them by G-ASYD, during 308 flights. The rest of the hours, 394, had been accumulated by the first three production aircraft, G-AVMH, 'MI, and 'MJ. The third aircraft, G-AVMJ, had first flown on 15 May and had remained based at Hurn as the definitive acceptance aircraft. BEA formally took delivery on 29 August, over a month early.

A BEA aircraft, G-AVML, took part in the flying display at the 1968 Farnborough SBAC exhibition. Also at Farnborough on 18 September, G-AVMK was officially named by Lady Freda Millward, wife of the BEA Chairman, Sir Anthony, as 'Super One-Eleven', a fleet name chosen by a joint BEA and BAC staff competition.

The much-modified G-ASYD and BEA's first production aircraft. Brooklands Museum

operations from rival companies led Thomson to start looking at the jet options available for these routes. Originally, Caledonian had strongly favoured the Boeing 737 and came very close to placing an order. The established relationship with Boeing, following the 707 purchase, had produced favourable terms and the airline was impressed with the 737's performance and passenger capacity. However, the Board of Trade indicated that heavy import duty would be imposed on the American aircraft. Concessions had finally been made to allow the 707s to be

aircraft. On completion of that work 'MH was mainly used to develop features particular to BEA and was principally involved in automatic approach and landing systems development. The aircraft conducted much of this work at Bedford, Gatwick and Liverpool. The second production aircraft, G-AVMI, was handed over to BEA on 8 July. Training was conducted at Wisley, Hurn and Teesside, for circuit pattern and night flying. Route training was conducted from Manchester, which had been designated the main UK base for the fleet.

BEA's West Berlin services had seen the introduction of Comet 4B jets as an interim measure to compete more effectively against Pan American's 727s in early August. The Comets had been released from London-based duties by the delivery of new Trident 2s and were eventually flying fourteen daily flights along the air corridors to and from West Berlin. Not particularly well suited to the corridors, with altitude restricted to 10,000 feet and the longest Tempelhof runway being only 5,266ft long, the Comets were never regarded as more than temporary stop-gaps. BEA began to

The first Series 510ED, G-AVMH remained with BAC until 1969. Brooklands Museum

Manchester was the UK home for the BEA Super One-Eleven fleet. Brooklands Museum

use the One-Elevens on an *ad hoc* basis from Berlin on 1 September, using G-AVMJ on Berlin–Hamburg and Berlin–Bremen services. Scheduled operations from Tempelhof began on 17 November.

Also on 17 November, 'Super One-Eleven' appeared on services from Manchester to London-Heathrow. BEA had been losing traffic on the Manchester–London route to new electrified train services and the One-Elevens were regarded as a major weapon in attracting passengers back to the air service. Fitted with an all-economy layout for 97 passengers, the seats were upholstered in bold bright colours, with softer tones on the fixed furnishings. This gave a much brighter, lighter feel than the previous, more staid, BEA interiors and had been designed by Charles Butler Associates of New York. This was an important break with tradition, with BEA having preferred British designers in the past. The standard all-economy layout for the Series 500 was actually for 99 seats, but in BEA service an extra bar unit occupied the space of two seats at the rear. In later years the bar unit was removed and the two seats installed in its place.

The decision to base the new fleet of jets at Manchester gave BEA's northern base a great boost in morale. Manchester's place in the BEA family had suffered a variety of highs and lows over the years. For the 1950s, the more important BEA base outside London was Liverpool, mainly responsible for a network of services over the Irish Sea and to domestic points in the UK. Manchester was served, but the service was erratic in the early years, with routes being closed as often as they were opened. Even-

tually though, the Liverpool base's routes were transferred to BEA's associate company, Cambrian Airways and BEA started paying more attention to their northern 'Cinderella' base at Manchester.

On the London service frequencies had already increased over the years, with Viscounts, and later Vanguards, offering a more practical schedule. More direct BEA services from Manchester to Europe were opened, allowing passengers to bypass London. Some of the continental services had actually been pioneered by the independent operators. Eagle Airways, in particular, had used Viscount 800s for a Manchester-centred network in the late 1950s. Their scheduled operations to Brussels, Copenhagen and Hamburg were discontinued though when the Viscounts were transferred to the more profitable Caribbean-based services in 1959. However, the loads on the pioneering Eagle flights did show that, given patience, the direct continental flights could possibly prove to be viable and BEA stepped in to replace the independent.

BEA jet services opened from Manchester in 1966, with Tridents operating to Paris. By the summer, six European destinations were served by the Tridents. As more 'Super One-Elevens' were delivered during the winter of 1968/69, they took over jet services from Manchester to Brussels, Copenhagen, Glasgow, Paris, via Birmingham and to Zurich. They also appeared on Irish Sea services to Dublin and Munich, Manchester became the servicing and maintenance base for the BEA One-Elevens and the 'Super One-Elevens' operation was promoted locally as Manchester's 'own airline'.

After signing a new 'pooling' agreement with BEA on 24 September, Air France withdrew from Berlin services from 1 April 1969. The Air France market share of the Berlin traffic had fallen to a hopelessly uneconomic 4 per cent, mostly as a result of being forced to operate from Tegel. Under the agreement BEA operated their One-Elevens under joint BEA/AF flight numbers on the routes from Tempelhof to Frankfurt and Munich, the Caravelle flights from Tegel being discontinued. Originally mixed BEA and Air France cabin crews operated over the routes and the aircraft's livery was adapted so that BEA's titles were less prominent. BEA had changed their established 'red square' colours in late 1968, the first One-Elevens still being delivered in the old livery. The new colours used a dark blue trim instead of black, a new Union Flag-based logo and new-style 'BEA' titles. On the One-Elevens though, to placate Air France, whose profile on the Berlin services had been almost submerged by the joint service agreement, the new fuselage titles were reduced in size and there was no logo on the tail. Instead the blue tail bore the simple legend 'Super One-Eleven' in white.

Charter 'Supers'

The Series 500s of BUA and Caledonian were to be an uprated version. They were powered by Rolls-Royce Spey 25 Mk.512DW engines, with a water-injection system to assist maximum take-off at hot and high airfields. This engine option

BEA's new image started appearing on production One-Elevens. Brooklands Museum

Caledonian flew their first One-Eleven to Prestwick for naming. Brooklands Museum

The Laird of Skye, Lord MacDonald of MacDonald, performed the naming ceremony for G-AWWX. Brooklands Museum

became standard on all subsequent Series 500s, with only BEA's Series 510EDs being fitted with the original, lower-powered Speys. The newer version also had new, drag-reducing flap-track fairings and improved brakes and anti-skid systems.

Caledonian named their first Series 500, 'Flagship Isle of Skye' in a ceremony at Prestwick on 24 March 1969. The company also unveiled a new image for its cabin crew with the arrival of the One-Elevens. From the beginning of operations, the Caledonian stewardesses had worn a distinctive 'Black Watch' tartan uniform. For 1969, this policy was modified in that the staff could pick one of nine different tartans to their own taste. All cut to an identical design, the variety of colour gave the airline an individualistic feel while retaining the decidedly Scottish flavour. Three One-Elevens were in Caledonian service by April, with the fourth due for delivery the next year. The aircraft operated from Gatwick, Glasgow and Manchester on IT work all over Europe and to North Africa.

New 501EXs and leased 416EK, G-AWKJ, joined BUA in 1969. Brooklands Museum

BUA had remodelled their image in 1966, with the rather formal black and red being dropped in favour of a brighter turquoise and sand livery, with bolder, much more modern BUA titles and logo in black. Between April and June 1969, BUA placed its five Series 500s into inclusive tour charter service, alongside the Series 200s. A single Channel Airways Series 400, in full BUA colours, was also leased for the 1969 summer season. This was acquired to replace Series 200, G-ASJJ which had been lost in a non-fatal take-off accident at Milan in January. Still in a high-density passenger configuration, the Channel One-Eleven was operated exclusively on charter work.

Autair International had also ordered Series 500s, signing contracts for five aircraft, later increasing the order to seven. These aircraft were to replace the Series 400s already operating on inclusive tour charter work with Autair and were to be fitted with no less than 119 passenger seats. This interior was achieved by severely reducing the space for galley units and a unique system of seat-back catering was designed. The cabin also featured face-to-face, non-reclining, seating areas over the emergency exit rows to help make the most of what space was available.

The Autair aircraft were also to be fitted with a new, re-contoured, wing leading edge, with a new range of flap settings, generating more lift at a lower airspeed. This would allow Autair to carry full loads out of its Luton base with no need to use water injection. As with the higher-rated engines, this option became a standard for later Series 500s.

In July 1969, Autair announced that it would close down the loss-making scheduled network from the end of October. Despite good load factors, the company was losing over £150,000 a year on running the scheduled routes and the decision was made to concentrate on the more profitable charter work with the One-Elevens. With the airline now specializing in holiday charter services, a new image was sought and it was announced that Autair would take up its parent company's name as Court Line Aviation. More noticeably, a whole new image was created, reflecting a more holiday-related atmosphere. The aircraft and crews were given a colourful new look, the previous two-tone blue livery and military-style uniforms would be swept away. Instead, the aircraft adopted bright new colours, inside and out, and the cabin crews were decked out in matching outfits.

The first aircraft to carry Court Line Aviation colours, pastel pink G-AXMF, 'Halcyon Breeze', arrived at Luton in December 1969, just under a month before the official name change on 1 January 1970. This was followed by vivid orange and turquoise examples, brightening up the Luton ramp no end. All but one of the

Court Line's new identity was revealed in late 1969. via Janine Redmond

G-AWBL was the only Autair One-Eleven to remain with Court Line. Aviation Hobby Shop

Series 400s were returned to BAC as the Series 500s entered service. The exception was Series 400 G-AWBL that spent one summer in the turquoise Court Line livery, for the 1970 season, before following its ex-Autair colleagues back to BAC.

In its first year as Court Line Aviation, the company flew holiday charters from Birmingham, Bristol and Cardiff, as well as the main base at Luton. The sole remaining Series 400, G-AWBL, 'Halcyon Dawn', opened the Birmingham programme on 14 March 1970 with a holiday flight to Palma. Barcelona, Faro, Ibiza, Malaga and Tenerife were also served from Birmingham. Alicante, Gerona, Ibiza, Palma, Rimini and Venice were served from Bristol and Cardiff. No less than sixteen holiday destinations were regularly served from Luton during the summer, as far east as Greece and Yugoslavia, as well as the usual Spanish and Italian favourites.

Court Line introduced a new method of in-flight catering designed to help busy cabin crews on the higher-capacity aircraft. Two small compartments were inserted in the back of the seat headrests, allowing passengers to help themselves to cold meals already stored there. The compartment meant for each sector was unlocked by the crew using a key before passengers boarded. The whole idea was that the cabin crew could spend more time on the profitable bar service and duty-free sales, instead of having half the flight time taken up with distributing meals. The space previously used for the galley units concerned with the meal storage could also be turned over to extra seating, or storage for more bar and duty-free goods.

The system was also adopted by some later operators of One-Elevens, and even other aircraft types with high-capacity configurations. Unfortunately, the locking system was far from reliable and pilferage by passengers of the meals meant for the next sector was common. Eventually the system fell out of favour as being more trouble than it was worth from a passenger-relations point of view. More and more extra meals, to cover the pilfering, had to be carried and their distribution was soon wiping out any time-saving. The increased demand for a hot meal service, as charter passengers became more sophisticated over the years, finally led to the death knell for seat-back catering.

Both old and new airline customers started to take an interest in the Series 500, once the stretched aircraft was finally on offer. Court Line Aviation was able to take advantage of one new One-Eleven customer in leasing out some spare winter capacity. Empressa Guatemalteca de Aviacion SA, of Guatemala, more usually known simply as Aviateca, had ordered a single Series 500 for its Central American network. Delivery was due in March 1971. In the meantime, a Court Line Series 500, G-AXMK, 'Halcyon Star', was wet-leased, reregistered TG-ARA, still in its colourful Court Line orange livery.

G-AMXJ, 'Halcyon Night' was one of the colourful Court fleet. via Author

Aviateca had been operating DC-3s, DC-6s and Convairs on their routes and had recently signed a co-operation agreement with Lufthansa. It had originally been planned that the German carrier would help the company acquire jet equipment and a number of Guatemalan staff had been sent to Frankfurt for training on Boeing 720s. However, following a diplomatic incident when the German Ambassador to Guatemala had been killed, the agreement was cancelled and Aviateca had to look elsewhere. The One-Eleven's success with other Central American operators had not gone unnoticed and a deal was signed with BAC.

Aviateca's own aircraft had been delivered. The British charter airline certainly left an impression on Aviateca, not least as the airline elected to adopt a Court Line Aviation style orange livery for its own fleet.

Bahamas Airways ordered two Series 500 aircraft at the end of 1968, and took out an option on a third. In the meantime, Bahamas was leased two Series 400s by BAC, until the 500s were delivered in July 1969. The 400s were configured for 79 passengers, the 500s for 99, the jets replacing long-established Viscount operations. The new aircraft were placed into scheduled, 'Flamingo Jet' service from the Bahamas to Florida, a notoriously competitive market.

mercial pressures and ceased operations on 9 October 1970.

The rise in popularity of the inclusive tour was not confined to the United Kingdom. Most Western European countries were just as enthusiastically transporting their citizens to the ever-growing range of resorts, for two weeks of sun and fun. As in the UK, airlines anxious to serve this market came and went with an often alarming frequency. As the industry gradually settled down after the pioneering and experimenting stages, more funds started to be invested in the charter carriers and they were able to look beyond acquiring their fleets second-hand. The scheduled, often state-owned,

Aviateca's TG-AZA arrived in a Court-style livery. Aviation Hobby Shop

As well as profitably leasing out the otherwise idle aircraft, Court Line also involved itself with Aviateca with managerial assistance and a general updating of procedures and practices. A number of Court Line crew members operated on the aircraft, alongside the locally based crews. The Court Line One-Eleven operated on daily scheduled flights from Guatemala City to Miami, Mexico City and San Pedro Sula, in Honduras, before returning to Luton in April at the end of the lease, once

Bahamas Airways had a long, but far from financially trouble-free, history. The airline had been sold on from one owner to the other, each one convinced it knew the secret to finally making the carrier profitable. An ex-British Eagle Series 300 joined the Series 500 fleet in April 1970. A third Bahamas Airways Series 500 was fitted with long-range fuel tanks for a proposed Nassau–New York route, but was fated not to be delivered, as the airline finally succumbed to com-

airlines were also just as happy to improve utilization of their expensive new fleets on charter flights in off-peak hours and were proving to be serious rivals to the private airline sector for these services. Many of the national carriers also set up their own charter subsidiaries or gained controlling interests in established operators.

The surviving charter airlines had to look seriously at improving their image, not least by operating newer equipment. Any new operator could certainly not hope

VP-BCZ, a 432FD, was leased to Bahamas Airways by BAC in 1968. MAP

Panair's 524FF, D-ALAT, 'Arno' joined the airline in 1969. via Author

Panair became Paninternational in 1970. Brooklands Museum

to have an easy time attracting business by offering a second-hand piston- or even turbo-prop-powered fleet. As with Clarksons and Court Line in the UK, many of the operators were bought out by, or even set up by the tour operators themselves, investing heavily in making their operations as 'in-house' as possible, with maximum control over their airline subsidiaries.

Worldwide Expansion

A One-Eleven customer which was part of this new style of airline ownership was a German charter airline, Panair, later renamed Paninternational. Owned by the tour operator, Paneuropa, their first Series 500 One-Eleven, of four eventually ordered, was delivered in June 1969. This was actually the first One-Eleven to be fitted with the redesigned leading edge. Until March 1970, the aircraft operated alone from Munich on IT charters, then being joined by two more. The fourth arrived in March

1971 and all the One-Elevens were operated in 109-passenger configuration, alongside a pair of second-hand Boeing 707s used for long-range and high-capacity services. Despite the rapid growth, or perhaps because of it, Paninternational was sadly forced into liquidation in October 1971.

Another West German One-Eleven operator which was fated to fare better than Paninternational was Germanair Bedarfsluftfahrt GmbH, of Frankfurt. Originally formed as Sudwest-Flug in 1966 by the Goetz textile combine group, the company was renamed Germanair in 1968. By then it was operating a single standard DC-6 and two slightly larger DC-6A/Bs, the latter being easily converted from passenger to cargo operations as required by charterers. The airline moved into jet operations on their inclusive tour services by leasing an ex-Swissair DC-9-15 in April 1969. In August this aircraft was replaced by a One-Eleven Series 400 leased from BAC, pending delivery of a fleet of three Series 500s, which finally

ousted the old DC-6s. Another Series 500 was later added to the order, all the 114-seaters being in service by May 1971.

The longest-established German One-Eleven operator, Bavaria, was flying no less than four Series 400s by 1970. Despite losing one in a take-off accident at Gerona in July 1970, the airline kept faith with the type and took delivery of three Series 500s in December. During 1969 and 1970 a twice-daily domestic scheduled service was flown on behalf of Lufthansa by the One-Elevens, between Munich and Hanover, with a Monday to Friday Hanover– Stuttgart service also operated. Previously, these flights had been operated by Bavaria's Handley-Page Dart Herald aircraft. Fitting of extra fuel tanks in the forward freight hold allowed the German operators to fly popular inclusive tour charters from various German airports non-stop to the Canary Islands and Cairo.

The increased passenger capacity of the Series 500 also appealed to the scheduled operators of the original short-bodied

Germanair's D-AMAT started flying German tourists in 1971. Brooklands Museum

Bavaria's aircraft could be fitted with extra fuel tanks. Brooklands Museum

Philippine Airlines 527FKs operated on busier domestic services. MAP

One-Elevens. Philippine Airlines actually replaced their Series 400s with the larger version from October 1971. The smaller aircraft were returned to BAC after the initial order for four of the 94-seaters were delivered. While the Series 400s had spent most of their time on regional schedules to neighbouring countries, with limited use on the domestic routes, the Series 500s saw much more use on the trunk domestic Philippine network. International destinations still served saw the use of the One-Elevens on new routes to Communist China, as well as to Vietnam and Brunei. An eventual fleet of twelve Series 500s was delivered to Manila by 1980.

Another established One-Eleven operator, Austral of Argentina, also upgraded their fleet by ordering Series 500s, with an order for three placed in November 1969. Two were delivered to Austral, the third to associate company ALA. The larger, 104-seat aircraft operated alongside the original Series 400s on the domestic and regional scheduled network centred on Buenos Aires Aeroparque. The Austral One Elevens also operated on behalf of the Chilean national airline, LAN, on a route from San Carlos de Bariloche, in Argentina, to Puerto Montt, in Chile, during 1970. Austral and ALA were finally merged into a single unit, Austral Lineas Aereas, in June 1971.

During 1970, one of Austral's Series 500s was leased to Brazilian operator Sadia, until the delivery of their own fleet of two

was delivered in October and December. Sadia had made great strides since it had been founded in 1954, initially to carry the parent company's processed meat products from Concordia in southern Brazil. Scheduled services had followed in 1956 with Douglas DC-3s and Curtis C-46s and by 1963 Sadia's routes stretched as far north as Fortazela and Recife. Leased turbo-prop Handley Page Dart Heralds entered service later that year and the company placed an order for five of their own Heralds in 1965.

The leased One-Eleven was operated in basic Austral red and black colours, with Sadia titles, the company's own aircraft being delivered in Sadia's own stylish gold and green livery. A dramatic change to the company's image took place in 1972 when

Sadia's first owned aircraft carried a green and gold livery. Brooklands Museum

it was renamed Transbrasil, to reflect the more nationwide nature of the airline's operation. The base was moved to Brasilia, the capital and a dramatic new livery adopted. The One-Elevens each wore their own colour variation on a basic two-tone pattern, designed to reflect a different aspect of

with a fourth acquired second-hand in 1974. The 99-seaters initially operated alongside the earlier Series 400s on regional schedules throughout the Central American and Caribbean area, operating as far north as Miami. LACSA also owned 49 per cent of Cayman Airways, based on the British

A UK scheduled carrier that had cancelled their original order for Series 300 One-Elevens came back into the fold when British Midland Airways ordered two Series 500s in mid-1969. An order for a third was placed a couple of months later. Based at East Midlands Airport, in Derbyshire,

The name change to Transbrasil brought more colourful schemes. Brooklands Museum

Larger 531FSs joined LACSA's original One-Elevens in 1972. Brooklands Museum

Brazilian life. Three were in service by September, wearing a brown (coffee), yellow (wheat), or orange (sun)-based livery. Later additions to the fleet wore green (Amazon), blue (water), and burgundy (wine).

Costa Rica's LACSA had also placed orders for the Series 500 and took delivery of the first of three in May 1971. The others followed in November 1972 and May 1973,

island of Grand Cayman. From 1970, a thrice-weekly service from Grand Cayman to Kingston, Jamaica, was operated on behalf of Cayman Airways using LACSA's Series 500s. In 1973 one of the LACSA fleet was painted in full Cayman Airways livery and introduced on twice-daily service to Miami, as well as increasing the frequency of the Kingston flights to four a week.

BMA had originally planned to operate two Series 300s on their growing scheduled network of European and domestic routes. British Midland had been operating as a scheduled and charter airline since 1947. Founded as a flying school, Air Schools, in 1938, the company had become Derby Aviation in 1949, later modified to Derby Airways. Shortly before the move from Derby's tiny airport at Burnaston to newly built East Midlands, in 1964, the company was again renamed, this time as British Midland Airways. BMA's founding fleet of DC-3s, Dart Heralds and Canadair Argonauts also flew extensive inclusive tour charters from various UK airports when not occupied with scheduled services.

Financial constraints had forced the cancellation of the Series 300 order in 1968 after BMA had begun to standardize the fleet on the Viscount, disposing of the surviving DC-3s and Heralds. The disposal of the aged, notoriously noisy, Argonauts was accelerated by the loss of one of the three aircraft in a well-publicized fatal crash at

Luton–Jersey service. The type also operated a thrice daily Teesside–Heathrow schedule from 4 May, the route being taken over from Autair International. Inclusive tour charters were also operated from East Midlands, Luton, Glasgow, Manchester, Belfast and Bristol. The inclusive tours were flown on behalf of Vista Jet, Clarksons, Horizon Holidays and Global Tours, among others. In its advertising for the One-Eleven services the company claimed to now have a 'sting in its tail', referring to the aircraft's rear mounted engines and auxiliary power unit. The arrival of the One-Elevens saw the withdrawal of the Series 700 Viscounts from BMA's fleet, although the larger 800

the company was merged with Caledonian Airways, with effect from 30 November 1970. The unlikely marriage of the predominantly scheduled operator, BUA, with Caledonian, an exclusively charter airline, was brought about by BUA's owner, Air Holdings, actively seeking out a buyer for the airline.

In one attempt to return BUA to profitability, Air Holdings had actually closed down another of their airline subsidiaries, Air Ferry Ltd, at the end of the 1968 summer season. Established at Manston Airport, near Ramsgate on the Kent coast, Air Ferry had operated a network of inclusive tour charters since 1963. The company had been bought from its original founders by

BMA's 523FJs were used on both scheduled and charter flights. Brooklands Museum

Stockport in late 1967. The remaining Argonauts were quickly replaced by additional Viscounts. With the cancellation of the earlier One-Eleven order, the Viscount continued to rule the roost at BMA, with nine in service in 1969. However, with several different versions of Viscount, with different passenger capacities and different marks of engine operated, the company could hardly have been enjoying the benefits of any standardization.

The Series 500 One-Elevens were delivered in February and March 1970, in a high-density 119-passenger configuration. The first scheduled service was over the East Midlands–Jersey route on 24 February. From East Midlands, the One-Elevens were to see service on the scheduled routes to Dublin, Jersey and Glasgow and the

and 810 Series of the turbo-prop remained in use on both the scheduled and charter networks.

BUA/Caledonian Merger

Swissair also returned to the One-Eleven family in 1970. As with the previous arrangement with the now defunct British Eagle, a leased aircraft was operated. A BUA Series 500, operated in a modified Swissair livery, flew schedules from Zurich direct to Nice and Stuttgart and, via Rotterdam, to Manchester. The lease was in operation from April to October 1970, after which the aircraft was returned to BUA at Gatwick. Within weeks of the Swissair aircraft rejoining British United,

the Air Holdings group in 1964. Air Ferry initially operated Vikings, Bristol Freighters and DC-4s, the former two types later being replaced by the ex-Hunting Clan/BUA DC-6As and a pair of Viscounts, leased from Channel Airways. The profitable IT work was supplemented by contract charters over Lufthansa's scheduled cargo network and a great deal of world-wide military cargo charter flying. By the time the Viscounts entered service in 1968, the small Air Ferry fleet was starting to look a bit old to charter customers, but plans were in hand to introduce second-hand Comet jets in 1969. However, Air Holdings felt that the still under-utilized BUA One-Eleven fleet would benefit greatly from the transfer of Air Ferry's IT contracts and the company was closed down in October 1968.

BUA's 501EXs were delivered in a modern new style of livery. Brooklands Museum

Both BUA and Laker based One-Elevens at Gatwick. Brooklands Museum

By 1970, BUA had been losing money on most of its scheduled services and had also experienced a certain amount of industrial unrest within its ranks. Political upheavals had decimated its once profitable operations to Central and East Africa. The Africargo service was no longer flown from Heathrow, being moved to Gatwick at the end of 1968 when extra VC-10 capacity became available and the Britannias used until then became redundant.

Despite these problems, compared with 1968, in 1969 BUA's total of passengers carried had increased by 53 per cent, to 1,400,000. On charter operations the increase was 58 per cent, mostly thanks to the addition of the ex-Air Ferry contracts, and scheduled services experienced a 44 per cent rise. The domestic 'Interjet' One-Eleven services had carried 180,000 passengers. 1970 had seen the arrival of a further three Series 500 One-Elevens and the further expansion of the inclusive tour network with Dubrovnik, Faro, Ljubljana, Pula, Tenerife and Zurich being served from Gatwick and services being flown from Birmingham to Ibiza and Palma.

The smaller operating divisions, the car ferry operation, the Channel Island and northern British-based local services had already been disposed of. British United Air Ferries had become British Air Ferries in 1967, based at Southend and Lydd with its specialized fleet of Carvairs and Bristol Freighters. British United (Channel Island) Airways eventually emerged as British United Island Airways in November 1968. This was not until after a great deal of contentious wrangling with the staff and unions concerned that, at one point, led to BUA management threats to close down the operation altogether. BUIA remained a division of British and Commonwealth Shipping and was not included in the sale of BUA to Caledonian. Later BUIA's operating name was modified to British Island Airways to further distance it from its BUA roots.

The state-owned corporations, BEA and BOAC had been approached to take over the relevant parts of BUA's operation. Government opposition to this move though saw Caledonian's Adam Thomson stepping in and paying £6,900,000 for BUA's assets. Initially the new airline was marketed as Caledonian/BUA, with the BUA aircraft eventually taking on Caledonian's Scottish-themed livery and BUA's female staff swapping their pale blue tailored uniforms for the Caledonian tartan.

The joint fleet comprised a total of thirty-one jet aircraft including eight Series 200 One-Elevens, the first production aircraft, G-ASJA having already been sold to the American company, E.T. Barwick Industries as an executive aircraft, in October, and the twelve Series 500s. Longer-haul flights were operated by four VC-10s and seven Boeing 707s. With the combined operation gaining government approval as a viable 'second force' airline, BOAC and BEA found themselves in the unenviable position of being forced by the licensing authorities to transfer a number of their routes to the new carrier in order to strengthen its position.

BOAC was forced to withdraw from services to West Africa and hand over its flights from London to Tripoli, in Libya. BEA found itself with a new competitor on

Yet another carrier showed an interest in the Series 500, with Phoenix Airways, of Basle, Switzerland, ordering a single 114-seater for delivery in April 1971. Phoenix Airways had only been formed In October 1970, to operate *ad hoc* and inclusive tour services. Switzerland had seen a number of charter carriers try and establish themselves in the country over the years. The independent operators, those without the benefit of being linked to the national carrier, Swissair, had enjoyed a very chequered past, often leading very shaky existences until finally being consigned to airline history.

One of the most famous of these was Globe Air, also based at Basle, which had built up a sizeable fleet between 1957 and 1967. Airspeed Ambassadors, Dart Heralds and Bristol Britannias had been operated on charter flights over the usual European

authorities were increasingly unhappy with the British-registered aircraft being operated from Zurich. Tellair was unable to finance the replacement of the Britannias and ceased operations in October.

This left Swissair and its charter subsidiary, Balair, with the Swiss airline market to itself again. Phoenix Airways AG came into being a year after the closedown of Tellair and immediately made clear its intentions of operating a modern, Swiss-registered fleet, in a serious attempt to exorcize the ghosts of past independent Swiss charter airline operations.

As well as the sole One-Eleven, an ex-Trans World Airlines Boeing 707 was bought in late 1972 and entered service on long-range charters. An order for a second One-Eleven was considered but the contract was never finalized and the order was

Caledonian/BUA took on the former's Scottish theme. Brooklands Museum

the London–Paris run, with Caledonian/BUA being awarded rights for a Gatwick–Le Bourget service. This opened on 1 November 1971, the same day the company's new name was changed to the more manageable British Caledonian Airways.

Alongside the scheduled network British Caledonian continued to operate extensive charter services both within Europe with the One-Elevens and worldwide with the Boeing 707s and, to a lesser extent, the VC-10s. Two more Series 500 One-Elevens were ordered after the merger was completed and extra aircraft were leased in at varying periods. New One-Eleven schedules were operated over an Edinburgh–Newcastle–Copenhagen route from November 1972, and a new service opened from Gatwick to Brussels in June 1974.

holiday routes, as well as to Africa and the Far East. The loss of one of their Britannias in a fatal crash at Nicosia in 1967 led to a detailed inquiry into the company's operations that showed up many doubtful practices and shaky finances, causing the airline to declare bankruptcy that October.

A successor, Tellair, was formed by some of the travel companies that had used Globe Air, although operations did not begin from Zurich until 1969. Originally, British Eagle had also invested in the new carrier and had planned to operate a pair of Britannias on their behalf. However, with the demise of the British airline, a pair of ex-British Eagle Britannias were leased and operated on behalf of Tellair by Caledonian. Tellair also operated its own Convair CV-440. Operations began in March 1969, but the Swiss

not placed before Phoenix sadly followed its independent predecessors into history, ceasing operations in 1974 following prolonged financial difficulties.

Rough-Field One-Eleven

With the established proliferation of the Series 500 throughout the scheduled and charter airlines of Europe, the Far East and Asia, BAC started to look at further development options for the One-Eleven. The Spey engine had reached the peak of its development, unless major, very expensive, changes were undertaken. However, BAC came up with another Spey-powered version, specifically designed for rough-field operations in under-developed areas.

Phoenix was one of a series of failed Swiss charter carriers. Brooklands Museum

BAC's 1972 Farnborough stand featured One-Eleven customers. Brooklands Museum

G-ASYD was 'shrunk' back to its original length as the 475. Brooklands Museum

By linking the new Series 500 wing, an uprated Spey with water injection and the short fuselage of the Series 400, the Series 475 was born.

Low-pressure tyres were to be fitted, which resulted in a redesign of the main gear wheel bay, actuation jacks, doors and

new version. Its fuselage plugs removed and back to its original length, G-ASYD flew its third 'maiden flight', now as the Series 475, on 27 August 1970.

The first order for the new type had been placed in June by the Peruvian domestic airline, Faucett SA. The Compania de

monoplanes that the airline had built itself, under licence from Stinson, in the 1930s.

Although it had been granted authority to operate full scheduled services to the USA as far back as 1960, the airline chose only to operate an international cargo service to Miami, operated by DC-4s.

Faucett's 475EZs took jet services to many. Peter Vine via Jennie Gradidge

fuselage fairings. The nose wheels were also wider and also used reduced pressure. An optional gravel runway kit, consisting of glassfibre coating on the underside of the belly, wings and flaps, as well as additional protection for the nose gear, antennae, beacons and draining masts, was offered for use in unpaved airfields.

The long-suffering G-ASYD, its Series 500 development work over, was chosen to become the aerodynamic prototype for the

Aviacion Faucett SA, to give the airline its full title, had been operating domestic services from Lima since 1928. Founded by a US citizen, Elmer J. Faucett, the airline was operating a single Boeing 727 jet, as well as a fleet of Douglas piston-engined aircraft, with DC-3s, DC-4s and DC-6Bs at the time of the One-Eleven order. Until recently, the company had also operated a few ageing survivors from a fleet of Stinson-designed Faucett F.19 eight-seat single-engined

Instead, Faucett concentrated more on their domestic network. Braniff Airways had become a minority shareholder in the airline in 1967, when it bought the operation of PANAGRA, a Lima-based subsidiary of Pan American which also held shares in Faucett. Faucett's first Series 475 One-Eleven was delivered in July 1971 and was quickly placed into service, bringing jet operations to many gravel strips at isolated cities and towns that the type had been specifically developed to serve. A second Series 475 followed two years later, bringing the benefit of jet service to even more regional Peruvian cities.

More orders for the Series 475 followed, with Air Pacific ordering two and Air Malawi signing for one aircraft during 1971. Air Malawi, one of the survivors of the long-dispersed Central African Airways Corporation, had actually leased one of the ex-CAA Series 200s from Zambia Airways from November 1970. The Series 475 was ordered to take over jet operation at the end of the lease, replacing Viscounts

years. As well as operating alongside the established fleet of HS.748s and DH Herons on scheduled inter-island routes, the One-Eleven was used to open Air Pacific's own services to Australia and New Zealand. Previously these had been flown jointly using QANTAS or Air New Zealand aircraft, with Air Pacific sharing capacity. The One-Elevens entered service in March 1972 and August 1973. One of the Air Pacific aircraft was leased to Air Malawi from July 1974 to November 1975, with an extra Series 400 being purchased second-hand in 1978.

400 leased from Philippine Airlines. The One-Eleven order was seen as a valuable breakthrough into the Australian domestic airline market that had been targeted as a possible customer for the aircraft as far back as the Hunting 107 days. The single aircraft was hoped to be the precursor for a much larger follow-on order. Unfortunately, it was not to be and the order lapsed without an aircraft being built. Ten years later, East–West went on to operate a number of Fokker F.28 jets, of similar size and operating capabilities as the One-Eleven Series 475, before being absorbed

Air Malawi's 481FW replaced Viscounts on regional routes. Brooklands Museum

on regional and domestic flights from Blantyre and Lilongwe.

Air Pacific had been founded as Fiji Airways in 1951. It not only served local business and community transport needs, but also acted as a feeder service to the trans-Pacific carriers, helping to open up new tourist markets for holiday-makers from the Americas, Australasia and even further afield. The Australian airline, QANTAS, had acquired control in 1957 and Air New Zealand and BOAC Associated Companies had also gained shareholdings over the

An order had been placed in December 1970 for one Series 475 by East–West Airlines Ltd, an Australian airline based in New South Wales. East–West, a fiercely independent carrier, was operating a large fleet of Fokker F.27s and had been an early post-war pioneer of both urban commuter routes on the heavily-populated New South Wales coast and longer-ranging flights to more isolated communities in inland Australia. In mid-1969 a series of demonstration flights to East–West had been undertaken by BAC using a Series

into the giant Ansett Group in 1991 and losing its identity.

The only other order for the Series 475 came from the Air Force of the Sultanate of Oman. Three aircraft were ordered for regional transport duties, configured for 79 passengers, and the first was delivered in December 1974. The last of the trio that arrived a year later, was delivered with a main deck cargo door fitted in the forward fuselage and a convertible cabin. The first two aircraft were similarly converted by BAC at a later date.

Air Malawi and Air Pacific's first 475s, fresh from the factory. Brooklands Museum

The success of the stretched One-Eleven, especially in the charter markets where cost-reducing is all, had given BAC a welcome boost during a lull that followed the introduction of the initial models. The corporation's designers were reluctant to rest on their laurels and produced the Series 475 to serve its own niche as a local service jet to more remote regions. Other versions of the One-Eleven, as well as completely new designs were constantly being studied and the resulting options were eagerly offered to the airline industry to gauge their likely response.

Aviation, though, especially the commercially driven sector, rarely stands still. Household names come and go, new routes are forever being opened and less successful services dropped. Hard-won reputations fall in the full glare of the media and new faces rapidly rise to prominence, often to fall in their own turn. Aircraft manufacturers can find customers of long standing vanishing overnight, or at least changing beyond recognition. BAC and the other aircraft builders around the world were constantly having to reappraise their product and were struggling to react to the increasingly flexible marketplace, preferably well ahead of their rivals.

Series 485FGs of the Oman Air Force featured cargo doors. Brooklands Museum

CHAPTER FIVE

Comings and Goings

Tenneco's executive N503T was the last Series 200 to be built. Brooklands Museum

While the first Series 500s had been rolling off the Hurn production lines, new, short fuselage aircraft continued to be built. Mohawk's last two Series 200s were delivered in January and May 1969. The very last Series 200 to be built, an executive version for Tenneco, was delivered in July.

Ten Series 400s were also delivered alongside the Series 500s in 1969. TAROM, the Brazilian Air Force, LACSA and Bavaria all took delivery of previously ordered aircraft, and new customers included Spanish charter airline TAE and Bahrein-based Gulf Aviation.

The TAE aircraft had originally been intended for Philippine Airlines but replaced by an order for Series 500s before delivery. TAE, Trabajos y Enlaces, based at Palma, Mallorca, operated three ageing DC-7s on inclusive tour work and had been formed, in its current guise, in 1967. Earlier incarnations had included the Bilbao-based company that ordered, but never took delivery of, the airline version of the Percival Prince. Apparently, however,

airliner salesmen have short memories and an order was accepted from TAE for two One-Elevens, the first entering service in March 1969. Operations saw the aircraft flying alongside the DC-7s on charter flights to many parts of Europe from the Spanish holiday resorts, throughout the year. The second aircraft was fated never to be delivered, the first being repossessed by BAC for non-payment in February 1970. The company carried on operations, using the DC-7s, until all flying finally ceased during the summer. TAE was eventually reformed three years later, using DC-8 and Caravelle jets, and operated, again on Palma-based services, until forced into bankruptcy yet again in 1982.

The delivery of a single Series 400 to Gulf Aviation was to a much sounder customer. At this time all Bahrein-based aircraft were under British registration, Gulf's first One-Eleven being G-AXOX, which had previously been leased to Bahamas Airways. Gulf Aviation had started commercial operations from

Bahrein in 1950 using a twin-engined Avro Anson. The airline's founder, F. Bosworth, initially operated wide-ranging charter services throughout the Middle East, usually in co-operation with the booming local oil industry. BOAC Associated Companies bought a shareholding in the company in 1951 and under their ownership Gulf Aviation entered the scheduled market, with local services opening to neighbouring states. By 1964 the airline was flying a single leased Viscount, four DC-3s, four DH Herons and a single Dove. Fokker F.27s were delivered in 1967 and took over the busier prestige services.

By 1968, a number of the busier local flights were being operated on behalf of Gulf Aviation by Kuwait Airways using their Trident 1Es. It was a matter of national prestige that Gulf Aviation should fly their own jets, and the order was place with BAC in July 1969 for one aircraft, with an option on another. Once in service, the One-Eleven, followed by the second, G-AXMU, in 1971, operated

TAE took delivery of only one of their two ordered 402APs. Brooklands Museum

schedules from Bahrein as far afield as Egypt, India and Pakistan, as well as numerous points throughout the Arabian Gulf area. A second-hand Series 400 was delivered in 1974 and further aircraft were

of the options proposed operation of a smaller fleet of One-Elevens and Britannias. One project involved the resurrection of British Eagle (Liverpool) Ltd, originally the old Starways operation, taken

surviving part of its business assets, goodwill and operating licences pertaining to the Liverpool-based operations.

A further £1 million would have been injected as operating capital by a consor-

G-AXOX flew for Bahamas Airways before joining Gulf Aviation. Brooklands Museum

leased in by Gulf at various periods when extra capacity was required.

The Series 300s rendered homeless by the sudden demise of British Eagle were also available on the second-hand market. Several rescue plans had been put forward for the possible revival of the airline. Most

over by British Eagle in 1964, that had been closed down a month before the bankruptcy of the parent company. As it had not been operating at the time of the parent company's demise, it still existed, at least on paper, in its own right. Offers were made to the liquidators for £25,000 for the

tium headed by Geoffrey Edwards and Mr J.O. Charleton, with £3 million available from merchant banks for the acquisition of three BAC One-Elevens. Two hundred and thirty ex-British Eagle (Liverpool) staff would have been re-employed, but sadly the dream never became a reality and the plans were scrapped after the liquidators, the consortium and the licensing authorities failed to come to a final agreement. Subsequently, the British Eagle One-Eleven fleet remained in storage.

However, two soon found their way to Canada when Quebecair took delivery in early 1969. A Series 400 had been leased from BAC for crew training from March to April. Based at Quebec City, the One-Elevens were used on schedules to Bagotville, Baie Comeau, Churchill Falls, Mont Joli, Montreal, Rouyn, Schefferville, Sept Iles, Toronto, Val d'Or and Wabush. They also operated charters throughout Canada, to the USA and the Caribbean. Previously a fleet of Fairchild F-27s and Douglas DC-3s were operated on the scheduled services. The arrival of the twin jets also coincided with a strike by Air Canada staff which had grounded the national carrier and the Quebecair aircraft were utilized on many extra sectors to carry stranded passengers, bringing much welcome revenue to the company.

Following their replacement by Boeing 737s, the Aloha Airlines fleet of three Series 200s were delivered to Mohawk in March and April 1969, bringing their fleet up to 20 by the summer. Three more were leased by Mohawk from Braniff in September, the newer aircraft introducing a new, more modern, tan and orange 'Buckskin' livery with an arrowhead style logo. The airline was now flying west as far as Chicago and Minneapolis, as well as internationally to Montreal.

Mohawk's Demise

All was certainly not well with Mohawk though, as several financial setbacks had placed the carrier firmly in the red, although the company was optimistic about its predicted results for 1970, its 25th year of operation. Three Boeing 727-200s were ordered for operation over new non-stop services, authority for which was expected to be granted that year. However, the new routes were not forthcoming and the 727s were sold on to California-based Pacific Southwest Airlines before delivery. To add to the company's misfortunes, a pilots' strike in November 1970 led to all 2,100 Mohawk employees being laid off until 1 April 1971. The previous losses and the devastating strike led directly to Mohawk's executives opening up merger talks with Allegheny Airlines, a

similarly sized regional carrier, also with a large network in northeastern USA.

Like Mohawk, Allegheny had started scheduled local flights shortly after the Second World War, as All American Airways. Until then All American had operated a unique mail-only service which included several cities that were served by automated pick-up and dropping equipment for the mail bags, eliminating the need for the aircraft to land. All American had started scheduled passenger flights,

Mohawk and American One-Elevens were in direct competition. Brooklands Museum

with a fleet of DC-3s, in 1949. Serving a dense network in the industrial heartland of the US, Allegheny, as the company became in 1953, prospered during the post-war boom years for the American economy. The airline introduced Martin 202s into the exclusively DC-3 fleet in 1955. The Convair 540, a British Napier Eland turbo-prop-powered version of the Convair 340 followed in 1960, and Fairchild F-27Js in 1965.

Allegheny's own choice for a short-haul jet was the DC-9, their first Series 30 entering service in 1968. As with Mohawk, the arrival of the jets saw a satisfying increase in Allegheny's loads and more routes were added, with authority being granted to link major points an the system directly, instead of being obliged to stop at smaller cities en route. This had also brought Allegheny in direct competition with the established trunk carriers, forcing the company to upgrade its passenger service standards. In 1968, Allegheny merged with the ailing Lake Central Airlines, considerably expanding its network and sphere of influence. As with other local service carriers at the time, Allegheny began to realize that they could take advantage of their position in being able to feed traffic from the local services into their new trunk routes. Thus, what was later to become known as the 'Hub and Spoke' style of operation developed.

(Above) **Short-haul cabin service on Mohawk could be a busy affair.** Brooklands Museum

Post-merger, N1136J in 'Buckskin' style livery with Allegheny stickers. via Author

Allegheny Airlines' discussions with the Mohawk management had begun during the latter airline's blackest hour, with the entire fleet being grounded throughout the network. The first Mohawk flights began to take to the air again on 1 April 1971, but it was too late to save the company. Mohawk's directors voted to approve the Allegheny merger on 5 April, but not before the departure of Bob Peach, who walked out of the board meeting that cast the fatal vote. Nine days later Peach resigned from the company he had personally guided from its DC-3 days. On 20 April, he took his own life at his home in Clinton, New York. As a tribute, one of the few original Mohawk One-Elevens to be painted in the new colours was renamed 'Robert E. Peach' and carried the name until the Allegheny merger was completed.

Even with the merger between Mohawk and Allegheny approved by the directors of both companies, it was to be a year before operations could finally be integrated. With Mohawk flying internationally, to Canada, Presidential approval was required, as well as the usual regulatory investigations and inquiries. Allegheny agreed to support Mohawk during this period, and to advance working capital, if required, of up to $4 million. In the end, Mohawk actually rallied and was able to pay off $3 million of debts and had $12 million cash in hand to pass on to Allegheny on 12 April 1972, when the merger finally took effect. From that date, all operations were conducted in Allegheny's name, with the Mohawk fleet having Allegheny stickers applied until they could be fully repainted.

Understandably, it had been surmised that Allegheny might dispose of the One-Elevens in favour of standardizing on the larger Series 30 DC-9s. However, Allegheny regarded the smaller One-Elevens as complementary to the DC-9 and no less than eight further Series 200s were obtained from Braniff by September 1972. Although Utica gradually became of lesser importance as an operations centre after the merger, the One-Eleven fleet went on

to form a valuable unit within the combined operation, most to eventually be based at Pittsburgh, Pennsylvania.

Braniff had first started to dispose of their One-Elevens from 1970, as more Boeing 727s were delivered to Dallas and took over most of the short-haul work. Braniff eventually standardized on the Boeing 727, operating both the -100 and -200 series throughout their domestic network. One One-Eleven was retained by Braniff as a corporate aircraft, in VIP configuration, after the rest of the fleet had left in 1973. The corporate One-Eleven was retained by Braniff until 1977.

American Airlines had also elected to standardize on the Boeing 727 for their short-haul network and had sold two of the

One-Eleven fleet as early as 1969. However, the withdrawal of their One-Elevens was far from an overnight affair, the remaining '400 Astrojets' being only gradually withdrawn, although all were finally out of service by January 1972. The aircraft were placed into storage at Tulsa, Oklahoma, American's Maintenance and Engineering Center. At the peak of One-Eleven operations, 230 sectors a day were being flown over a network encompassing twenty-one cities. The One-Eleven fleet was only one victim of American's new standardization policy. The remaining Electra turbo-prop and the medium-haul Convair 990A jet fleet were also beginning to be withdrawn at about this time, soon followed by the similar sized Boeing 720Bs as more Boeing 727-200s were

(Above) **Allegheny kept and expanded their fleet.**
D. Lucabaugh via Jennie Gradidge

American chose to replace their One-Elevens with larger Boeings. via Author

delivered. This reducing of the number of different types in the diverse fleet was also helping to make way for the wide-bodied Boeing 747s and DC-10s due to start American Airlines' service in the early 1970s.

Although the '400 Astrojets' were only in service with American Airlines for a comparatively short time, the airline still regarded their use as a successful operation. The cabin crews did complain about the limited size of the galley, understandably if compared to the wide-open spaces of a Boeing 707, and the high landing speed took some getting used to. However, if anything, the American One-Elevens

British airlines, operating a small scheduled network, as well as countless inclusive tour and *ad hoc* charters throughout Europe. By 1969, the company was flying a varied fleet, ranging from DC-3s, which had been with the airline since its foundation in 1953, Airspeed Ambassadors, a single DC-7 freighter, and the first half dozen of what, over the years, was to become a substantial fleet of second-hand DH Comet 4 jets of various versions.

Barely a little over two years old when purchased by Dan-Air, the One-Elevens were initially acquired to service new charter contracts signed with Lunn-Poly and

the first aircraft finally arrived at Dan-Air's maintenance base at Lasham in Hampshire on 14 March 1969. Following extensive engineering and conversion work to make the aircraft ready for UK operations, the first one had its Certificate of Airworthiness issued just nineteen days later. In the meantime, not only had the cabin been fitted with 89 high-density seats, a toilet was moved from the front to the rear of the cabin, new galley units installed and fuel indicators, as well as much of the other flight deck instrumentation, replaced to show European instead of American readings.

400 Astrojets did remain active in the American fleet until 1972. Tim Kincaid collection

were victims of their own success with the now clearly demonstrated demand for seats on short-haul flights soon outstripping their limited capacity. Had a larger One-Eleven been available earlier for American's consideration, it may have been a different story. As it was, by the time the Series 500 was finally available, the airline had already decided to standardize on the Boeing 727 on shorter flights and the British twin jets' days were numbered at American.

Dan-Air Debut

An early customer for the first of the ex-American One-Elevens was Britain's Dan-Air Services Ltd, based at Gatwick. Dan-Air was one of the leading independent

Everyman Travel. Both travel companies had been left looking for a new airline to carry their customers after the collapse of British Eagle. Interestingly, Dan-Air elected to open a new London operating base for the One-Elevens at Luton Airport instead of their main headquarters at Gatwick Airport. Gatwick was not left out of that year's jet fleet expansion though, with two more Comets joining the fleet there, as the One-Elevens arrived at Luton. A single Comet also operated alongside the One-Elevens on charters from Luton for the 1969 season and a Luton-based HS748 service was operated to Leeds/Bradford and Glasgow as part of the 'Link-City' scheduled domestic network.

The delivery of the One-Elevens from the USA was held up by a strike by American Airlines' mechanics. Nonetheless,

The new Luton operation saw summer season departures to Alghero, Alicante, Djerba, Gerona, Ibiza, Istanbul, Luxembourg, Mahon, Malaga, Palma, Pisa, Rimini, Santiago de Compstela, Split, Tunis and Venice. An extra One-Eleven, an ex-British Eagle Series 300, arrived in October, followed by a second Series 300, also ex-British Eagle, in early 1970. The Bavaria series 400 that had crashed on take-off from Gerona on 19 July 1970 was rebuilt at Hurn and delivered to Dan-Air in December 1971.

For the same political reasons that saw BEA and Pan American flying scheduled domestic services into West Berlin, holiday charter flights from the beleaguered city had to be operated by airlines of the 'occupying powers' as well. Both the scheduled carriers participated in this

Dan-Air's One-Elevens opened their new base at Luton. Jennie Gradidge

West Berlin was never treated to the colourful Orientair livery. via Author

market to a limited extent, but as in their home countries, the majority of this work was undertaken by the specialist charter operators. UK One-Eleven operators Channel Airways, Dan-Air and Laker Airways all signed valuable contracts with German travel companies, such as Flug Union, GUT, Neckerman and Stolle, for seasonal holiday charters and based aircraft at West Berlin's Tegel Airport to operate these flights.

The British operators were certainly far from having this market to themselves. American carriers such as Aeroamerica, Capitol International Airways and Modern Air Transport also bid for contracts

and soon established their own Berlin operations from Tegel. Channel also operated a Trident 1E from Berlin, and Dan-Air also operated Comets and, later, Boeing 727s alongside their One-Elevens. Laker based at least two One-Elevens at Berlin during the summer season. Another ex-British Eagle One-Eleven Series 300 found a new home, this time with Laker, to help operate these lucrative contracts.

One new British operator was founded with the express aim of exploiting the Berlin inclusive tour market. Orientair Ltd was registered by an ex-Channel Airways pilot, Captain Lockwood, in late 1971. Contracts were negotiated for 1972

operations from West Berlin and an ex-American Airlines Series 400 was acquired and registered G-AZMI following overhaul and repainting by BAC at Hurn. The aircraft had been scheduled for delivery to Orientair on 15 March 1972, with a second ex-American One-Eleven due on 17 May. However, before the delivery of the fleet could be carried out, Orientair sold the Berlin contracts to Dan-Air and no commercial flying was undertaken by the carrier. G-AZMI, still named 'City of Berlin', ignominiously found itself remaining in storage with BAC at Hurn in Orientair's yellow and black livery.

Channel's One-Elevens rarely achieved profitable utilization. via Author

Channel's Rocky Road

Despite holding a number of important charter contracts and operating an extensive short-haul scheduled network, all was not well at Channel Airways by the early 1970s. Complaints of noise and operating restrictions at the original main base at Southend had seen the jet operations forced to move to Stansted Airport, expensively splitting the company into separate jet and propeller units. After much legal wrangling and numerous appeals to the licensing authorities, Channel had been awarded a route from Stansted to Glasgow, although permission to operate additional schedules from Stansted to Belfast and Newcastle had been refused. Unfortunately, before operations could begin on the Glasgow route, the approval was reversed and plans for the service had to be abandoned. The One-Elevens did open a scheduled service from Stansted though, beginning a weekly night-tourist flight to Rimini on 25 May 1971. This route had previously been operated by British Eagle from Heathrow.

Bold plans to acquire more One-Elevens and Tridents fell by the wayside, along with even more ambitious visions of operating Boeing 707s on trans-Atlantic charters, as financial problems began to worsen. Of the five Trident 1Es ordered, only two were placed into service and one

of those spent most of its time idle and engineless at Stansted, being stripped for spares to keep the other aircraft flying out of Berlin. The three remaining Tridents were sold before delivery, one to Air Ceylon, the other two to BKS Air Transport, owned by British Air Services, a subsidiary of BEA that had previously been negotiating for a pair of Series 500 One-Elevens until the Tridents became available.

A quick-fix solution to their continuing operational problems had been hoped for when Channel took delivery of a fleet of ex-Olympic Airways and BEA Comet 4Bs, but a shortage of spares led to two disastrous summer seasons in 1970 and 1971. Endless expensive delays and sub-chartering of flights to other carriers saw both the tour companies and creditors rapidly beginning to lose patience with the airline. Both Tridents were sold off to BEA at the end of 1971 in an attempt to stabilize the situation.

In 1971, 386,400 passengers were carried on the inclusive tour flights, with only 155,600 on the scheduled services, approximately the same totals that had been carried on a smaller fleet of Viscounts and HS 748s five years earlier in 1966. The two One-Elevens in service during 1971 had averaged only 1,173 hours each that year, barely three hours a day of utilization. Eventually, all jet operations came to an end on 15 February 1972, two weeks after the company entered receivership. Propeller aircraft operations,

with a handful of Viscounts and DH Herons at Southend, continued for a couple more weeks but Channel Airways finally ceased to exist on 29 February.

While BAC had been unable to close the deal to sell a pair of Series 500s to BKS Air Transport, the sister company to BKS, Cambrian Airways, based at Cardiff, was to become a One-Eleven operator in 1970. Both BKS and Cambrian had started life as independent operators. BKS concentrated on developing scheduled and charter services from the northeast of England, after starting life at Southend in 1952. Cambrian Airways, promoting itself as the Welsh national airline, had been almost exclusively a scheduled operator although inclusive tour and *ad hoc* charters were forming a valuable part of its operations by the late 1960s.

Both airlines were brought together under the banner of British Air Services Ltd, wholly owned by BEA, after financial pressures had almost closed them both down in the early part of the decade. With BEA's patronage and support both companies managed to weather several financial storms and were regarded as reliable, quality operators. By 1969, BKS was flying the pair of Trident 1Es plus four Bristol Britannias, several Viscounts and the sole survivor of a once large fleet of Airspeed Ambassadors on scheduled networks centred on Newcastle, Leeds/Bradford and London-

British United's G-ASJA. Aviation Hobby Shop

RAE's XX105 at Fairford. Steve Edmunds

SAS' G-ATPL on lease from British Eagle. Aviation Hobby Shop

(Top) **Dan-Air's G-ATTP at Bristol.** Martyn East

(Middle) **Braniff's bright red N1548 at Tulsa.** Tim Kincaid collection

(Bottom) **Evening arrival for American's N5020.** Tim Kincaid collection

(Top) **Birmingham European's G-BBME at Amsterdam.** Steve Bunting

(Middle) **USAir's N1123J.** Aviation Hobby Shop

(Bottom) **Quebecair's C-GQBP in the later blue livery.** MAP

Laker Airway's G-AVYZ. MAP

(Below) **Air Bristol/Air Belfast's fleet of 510EDs.** AB Airlines

G-AVMY at its Manchester home base. Steve Bunting

G-AXMU landing at Bristol on lease to Airways Cymru. Martyn East

Paninternational's 515FB, D-ALAT. Aviation Hobby Shop

Monarch's G-BCXR at Manchester. Steve Bunting

Court Line Aviation's turquoise G-AXMJ. Aviation Hobby Shop

Phoenix HB-ITL at Basle. Aviation Hobby Shop

(Top) **G-AZPZ joined BCal in 1982.** Steve Bunting

(Above) **G-OBWC after starting a new career with British World.** MAP

(Below) **Air Pacific's 479FU, DQ-FBQ in flight.** Brooklands Museum

(Top) **VIP 488GH, HZ-MAM under construction.** Brooklands Museum   *(Above)* **ROMBAC One-Eleven, YR-BRD went on to fly with Aero Asia.** Steve Bunting

Heathrow. Inclusive tour contracts were very important to BKS, with all three operating bases servicing sizeable contracts from the travel industry.

Cambrian Airways had become an associate of BEA after the corporation saved the Welsh airline from impending bankruptcy in 1958. At the beginning of 1969, Cambrian was operating a respectably sized Viscount fleet, of no less than eleven ex-BEA Series 700s. With its head office at Cardiff, an operating base was also established at Liverpool following the transfer of BEA's Irish Sea services in 1963. There was also a smaller crew base at London-Heathrow. When British Eagle had folded, Cambrian found itself the sole operator on the important Liverpool–London route.

When Autair International became Court Line Aviation and replaced their Series 400s with the higher-capacity Series 500s, Cambrian immediately acquired two of them, G-AVOE and G-AVOF. The Welsh airline took delivery of 'OF in December 1969, with 'OE following a month later. A third ex-Autair One-Eleven, G-AVGP, was delivered in July 1970. Initially the One-Elevens, after completion of crew training duties at Liverpool, were used almost exclusively for inclusive tour services, especially over the Bristol–Palma route. From April, the jets were also operating scheduled services for Cambrian from London–Heathrow to Cork, the Isle of Man and Liverpool, and from Liverpool to Dublin.

Cambrian's ex-Autair One-Elevens made their debut on charters. Brooklands Museum

April 1970 saw Cambrian's One-Elevens on scheduled routes. MAP

One barrier to the operation of the jets on more scheduled services was the restricted runway at Cardiff Airport, serving the Welsh capital as well as being Cambrian's head office and prime scheduled and charter services base. This was remedied in 9 March 1979 when a new 7,000ft runway was finally ready for use. Cambrian had planned to position a One-Eleven over from Bristol at 10am, to gain the distinction of being the first jet to land at Cardiff. Great civic ceremonies were planned involving local and national dignitaries. Unfortunately, the weather intervened and the cold frosty dawn saw the

to Alicante, Barcelona, Ibiza, Malaga, Palma and Venice. Cambrian Air Holidays also chartered Cambrian Airways Viscounts for holiday services to Ostend from Bristol and Cardiff.

The Cambrian One-Elevens were also leased out, on rotation, with full crews, to BEA for much of 1970, and on several subsequent occasions up until 1972. Wearing BEA stickers, the Cambrian aircraft flew out of West Berlin on the scheduled domestic network. The crews were based there for up to three weeks at a time, with several of the cabin crew initially being confused by the unusual folding style of German news-

changing the carrier's name to Northeast Airlines, better reflecting its sphere of influence in northeastern England. Northeast's version of the new BAS livery was identical to Cambrian's, except their cabin roof was bright yellow, but with the company titles and new logo in black, as on Cambrian.

It had been intended that the new image for the British Air Services companies would be expanded. From the beginning of the 1970s, the BEA Viscount fleet had been operated by two new divisions, BEA Scottish Airways was based at Glasgow and BEA Channel Islands, perhaps a little less logically, was based at Birming-

The new Cambrian livery gave the company a much more modern image. MAP

Cambrian jet thoroughly ice-bound on the ground at Bristol's Lulsgate Airport, a tantalizing five-minute hop away over the Severn Estuary. Engineers at Bristol did their best, but the One-Eleven was not able to beat an Aer Lingus Boeing 737 that arrived at Cardiff ten minutes before it, on a normal scheduled service from Dublin.

To get more profitable utilization out of their expensive new jets, Cambrian set up its own holiday company, Cambrian Air Holidays, offering over 16,000 inclusive tour seats in its first 1970 brochure. The 'Cambrian Luck' continued though, with the inaugural flight to Malaga being diverted to Seville, following torrential rains and flooding in southern Spain. Once things settled down though, Cambrian was operating One-Eleven holiday flights from Bristol, Cardiff and Liverpool

papers. One stewardess found she had mistakenly distributed just one page each to the planeload of rather bemused German passengers! During 1970, BEA also wet-leased Cambrian One-Elevens for a number of scheduled services from Dublin to Birmingham and Manchester.

The arrival of a fourth One-Eleven, Court Lines sole Series 400, G-AWBL, in early 1971, coincided with a change in image for Cambrian. The plain red white and blue British Air Services livery, also worn by BKS, was swept away by a modern new colour scheme, consisting of a deep orange roof, white cheat-line and grey underside. Large Cambrian titles in black were complemented by an updated Welsh Dragon logo carried on the tail, also in black. Sister British Air Services airline, BKS, had also updated their image,

ham. Scottish Airways also flew DH Herons, later replaced by Short's Skyliners, on local Highlands and Islands services. Channel Islands operated one of the two ex-Channel Airways Trident 1Es bought by BEA, the other passing to Northeast, although the Trident only carried normal BEA titles, without the 'Channel Islands' suffix. It was expected that the two operating divisions would join BAS as new separate airlines. It was even proposed that Scottish aircraft would wear a blue version of the BAS design, and the Channel Island fleet, a green-based styling. However, national events overtook these ambitious plans that would eventually see the total disappearance of British Air Services, Cambrian, Northeast, Channel Islands and Scottish Airways from the airline scene.

A re-merger between British European Airways and British Overseas Airways, BEA and BOAC, had been mooted for many years. Almost, indeed, since 1946, when BEA had been split away from BOAC in the first place. The proposal had been resisted by the corporations for years, both carriers claiming that specialization in their own fields was better for all concerned. Eventually though, politics intervened and, on 1 April 1972, the British Airways Board came into being, bringing the operations of BEA, BOAC and BAS under their control and creating the new British Airways. Any plans for their transfer to BAS control abandoned, Channel

1972, flying inclusive tour charters on behalf of BEA Airtours. From October 1973 to June 1974, G-AWBL was wetleased, complete with both flight-deck and cabin crews, to Gulf Air as Gulf Aviation had become. Joining Gulf's own One-Elevens on regional scheduled services, G-AWBL continued to wear the orange Cambrian colours, with green Gulf Air titles on the cabin roof in English and Arabic. G-AVOF was also leased out to Gulf Air for October and November 1974. On its return to the UK, G-AWBL continued to carry the Gulf Air titles for several months, confusing the Liverpool–London passengers no end.

opened Cardiff–Bristol–Brussels route being swiftly dropped before it lost even more money. Gradually, other services followed until only Belfast, Dublin, Guernsey, Jersey and Paris flights were operated from Cardiff by the Viscount fleet. The One-Elevens still flew from Liverpool and London in their new BA liveries, until the total merger of Cambrian and Northeast into British Airways Regional Division on 1 April 1976 took place.

While their old Series 400 One-Eleven fleet members were establishing themselves at their new home with Cambrian, Court Line Aviation was building up its colourful Series 500 operation at Luton.

Cambrian's identity was soon being smothered by British Airways. MAP

Islands and Scottish Airways continued their semi-autonomous operations as before. Eventually, Cambrian, Channel Islands, Northeast and Scottish came under the control of the newly founded British Airways Regional Division although Cambrian and Northeast initially continued to operate under their own names. A final show of resistance within Cambrian and Northeast towards full integration into British Airways saw female staff of both carriers adopting an identical brown and orange uniform, totally different from the new British Airways outfit.

Despite all the political upheavals going on around them, Cambrian had still expanded their One-Eleven services, with new scheduled routes from London to Dubrovnik and Lyons. One One-Eleven had been based at Gatwick for most of

From 1974, the Cambrian and Northeast aircraft started to carry full British Airways titles, with their own company names, much smaller, on their lower fuselages. One by one the aircraft were completely repainted in full British Airways colours and their individual airline identities started to fade away in the public consciousness, although British Airways-Northeast continued to handle their own and British Airways-Cambrian movements separately at Heathrow for at least another year.

The base at Cardiff suffered greatly from the loss of Cambrian's identity. Services from there had rarely been profitable, but that the Welsh national carrier would withdraw totally from the Principality's capital was unthinkable. British Airways though had no such qualms. The most unprofitable services were withdrawn first, with a newly

Two new aircraft arrived in early 1971, following the disposal, to Cambrian, of the last Series 400, G-AWBL. Two more second-hand aircraft arrived later in the year, and another new one in early 1972. 1971 had seen the lease of an Austral aircraft, and 1972 saw the lease of two of British Midland's Series 500s, at separate times. until September 1973.

Court Caribbean Adventure

Following the success of the winter lease of an aircraft to Aviateca in 1970–71, another Series 500 was leased to LANICA, of Nicaragua from December 1971 to March 1972. The aircraft was needed to temporarily replace LANICA's Series 400 which had been ferried to Hurn for repair by BAC. During an attempted hijack, the aircraft's interior had been damaged by fire. Still in the pink Court Line livery, G-AXML became AN-BHJ for the period of the lease. The Series 500 was replaced by an ex-American Airlines Series 400, also on lease, until a pair of Convair 880 jets took over the One-Eleven services, LANICA's own aircraft being sold on as soon as it had been repaired.

The Convairs were owned by the Hughes Tool Company that had recently purchased a large shareholding in LANICA. The Convairs had originally been leased by Hughes to TWA and Northeast Airlines in the US, but found them difficult to place once the original leases ended. Hughes was pleased to find a new home for their redundant fleet of Convair jets as

the network. By 1960, four Beechcraft Bonanzas and two DH Herons made up the fleet and the headquarters had been transferred from Monserrat to Antigua.

Delisle initially continued to control LIAT and, in 1965, the airline put its first turbo-prop, a HS 748, into service. A pair of DHC Otters were soon replaced by Britten Norman Islanders, a total of five of which were eventually operated. An extra 748 was leased from Autair each winter from 1967. Court Line's initial 75 per cent holding in LIAT was increased a year later to 100 per cent in October 1971. Court Line had already invested in the building of several new hotels in the islands and were anxious to acquire a foothold in the local airline industry to carry their clients to the resorts.

aircraft concerned was the same one that had been leased a year before to Aviateca, G-AXMK, and was re-registered locally as VP-LAK, although it retained its Court Line fleet name of 'Halcyon Star'. Both the ex-Autair 748s followed the same month and the 'new look' LIAT was soon making its colourful presence felt throughout the Caribbean.

The original aircraft was replaced by VP-LAN that had been ordered by Court Line specifically for use by LIAT, arriving in June 1972. Another One-Eleven, VP-LAP, ex-G-AZEB, joined 'AN in November 1972, and an extra aircraft, VP-LAR, ex-G-AZEC, arrived in December 1973. In LIAT service, the cabins were reconfigured from the 119-seat inclusive tour layout to 99-passenger scheduled service standard.

Lanica 412EB, AN-BBI, was replaced by Convair CV-880s. Aviation Hobby Shop

part of the deal with the airline, although the operating economics of the larger four-engined aircraft, compared to the twin-jet One-Elevens, were dubious over LANICA's small, mostly regional network.

In 1971 Court Line had purchased a 75 per cent shareholding in Leeward Islands Air Transport, of Antigua in the Caribbean. LIAT had been operating a scheduled network of great social worth, if questionable profitability, since its formation by Frank Delisle of Monserrat in 1956. Delisle's single aircraft operation was acquired by British West Indian Airways the following year, continuing operations in its own name as a separate subsidiary. The fleet expanded over the following years as more of the islands were added to

Part of the purchase agreement saw Court Line permanently transferring its two ex-Autair 748s, plus the seasonal transfer of one of the Court Line Aviation One-Elevens, to the Caribbean operation. It was envisaged that LIAT and Court Line Aviation would, in effect, become one carrier with two different spheres of operation. The fact that both operational areas had opposite annual peak and trough seasons was regarded as a definite bonus. LIAT also took on Court Line Aviation's multi-coloured image, repainting the existing fleet in the all-over pastel shades that did, perhaps, seem to suit the Caribbean climate a bit better than windswept Bedfordshire.

The first Court Line One-Eleven was delivered to LIAT in November 1971. The

The aircraft were used throughout the LIAT system on a network that stretched from Puerto Rico, in the north, through the Leeward Islands, down to the Windward Islands and Trinidad in the south.

As part of the planned integration of the two airlines, there was a considerable amount of exchange of information and personnel between LIAT and Court Line Aviation. Staff members of both carriers took part in base exchanges, learning a great deal from each other's different style of operations. As part of their One-Eleven conversion courses, LIAT stewardesses also operated on some of Court Line's UK-based charters during the summer. They had obtained permission to shorten the already skimpy Court Line Aviation uniform skirt to a length more in common with what they were used to wearing with LIAT in the Caribbean. In the less politically correct 1970s, this certainly helped make them popular additions to the crew, at least among the male passengers and airport workers.

The seconded Court Line Aviation One-Eleven flight-deck crews in the Caribbean were certainly experiencing a totally different flying environment from their more usual European operations.

pany had been hoping for. Court Line was determined that fares would have to increase in order to make the LIAT operation profitable. The island governments were just as determined that fares would not rise and refused to sanction the increases. Court Line actually carried out a threat to withdraw the LIAT One-Elevens on 15 October 1972. Faced with the loss of prestige to their national carrier, fare increases were finally agreed by the Council of

make economies in all areas. In April 1974, at the end of that year's Caribbean tourist season, LIAT withdrew the One-Elevens again, returning the aircraft to Court Line at Luton for use on that summer's European holiday programme.

LIAT had no plans to abandon jet operations entirely, with studies being made of the then new Hawker Siddeley HS146 project as a long-term One-Eleven and HS 748 replacement. By July 1974, however,

Court Line Aviation's influence on LIAT was obvious. Aviation Hobby Shop

VP-LAN was diverted to LIAT from Court Lines. Peter Vine via Jennie Gradidge

Runways in the islands were of widely varying standards and not always of ideal length. Landing at Grenada called for full reverse thrust and very hard braking, assuming that they had landed before the white line painted across the runway as a guide for the pilots, with a view to them not ending up overrunning into the sea.

The use of the One-Elevens did not provide the higher load factors that the com-

Ministers in January 1973 and jet services began again. More fare increases followed over the next year, but were still regarded as inadequate and the international fuel crisis of 1974 did nothing to ease the situation.

When the Oil Producing and Exporting Countries (OPEC) put huge price increases into place, the era of cheap aviation fuel was over. LIAT, in common with most airlines around the world, was having to

the Court Line Board had made the decision to dispose of LIAT, following increasing losses to the parent company in maintaining the Caribbean operation. The Board of Trade was informed of the decision, but events rapidly overtook any such actions being planned.

Back in Europe, the inclusive tour industry was growing fast, perhaps too fast. Vertical integration, with the tour companies being major shareholders in the airlines was rife and did effectively contribute to reduced costs, leading to cheaper and cheaper holidays. In no time this erupted into a rabid price war, with holiday companies vying with each other to offer the best deal and fill the most hotel rooms and aircraft seats.

British Midland had found it impossible to tender for contracts at economic rates and finally withdrew from mass inclusive tour work in 1972. Initially, of their three-aircraft One-Eleven fleet, one aircraft was leased to Court Line, one sold and the third retained for use on scheduled services and a much reduced charter programme, mainly from East Midlands. In early 1974, the remaining aircraft were sold on to Transbrasil, with BMA receiving three of their Handley Page Dart Heralds as part of the deal. With these, and an

enlarged Viscount fleet, the airline decided to concentrate on building up its scheduled service network.

Court Line and Clarksons were major players in the price war and the group was determined to take as much market share as possible. Being the leaders in mass travel was their vision and larger aircraft were needed to fulfil this dream. Various types were studied, including yet larger versions of the One-Eleven, as well as the original Airbus A300 designs. In the end, an order was placed for two leased Lockheed L1011 Tristars in August 1972, with options taken out on three more. The original letter of intent for the Tristars had been signed as far back as July 1970.

Configured for no less than 400 inclusive tour passengers, the first Tristar, the bright orange 'Halcyon Days', arrived at

Luton in March 1973, followed by a second, an equally bright pink 'Halcyon Breeze', two months later. As the first European operator of the Tristar, Court Line Aviation suffered a great deal from the teething problems of the advanced and largely untried aircraft. Most of the provincial Mediterranean resort airports the aircraft served were simply not properly equipped to deal with the influx of 400 passenger off one aircraft. Attempts had been made to alleviate the problem, with electrical conveyors being fitted in the aircraft hold, as containerized baggage handling was almost unheard of except at a few major airports at this time. Large fresh water tanks were fitted, to allow sufficient return supplies to be uplifted in the UK before departure and much of the rear hold was given over to house a retractable

(Above) **Court Line Aviation's fleet continued their UK-based operations.** Aviation Hobby Shop

(Below) **The Court Tristars could carry up to 400 passengers.** Aviation Hobby Shop

airstair for use at airports unable to provide steps for the wide-body.

Despite the early problems, the aircraft did eventually settle into European holiday charter work alongside the One-Elevens. With the arrival of winter, the 400-passenger capacity was definitely not required in Europe, but a number of long-range charters to Kingston, Jamaica, Hadj flights from Malaysia to Mecca, a Lockheed and Rolls-Royce-sponsored demonstration and sales trip to Moscow and a couple of Munich–Puerto Rico charters kept the aircraft busy enough. For the long-range work, the Tristar's configuration was reduced to 350.

Even before acquiring the LIAT operation, Court Line had already purchased or built several new hotels in the Caribbean. Hoped-for loads of American and Canadian tourists had not materialized and it looked to Court Line Aviation to provide it with extra clients by flying them in from Europe in the new Tristars. Up until then, any UK originating clients had been expensively flown on BOAC scheduled services, which was far from the spirit of vertical integration. The arrival of the Tristars meant that Clarkson's 'Go-Caribbean' passengers would be carried on their own company's aircraft for the 1974 season, with regular flights arranged from Luton to St Lucia and Antigua.

One travel company that floundered in the price war was the highly respected Horizon Holiday Group. Horizon Holidays had actually been one of the first companies to offer the 'Inclusive tour' concept using chartered aircraft. In 1949 the first series of charter flights carried over 300 holiday-makers to Corsica, by Air Transport Charter Ltd DC-3. However, despite its pioneering work and subsequent rapid growth, by early 1974 it was in a very precarious financial situation. Horizon was finally saved by Court Line buying it out and operating it as a partner to Clarksons. Horizon, with sister companies Four S Travel, Horizon Midlands and Scottish and Irish subsidiaries, had contracted most of their flying to British Caledonian. Naturally, Court Line wanted its own in-house airline to take over the work. The prospect of losing the valuable contract, sufficient to keep three of their One-Eleven fleet busy, was an alarming one to British Caledonian. Already suffering as much as everyone with the international fuel crisis, BCal fought to hold on to the business and eventually managed to retain at least part of it.

All Court Line Operations suddenly ceased in August 1974. via Author

Court Line struggled through the first half of 1974, battling to operate economically against higher priced and increasingly scarce fuel supplies, as well as falling holiday sales caused by the generally bad financial situation in the country as a whole. With unemployment and lay-offs common, people were simply unwilling to commit themselves to an expensive trip abroad. Prices were slashed again, in an attempt to attract what little business there was and the holiday companies were soon selling their wares at a huge loss.

In an attempt to ease the situation Court Line had managed to arrange potentially profitable leases for two of their One-Elevens, one each to Germanair and Cyprus Airways, and the Tristars were operated more out of Gatwick, which was better equipped to deal with the larger aircraft than Luton. It was still a situation that could hardly be expected to go on for long. In June 1974, it was announced that the UK government would pay £16 million for Court Line's shipping interests, in the hope that the injection of cash would keep the leisure-based group afloat. It succeeded in this only until 22.00 hours on 15 August. At that time, all operations of Court Line Aviation and the Court Line Leisure Division that encompassed Clarksons, Four S Travel, Halcyon Holidays, OSL Travel, Air Fair and Horizon Holidays, ceased immediately. This had the effect of stranding 50,000 clients abroad and cancelling holidays for 150,000 others. The very last commercial flight by Court Line Aviation was the completion of a Tristar charter from St Lucia, which arrived at Luton on the morning of the 16th.

Most of the remaining One-Elevens were present in the UK before the axe fell in the late evening of the 15th, that evening's night charters being in the first to be cancelled, stranding their passengers at airports with tickets for holidays that would now never take place. Most of the aircraft were soon home at Luton, except for G-AYOR, impounded by the airport authorities at Cardiff and G-AXMF suffering the same ignominy at Manchester, held against outstanding debts to the airports. The aircraft leased out to Germanair continued to operate for its temporary owner for the period of the lease contract. G-AXMG, leased out to Cyprus Airways as 5B-DAF, was even less fortunate. Even before the collapse of Court Line, it had already been stranded at Nicosia Airport by the Turkish invasion of Northern Cyprus in July, only two months after having entered service with Cyprus Airways, operating alongside their Trident fleet. It was to be over a year before it was eventually released and returned to BAC at Hurn in December 1975.

Although still officially owned by the now defunct Court Line, LIAT was quickly reformed by the island government as LIAT (1974) Ltd and continued to operate a fleet of HS 748s and Islanders. Although the HS146 jet order never materialized, LIAT (1974) Ltd managed to survive as a turbo-prop operator, maintaining the vital inter-island links.

The One-Eleven still maintained a presence in the Caribbean, with the established Cayman Airways and Central American operators continuing to fly the type on their scheduled routes throughout the region. In July 1971, Flamingo Airlines of Nassau in the Bahamas, leased a Series 200, N1543, from Braniff for operation on their scheduled routes from Nassau to Freeport and Port au Prince. Flamingo had been established by private investors in March 1971, to take over the local services of Bahamas Airways. The Flamingo One-Eleven operation only lasted until May 1972, with services afterwards being flown by an established fleet of two Lockheed Electras and a single Convair 340.

Out Island contributed VP-BDI to Bahamasair. D. Spurgeon via Jennie Gradidge

However, another Bahamian carrier, Out Island Airways, purchased two of the ex-American Series 400 fleet the following year. Out Island had operated a small fleet of Twin Otters, a variety of light aircraft including several amphibians, and a single Fairchild FH-227. Re-registered locally as VP-BDI and VP-BDJ, the first of the two One-Elevens entered service in local inter-island schedules in March 1973, followed by the second in June.

On 1 July, Out Island Airways and Flamingo Airlines were merged to form a new national carrier, Bahamasair. The One-Elevens continued with the new carrier, with two more arriving from American in November and December, although one of the original pair was sold after the December arrivals. The aircraft continued to operate within the Bahamas, as well as operating new scheduled flights to Miami and Atlanta. Bahamasair took delivery of its first leased Boeing 737 in 1978, and the type gradually replaced the original jets, until the last of the One-Elevens left the fleet in 1984. Bahamasair continued to enjoy chequered fortunes over the years, with the airline reverting to an all turbo-prop operation on occasion.

The fuel crisis and worsening financial climate had led to British Caledonian employing drastic measures to stop themselves following Court Line into oblivion. On the plus side, the One-Eleven service to Paris had transferred its operation from Le Bourget to the new Charles de Gaulle Airport on 20 March 1974. A trans-Atlantic network, with daily departures from Gatwick to both New York and Los Angeles

had opened in 1973, using the Boeing 707 fleet. The ex-BUA VC-10s had been withdrawn in deference to the American aircraft the previous year. Early in 1974, two of the BCal Series 500s found themselves temporary new homes in South America, being leased out to Austral and Transbrasil.

The One-Eleven service from Gatwick to Brussels had opened in June and the Gatwick–Manchester route was finally in operation, after years of hearings and appeals. However, the latter route was not initially operated by the One-Elevens, BCal using chartered British Island Airways Dart Heralds instead. The British Island Airways Dart Herald fleet also took over operation of the Gatwick–Le Touquet 'Silver Arrow' service on behalf of BCal.

British Caledonian soon found itself losing money at an alarming rate though and serious action had to be taken. On 31 October 1974, the scheduled trans-Atlantic network was axed, having failed to achieve the hoped-for load factors. The Gatwick–Belfast service was dropped and taken over by British Midland Airways, using Viscounts, with the Glasgow–Southampton One-Eleven route being handed over to British Airways, who placed their Viscounts on the service. Also closed down were One-Eleven-operated scheduled routes from Gatwick to Gibraltar and Tunis, and the Edinburgh–Newcastle–Copenhagen flights. The multi-stop One-Eleven service to West Africa, operated since the introduction of the type by BUA, was also dropped, the cities on the route still being served by Boeing 707s on direct flights to Gatwick.

A great number of British Caledonian's staff and management found themselves made redundant and several of the One-Eleven fleet were also surplus to requirements. Allocation of more of the aircraft to charter services, and further leasing out of Series 500s to Air Malta and Austrian Airlines helped, although some of the fleet still found themselves in temporary storage. On the remaining routes, special promotions were inaugurated in an effort to increase loads. In the winter of 1975, a special fare was introduced on the routes from Gatwick to Edinburgh and Glasgow, with half-price weekend fares available, provided the booking was not made until the Friday immediately before the flight.

BA One-Eleven Expansion

Even before acquiring the Cambrian Series 400 fleet, British Airways Regional Division had already made plans to expand operations of the type, as at least partial replacements for their still large fleet of Viscounts. Three second-hand Series 400s, from various sources, were bought by the British Airways Board for use by the Regional Division in late 1973. The ex-Orientair aircraft, G-AZMI, found its way to British Airways from storage at Hurn, becoming G-BBME. The ex-Channel G-AWEJ, converted from its high-density layout, followed, reregistered G-BBMG, and ex-American and Bahamasair G-BBMF completed the trio in December. Unfortunately, G-BBMF disgraced itself a year later in December 1974, being forced

BCal's Series 500s began to be seen more on scheduled services. MAP

Series 201ACs continued to be the backbone of the BCal One-Eleven fleet. MAP

to make a landing on foam at Hurn after the nose-gear failed to extend. There were no injuries to the occupants and the aircraft was repaired and returned to service.

The British Airways Series 400 aircraft were operated mostly from Birmingham, replacing some of the older Viscounts and the single Trident 1E which was passed on to Northeast Airlines. With the three other Northeast Trident 1Es, the aircraft continued to operate in its BEA livery, with British Airways main titles and 'Northeast' in small letters on its lower fuselage.

The BEA Super One-Eleven Division Series 500s had, of course, also become part of the British Airways fleet after the merger between BEA and BOAC. The BEA/Air France agreement for joint operations from Berlin had ended in October 1972. The result of this was that many of the One-Elevens were decorated in full BEA colours for the first time, but then British Airways titles started to be applied over the BEA livery. Still operating mostly from Manchester and Berlin, the Series 500s were also now seen on more regional services from Glasgow and Jersey.

After full integration into British Airways Regional Division, the ex-Cambrian One-Elevens also started to be based at Birmingham. This followed BA's commercial operations at the ex-Cambrian bases at Liverpool and Cardiff being gradually run down over the years as financial recession hit both the local business and leisure traffic. British Airways Regional Division itself was to disappear following a reorganization within BA in 1977. When the BA livery was later changed from white to grey roofs, British Airways Series 400 One-Elevens were all given individual 'County' names reflecting the Midlands area and their extensive use on European and domestic flights from Birmingham, the largest city in the region served by BA.

BA gathered a trio of Series 400s together for regional services. via Author

BEA's Super One-Elevens continued in BA service as before. MAP

Although there were commercial casualties along the way, by the mid-1970s the inclusive tour and charter industry had changed beyond all recognition from only ten years before. The use of more modern aircraft like the One-Eleven made the whole process much more attractive to the travelling public and expanded their horizons. It also increased their expectations and charter airlines were having to match their service standards closer to the scheduled carriers. There were few inclusive tour companies daring to try and sell holidays using propeller-driven aircraft by 1976. The last of the once seemingly giant Bristol Britannia turbo-props no longer carried capacity loads to the Mediterranean holiday resorts and were either long scrapped or flying freight. Once omnipresent Vickers Viscounts were confined to shorter or low-capacity scheduled services and piston types had all but vanished.

The airlines of the world were starting to look for their third generation of jet transports. The One-Eleven, Caravelle, DC-9 and Boeing 737 had proved the viability of twin-engined jets on short-haul services. The OPEC crisis had made fuel economy a top priority and a new interest was being taken in noise levels around the airport as much as it once was in the passenger cabin. These were the new concerns that all the world's aircraft manufacturers would have to address. New types and versions of the One-Eleven and the other twin-engined jets were on the way, but which would the airlines sign orders for?

The enlarged Series 400 fleet linked many UK regional points. Steve Bunting

CHAPTER SIX

False Starts, False Hopes

Although the Series 475 had only managed to attract limited interest from potential customers, BAC was still trying to come up with the right combination of power, capacity, range and operating economy that would sell more aircraft. Main rival to the Series 475 was undoubtedly the Fokker F.28 Fellowship that, following a protracted gestation, had finally managed to establish itself as a successful twin-jet airliner of Japan. Due to the nature of the mountainous terrain of the Japanese island group, many of the airports were in very restrictive locations and the airlines were confined to operating prop-jet or even piston-engine-powered aircraft into quite major cities. The Japanese aircraft industry had produced a turbo-prop airliner, the NAMC YS-11, specifically to serve these markets and large fleets were operated by the major Japanese domestic airlines, the aircraft having entered service in 1965. Powered by two Rolls Royce Darts, the 50–60-passenger NAMC YS-11 also managed a limited number of foreign sales, with aircraft being exported to Philippine Air Lines and the US regional carrier, Piedmont Air Lines. With a view to possible Japanese orders as a YS-11 replacement, the Series 475 design was modified, the long-suffering development aircraft, G-ASYD, being trundled back into the hangar yet again. Although G-ASYD, as the Series prototype, had already made a successful series of demonstration flights in Japan, operating from some runways as short as 4,000ft, the Japanese authorities insisted on improved performance margins before they would consider certifying the aircraft for local Japanese airline operations.

Initially proposed as the Series 475D, the changes to the aircraft included an extension of the trailing edge flap chord by 4.65

G-ASYD was demonstrated in Japan as both the Series 475 and 670. MAP

design. Rough-field versions of the Boeing 737 were also available and also had a limited sales success. While the One-Eleven Series 475 and modified 737 had been adapted from original main-line aircraft to make them suitable for rough-field airports and other extremes, the Fokker aircraft had been designed from the outset to cope with such conditions. This gave the F.28 a definite edge in the minds of many airline executives searching for an airliner to spread jet service to more remote regions.

The short-field potential of the Series 475 was promoted heavily to the airlines

per cent and a redesign of the wing leading edge. Wind-tunnel testing found that these modifications would have reduced the maximum weights and a new solution, involving a more limited redesign of the wing only from the wing root to the wing fence was found to be all that was required to solve the problem if a triangular fillet was fitted to the leading edge. A Hydrol Mk 111A anti-skid system, automatic braking and deployment of lift dumpers and an improved silencing system in the area of the engines' exhaust were also proposed in an effort to gain Japanese certification.

The development aircraft was redesignated the Series 670, in an effort to distinguish it from the earlier versions and emphasize the new improvements. G-ASYD first flew in its new guise on 13 September 1977, followed by an extensive flight trials programme. Despite the design changes proving successful in the trials, no Japanese certification, or airline orders were forthcoming.

The Series 700, an even more stretched Series 500 powered by Spey 606s, carrying 119–134 passengers was also proposed. As well as production as a new aircraft, the Series 700 was also offered as a conversion of existing Series 500s. A 700J version, with a new technology high-lift wing was developed with the ever elusive Japanese market in mind. Once again though, it failed to arouse sufficient interest to lead

to orders, despite offers of joint development and production with the Japanese aerospace industry. An even bigger stretch of the Series 500, the 144–161-passenger Series 800 was also on offer off the drawing board. The first non-Rolls-Royce Spey-powered One-Eleven, the Series 800 would have been fitted with two General Electric/SNECMA CFM56s of 22,000lb static thrust. A maximum take-off weight

The proposed Series 700 was a further stretch of the 500. Brooklands Museum   *(Below)* **Both scheduled and charter configurations were on offer.** Brooklands Museum

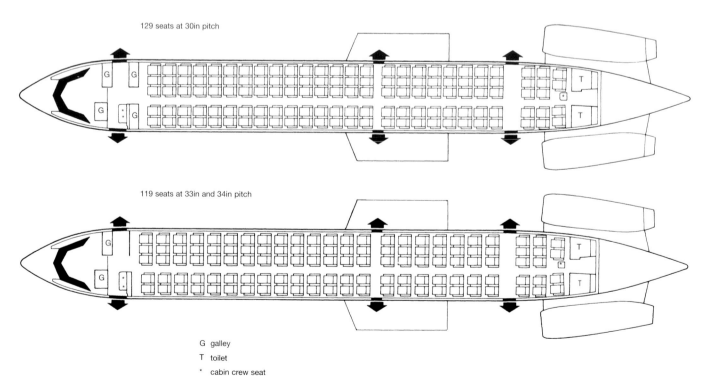

129 seats at 30in pitch

119 seats at 33in and 34in pitch

G galley

T toilet

* cabin crew seat

The Series 800 would have been the first non-Spey powered One-Eleven. Brooklands Museum

of 137,000lb and a range of 2,400 miles would have been achieved with a ten-foot increase in wing span over the Series 500.

Beyond the One-Eleven

Although not strictly developments of the One-Eleven, BAC had also put forward speculative designs for two much larger aircraft which were, at least, to be numbered in the same sequence as the Two-Eleven and the Three-Eleven. As early as the mid-1960s the first of the proposed new designs, the BAC Two-Eleven, was attracting some airline interest.

The wing, fin and tailplane of the Two-Elevens were directly scaled up from the One-Eleven and the fuselage was not only stretched, but also widened to permit comfortable six-abreast seating. With a fuselage length of 165ft, a wingspan of over 125ft, an overall height of 35ft and a wheel-base of over 78ft, the Two-Eleven would have been a formidable aircraft for its time, capable of carrying 176 passengers in a scheduled service, mixed-class layout. Up to 219 charter passengers could be carried on medium and short-haul services.

Autair actually placed firm orders for the Two-Eleven. Brooklands Museum

The powerplant chosen was to be the new Rolls-Royce RB211-08, still under development, a pair of which would be installed on the rear fuselage, in the same fashion as the One-Eleven's Speys. Autair International Airways had just placed a firm order for three aircraft when, as is so often the case, politics intervened. The Labour Government of the day announced it would not offer financial support for the Two-Eleven project and BAC was forced to withdraw the proposal.

A similar fate was to befall the Three-Eleven, an even more ambitious new option from BAC. Designed to fulfil the growing airline interest in wide-bodied short-haul aircraft, it was planned that the Three-Eleven was also to be powered by two rear-mounted RB211 engines. A typical mixed class configuration allowed for 36 first-class and 168 economy class seats, or up to 300 passengers could be accommodated in a nine-abreast charter layout.

The market for the wide-bodied short-haul airliner was still regarded as a limited one at the time. With US giants Lockheed and McDonnell-Douglas already offering their L-1011 Tristar and DC-10 tri-jets, the European aircraft manufacturers were having trouble getting sufficient interest generated in their own designs for the new market. The European manufacturers came to recognize that, in order to fight the American companies, they would have to join forces and offer a combined proposal.

France's Sud-Aviation already had a 300-seat wide-bodied design, the Galion, under study. In 1966, the French design was used as the basis for a slightly smaller, 260-passenger aircraft, the HBN 100, to be designed and built jointly by Hawker Siddeley and the other European partners. This was further refined to emerge as the A300. A joint French/British study into the potential market for such an aircraft led, in 1970, to the formal establishment of the Airbus Industrie consortium, with the aerospace industries of the UK, France and West Germany joining together to produce the aircraft and compete as a united force against the giant American manufacturers.

Before the formal establishment of Airbus, the financially stretched British government once again changed its mind and decided to withdraw its investment support for the European project. Unfortunately, this was after the Three-Eleven design project had already been abandoned

by BAC, in anticipation of potential British interest in developing the European aircraft. Luckily Hawker Siddeley Aviation elected to remain in the Airbus group, as a private investor, without government backing and maintained UK participation in the consortium.

Over the next few years Airbus was to suffer a great deal of difficulty in establishing itself, as well as the triumphs of finally managing to break into the US market. After a very long period of struggling to obtain only a small number of orders, a major coup was eventually enjoyed by Airbus, by selling a fleet of A300s to an established Lockheed Tristar customer, Eastern Airlines. A few years later, both A300s and slightly smaller A310s were sold to ultra-loyal supporter of the American aircraft industry, Pan American World Airways. By exploiting its strengths as a diverse consortium, Airbus Industrie found it was able to adapt itself to changing trends and to become a

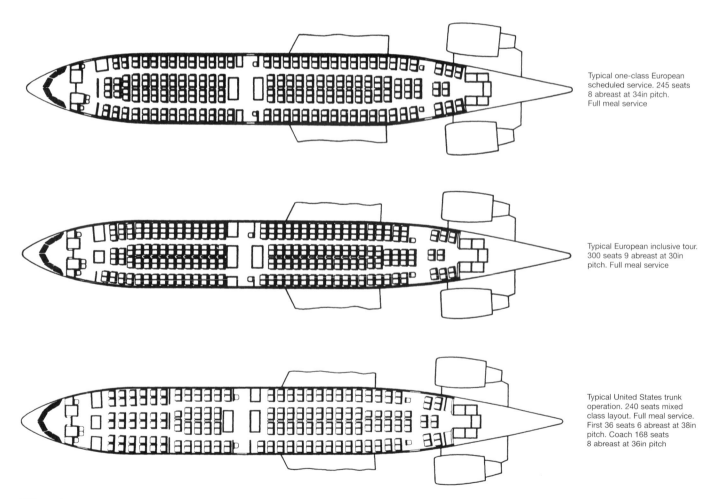

Typical one-class European scheduled service. 245 seats 8 abreast at 34in pitch. Full meal service

Typical European inclusive tour. 300 seats 9 abreast at 30in pitch. Full meal service

Typical United States trunk operation. 240 seats mixed class layout. Full meal service. First 36 seats 6 abreast at 38in pitch. Coach 168 seats 8 abreast at 36in pitch

Different layouts were available on the wide-body Three-Eleven. Brooklands Museum

Laker was one of several carriers interested in the Three-Eleven. Brooklands Museum

highly successful joint European venture offering a wide portfolio of aircraft to the world airliner market.

Even the US manufacturers were having a hard time in the early 1970s. Both Lockheed and McDonnell-Douglas experienced problems with their medium range wide-body offerings. Financial problems within the Rolls-Royce group led to delays in the production of the L-1011 Tristar's RB211 engines, costing several potential orders and the whole project came close to cancellation a number of times. The DC-10, once it entered service, experienced catastrophic structural problems, leading to at least three major fatal crashes. Although later managing to redeem itself to a certain extent, the DC-10's reputation with the travelling public was to be seriously tarnished for several years.

Despite managing to rally a healthy number of sales after surviving the Rolls-Royce crisis, Lockheed was to make a resounding loss on the L-1011 Tristar project as a whole. The company eventually pulled out of the civil aircraft market altogether after closing down the L-1011 production line when the last aircraft was delivered in 1984. This brought to an end over sixty years of airliner production by Lockheed, a line that had included some

Ideas from several European makers emerged as the Airbus A300B2. M.L. Hill

of the most elegant and stylish designs to grace the world's airport ramps.

Bigger is Better – Again!

While One-Eleven 475 prototype G-ASYD was being modified for its new rôle in what was to turn out to be the sole Series 670, the British Aircraft Corpora-

tion quietly ceased to exist. At midnight on 29 April 1977, the assets of BAC, Hawker Siddeley Aviation, Hawker Siddeley Dynamics and Scottish Aviation were purchased by the British Government and merged to form British Aerospace, a new nationalized corporation. In 1979, British Aerospace was welcomed back as a partner in Airbus Industrie, with a 20 per cent holding.

With the participants in the wide-body airliner market going through such traumatic, expensive times, the new British Aerospace elected to concentrate on developing their established markets. In the airliner field this was now firmly in the short to medium-haul aircraft bracket, the VC-10 production line having closed down. The last Super VC-10, the last long-haul, all-British commercial jet airliner, had been delivered by BAC to East African Airways in 1970. Ironically, although British commercial long-range jet transports were no longer being produced, a derivative of the very first was still being built. The Nimrod, based on the De Havilland Comet 4, was used by the RAF on long-range maritime reconnaissance duties and was still being built by the Hawker Siddeley factory at Chester.

As with the De Havilland/Hawker Siddeley/Avro and Vickers/Bristol/Hunting mergers over twenty-five years earlier,

British Aerospace now found itself the owner of several aircraft designs with conflicting potential customer bases. Hard decisions had to be made as to what was to be kept and what was to be dropped. Unfortunately for the One-Eleven, this time one of those decisions was to go against it.

In the aftermath of the Oil Crisis, fuel economy was to become a much more important issue in airliner operations. With a new worldwide interest in ecological matters and increasingly vociferous protests over aircraft noise levels from those living in the vicinity of the world's airports, any new aircraft also had to operate more efficiently and quietly, as well as making significant savings in fuel consumption. Of the airliner proposals now on offer from BAe's commercial portfolio, the One-Eleven was looking less and less likely to offer these requirements to airline managements.

Although the rear-engined One-Eleven was always marketed as a quiet aircraft

from the passengers' point of view, the aircraft could never seriously be regarded as a 'good neighbour'. As well as being one of the noisiest aircraft on take-off, an equally noisy reverse thrust on landing and even the characteristic banshee-like whine on engine start-up that could carry for miles, did little to endear it to local noise control groups. The One-Eleven's rivals were just as guilty, the Caravelle and early Boeings and DC-9s being nearly as noisy or even worse. However, the Caravelle was rapidly nearing the end of its production life and the Boeing 737's and DC-9's later versions had done much to improve their noise profiles over the years.

A likely contender for a One-Eleven successor had emerged from BAe's Hawker Siddeley predecessor. As far back as the 1950s, De Havilland had been studying designs for the ever-elusive 'DC-3 replacement', long sought by the world's airliner manufacturers. By 1959 De Havilland was offering the DH123, a high-wing 32–40 seater turbo-prop, similar in size and layout to the French Nord 262. At the 1959 SBAC display at Farnborough, De Havilland presented the design as the 'Branchliner'. The absorption of De Havilland into Hawker Siddeley saw an end to that project, as it competed directly with the Avro/HS 748, already in production. A pure-jet version of the 123, the 126, was proposed instead. With a low wing and rear-mounted engines, the design resembled the DH/HS 125 executive jet with an enlarged fuselage that would carry up to 32 passengers.

With its intended operations encompassing very short stages from airfields with runways as short as 3,000ft, the DH126 attracted a great deal of interest from the Australian domestic airlines. However, lack of a proven jet engine of the right size in the commercial sector eventually led to the shelving of the 126. In the meantime the One-Eleven and its contemporaries were introducing jet travel to the short-haul market.

Hawker Siddeley continued to look at short-haul jet projects and in 1963–1964 was offering the HS131, a pure-jet using many components of the successful HS748 turbo-prop. Another study, the HS136, was offered in 1964, this time with rear-mounted engines and a T-tail. By 1966 the aircraft had grown to a 50-seater and increased the next year to 57 seats. Hawker Siddeley was now aiming the aircraft more in the Convair/Viscount replacement range, instead of the few remaining DC-3 operators.

Spey noise levels were starting to cause concern by the 1980s. Brooklands Museum

The enlarged HS136 was to be powered by the Rolls-Royce RB203 Trent, a new engine developed as a more fuel-efficient successor to the Spey for the 1970s. The proposed use of the Trent saw a reconfiguration of the design, with the engines now positioned on the wing. By 1968, versions of the HS136 seating up to 93 passengers were being considered. When the HS136 study was superseded by a new project, the HS144, in 1969, the engines were positioned back to the rear fuselage and the T-tail made a reappearance. The HS144 was to carry up to 80 passengers in its larger version, with operating specifications close to those of the Fokker F.28 Fellowship.

The American manufacturer Fairchild, that had built the Fokker F.27 under licence in the USA, had planned to produce a new, stretched version of the F.28, the Fairchild FH-228 and it was for this project that much of the development of the Rolls-Royce Trent was undertaken. However, in 1968, Fairchild abandoned their plans for the FH-228 and the work on the Trent was wound down. Following the near bankruptcy of Rolls-Royce after their financial crisis, the Trent design work was scrapped altogether. Once again the Hawker Siddeley plans had to be put to one side for lack of a suitable engine.

It was to be 1971 before the short-haul jet airliner design was to be revived by Hawker Siddeley, as the HS146. The lack of powerful enough engines was solved by using four, instead of two, of a more modest engine, the Avco Lycoming ALF 502 turbofan. In order to cut down the chance of foreign matter ingestion, the wing was redesigned in a 'shoulder' position, with engines mounted underneath it on pylons. A major advantage that emerged, however, from the use of four engines was a great improvement in the take-off field performance of the aircraft. Unlike many of the previous jet projects, the HS 146 would be able to operate from airports then currently only able to take the HS748s, Fokker F.27s and similar twin turbo-props for which the new aircraft was now being seriously offered as a viable jet replacement.

Fourteen years of project studies apparently came to a successful conclusion on 29 August 1973 when Hawker Siddeley announced it would go ahead with production of the HS146, following the provision of some £40 million in risk-sharing government support. Hawker Siddeley was investing a similar amount of its own money in the aircraft. The company estimated that there would be a requirement for over 1,500 aircraft in the HS146 category by 1982 and expected to provide at least 420 of them.

The HS146 was competing head-on with the established Fokker F.28 and a new joint Dutch/West German design, the VFW/Fokker VFW614. The 40-passenger VFW614 was never to sell in any great numbers, despite high hopes early on and a great deal of Third World interest in particular. The much more successful Fokker F.28 was now being offered in several different versions, with passenger seating now reaching One-Eleven figures in the stretched models.

Following the official launch of the HS146, a full-scale wooden mock-up was built at Hatfield, with its passenger cabin fitted out with Boeing 747 seats. The first flight was planned for December 1975. Work continued apace throughout 1973 on the design, with representatives of nearly thirty airlines contacting Hatfield to look at the project's proposals. Thirteen of them expressed a definite interest, with others requesting information on route studies and performance, although no actual firm orders were forthcoming at the time.

Another wooden mock-up was built of the nose, for experimenting with different flight-deck layouts and an extensive metal engineering mock-up was built beside the Trident production line at Hatfield. Sub-contract work was awarded to Shorts, at Belfast, for engine pods and SAAB-Scania, of Sweden, were to build the tailplane, elevators, rudder, ailerons, spoilers and all other moveable control surfaces.

Two elections in 1974 brought the Labour party to power. Among their campaign promises was one to nationalize the British aircraft industry. The alarming prospect of losing its independence and the emerging world-wide recession which followed the OPEC fuel price rises, all managed to contribute to Hawker Siddeley's management having a serious crisis of faith in the future of the HS146. All work on the project stopped on 21 October 1974, among a great deal of protest from employees, who faced redundancy, and the

Plans for Fairchild to produce a stretched F.28 were shelved. via Author

new government that accused Hawker Siddeley of being in breach of contract.

A union committee was formed with a view to saving the aircraft and to lobby for political support for the programme. This led to the then Secretary for Industry, Tony Benn effectively ordering Hawker Siddeley to put the HS146 on hold. Although work on the project had ceased, none of the work already carried out on jigs and tools was dismantled and the design capacity was maintained, to allow the situation to be reviewed at short notice at a later date. However, all sub-contract work, including an order for 100 engines, was cancelled. This situation was to continue through until the absorption and nationalization of Hawker Siddeley and BAC into British Aerospace on 19 April 1977. From then on the design was redesignated the BAe146.

A year later, the economic situation had improved enough for BAe to consider reopening the BAe 146 programme. The official relaunch took place in July 1978, with both civil and military versions being launched. New sub-contract agreements saw the programme taking on an even more multi-national nature. Avco, the engine supplier, took on the design and manufacture of the wings as a risk-sharing partner. SAAB-Scania returned to the fold in its previous rôle as supplier of moveable control surfaces, with other elements of BAe taking other components of the aircraft under their control. The increased interest of the American company was regarded as important for improving the chances of sales to US customers. Recent sales of Airbus aircraft to American carriers, in preference to their own domestically produced airliners, had caused a great deal of adverse comment and bad feeling. The considerable amount of US jobs tied up in the BAe 146 was seen as a useful

counter-measure to any such criticism that might come BAe's way in the future.

Improvements included the inclusion of a wing centre-section fuel tank as standard and extra tankage being available in the wing-root fairings as an option. Systems and structures had been refined and better materials selected while the relaunch was awaited. Finally, on 20 May 1981, the first BAe 146-100, G-SSSH, was rolled out. Like many aircraft of the time, initial sales were slow but steady, as the world-wide recession took its time in ending. However, following a further redesign and relaunch as the RJ (Regional Jet), series, BAe later revived the old name of Avro to market the improved version that was, at last, beginning to enjoy long-awaited sales success. Quite what the wraith of the late

Sir Geoffrey de Havilland makes of an aircraft originally conceived by the company he founded being named after one of his greatest rivals can only be imagined.

Production of the One-Eleven actually came to a temporary halt after the delivery of the last Oman Air Force series 475. Despite the successful development programme flown by G-ASYD, the Series 600 attracted little if any airline interest and no orders at all resulted from all the hard work. When work began again on the BAe 146 programme, it became increasingly obvious that the new aircraft, especially in stretched versions planned for the future, would become a direct rival to the One-Eleven. The financial problems at Rolls-Royce which almost led to the bankruptcy of the much-respected aero-engine manufacturer

TAROM's order gave the Hurn production line a welcome boost. Brooklands Museum

YR-BCR was kept busy flying One-Eleven components to Bucharest. Brooklands Museum

also helped bring an end to any further One-Eleven development by BAe. As well as work ceasing on the Trent, plans for the uprated version of the Spey, the 67C, that would have powered production Series 600 and 700 One-Elevens, were also scrapped.

Five Series 500 One-Elevens had been ordered by TAROM, to supplement the established fleet of Series 400s that had been operated on the Romanian airline's European network for some time. The One-Eleven production line had already been drastically run down in the intervening period, with no new deliveries at all having taken place in 1976. Unlike earlier years, where aircraft had been built strictly to order, the company started to build in authorized batches, not necessarily with all the aircraft sold before construction began. Although giving the manufacturing side of the business the advantage of a little more stability, it certainly gave the sales division a few sleepless nights as unsold aircraft neared completion.

Last British Batch

However, the Romanian order did give BAC the confidence to start work on a further ten aircraft. Having the aircraft

already under construction did lead to early delivery for any sale that was forthcoming. All five TAROM aircraft were delivered in 1977. The TAROM aircraft were the first to be delivered new fitted with 'hushkits', in an attempt to reduce noise problems that were associated with Spey-powered aircraft.

First flown on G-ASYD in 1974, the hushkit was developed jointly by BAC and Rolls-Royce. The hushkit consisted of intake duct linings, acoustically lined jet pipes and a six-chute exhaust liner. Despite the extra 400lb weight and a performance penalty, a number of earlier aircraft were fitted with the system in an attempt to extend their operational lives, with tougher noise regulations threatening to ground commercial One-Eleven services in some markets.

The delivery of the TAROM fleet of Series 500s also heralded the next phase in the production life of the One-Eleven. Shortly after the formation of British Aerospace, in May 1977, a co-operation agreement was signed between BAe and the Romanian Government. This was intended to lead to the gradual transfer of technology, leading to One-Eleven development and production being undertaken by the Intrepinderea de Reparat Material

Aeronautic, from the Romanian Government Aircraft factory at Baneasa Airport, near Bucharest.

With the increasing emphasis being place on the BAe 146 as the British aviation industry's current offering for the short-haul jet market, the original co-operation agreement was further endorsed a year later. The final contracts for Romanian licence production of the One-Eleven, the company now using the simpler marketing name of ROMBAC, were signed in 1979. Romania had also signed a similar agreement for licence production of the Britten Norman Islander. Initially two Series 500 One-Elevens were to be supplied by Hurn, to be used as 'pattern' aircraft. A single Series 475, equipped with a freight door, was also supplied by Hurn under a similar arrangement.

Operated by TAROM, the Series 475 freighter was used for the transport of a number of One-Eleven components and equipment from Hurn to Bucharest. From then on, British components were supplied in kit form and would gradually be replaced by Romanian-built items until, from aircraft number 22 of the Romanian line, all-Romanian built aircraft would be supplied. The One-Eleven production jigs would also be transferred to Bucharest from Hurn. The Spey Mk.512DW engine would be built in Romania to power the aircraft and a licence agreement was reached between Rolls-Royce and the Turbomecanica company, set up for production of the Spey in Bucharest.

As well as the Romania-bound aircraft, BAe continued to sell aircraft from what was to be the last batch of British-built

and a single leased One-Eleven had finally been rescued after protracted negotiations but were not returned to the airline. The Tridents went on to fly for British Airways Regional Division and the One-Eleven returned to BAe.

Jet operations were restarted when leased Boeing 720B and DC-9 equipment took over from the Viscounts in 1975. A

Cyprus's own Series 500s were delivered in December 1977 and January 1978. A third aircraft was also ordered for October 1978 delivery, but this aircraft was immediately leased out to British Airways for eighteen months.

The remaining two ex-Transbrasil aircraft were sold to another eastern Mediterranean carrier. Arkia Inland Airways was a

Leased DC-9s were used by Cyprus Airways to restart jet services. via Author

Cyprus One-Elevens took over from the leased Douglas aircraft. Aviation Hobby Shop

production aircraft. Cyprus Airways, grounded since the Turkish invasion of the island, had restarted operations from Larnaca in January 1975, using Viscounts leased from British Midland Airways. The airline was unable to utilize its old base at Nicosia as the cease-fire line ran right through the airport. The flyable remnants of the old Cyprus Airways fleet of Tridents

DC-8 was also leased in early 1976. That October, a single One-Eleven 500 was leased from BAe, pending delivery of Cyprus Airways' own pair of newly-ordered aircraft. Replacing the DC-9, the first One-Eleven was joined by a second aircraft, also leased from BAe, in February 1977. The second aircraft was one of three purchased back by BAe from Transbrasil.

regional subsidiary of El Al, the Israeli national carrier and operated a fleet of turbo-prop Viscounts and Dart Heralds on local scheduled flights within Israel. The arrival of the pair of One-Elevens, refurbished by BAe at Hurn, saw a huge increase in the company's capacity and they were placed into scheduled service on the busy route from Tel Aviv to Eilat, an important port and resort area in the far south of Israel. In addition, numerous charter flights were operated throughout Europe and Arkia also used the One-Elevens to operate a number of Tel Aviv–Larnaca scheduled services on behalf of El Al.

Unfortunately, passenger figures on the domestic network did not rise as fast as anticipated and Arkia lost a large section of their route network when the Sinai was returned to Egypt. The ever-rising fuel costs soon started to affect the One-Eleven jet operations, making their use on the remaining domestic routes uneconomic and affecting revenues on the charter services. Finally, at the end of 1979, El Al and the Histadrut Labour Federation that jointly owned Arkia, voted to dispose of the One-Elevens and sell the airline off to private investors.

A single VIP configured Series 475 was supplied by BAe to a private Saudi Arabian customer in May 1978. This was the only new executive version of the 475 series to be exported by BAe. Three extra Series 500s were also built for British Airways, to augment their ex-BEA fleet of 'Super One-Elevens'. The new aircraft actually differed from the original BEA Series 500 aircraft in that they were standard production aircraft and fitted with Spey Mk.512DW engines. Delivered in March, June and August 1980, the three aircraft were based at Birmingham and replaced two of the Series 400s that were traded in to BAe in part exchange for the new aircraft.

Following the delivery of the last complete aircraft, a Series 500 for TAROM in March 1982, Hurn was now running down the One-Eleven work, in preparation for the transfer of all jigs and equipment to Romania. Apart from building parts for the Romanian production line, the staff were

4X-BAR operated only briefly from Tel Aviv. D. Spurgeon via Jennie Gradidge

Tradewinds CL-44s were used to transfer equipment to Bucharest. Brooklands Museum

mostly busy with the refurbishment of second-hand aircraft and repair work on damaged airframes. Two more Series 475s were under speculative construction without any customers having ordered them. There had been great expectations that these aircraft would have been bought by the RAF for VIP use by The Queen's Flight. Unfortunately nothing came of these expectations and both aircraft were stored at Hurn for nearly two years. When the RAF did finally make a decision on the VIP jet aircraft, the order still went to BAe, but for BAe 146s. Eventually the last pair of One-Elevens were sold to McAlpine Aviation for executive charter work from Luton. A rather uninspiring end to the production facilities that, since 1945, had produced 940 airliners, including the 235 British-built One-Elevens.

Progress on the Romanian production lines at Bucharest was painfully slow, but the first ROMBAC assembled One-Eleven was finally rolled out on 27 August 1982. It made its first flight on 18 September and was delivered to TAROM on 24

McAlpine Aviation's G-BLDH was the last UK built One-Eleven. Martyn East

December. Difficulties caused by lack of hard currency were compounded by inefficiencies and a lack of enthusiasm in the responsible Romanian government departments which was bringing about even more delays to the programme. The planned production rate of six aircraft a year was drastically reduced to an uneconomic reality of barely one on average.

Only nine One-Elevens were completed by ROMBAC by 22 December 1989, when political upheaval in Romania,

along with most countries behind the then crumbling Iron Curtain, led to the ousting of the long-established communist dictatorship of Nicolae Ceausescu. Romaero, as the company had become, had already all but ceased to function and was desperate for new capital to be able to continue to exist. All the ROMBAC One-Elevens were delivered to TAROM. A Series 475 with a cargo door, ordered by the Romanian Army, was 85 per cent complete, with another Series 500 70 per cent ready.

Components were reportedly in existence for no less than 22 other One-Elevens.

Although only a handful of the planned Romanian production One-Elevens were ever to take to the air, the aircraft themselves proved to be sound examples of the type. With TAROM, the aircraft operated alongside their UK-built predecessors throughout both eastern and western Europe and to the Middle East. When the rapidly changing political situation within Romania led to major upheavals in the

Rombac One-Eleven, YR-BRC was displayed at several airshows. Jennie Gradidge

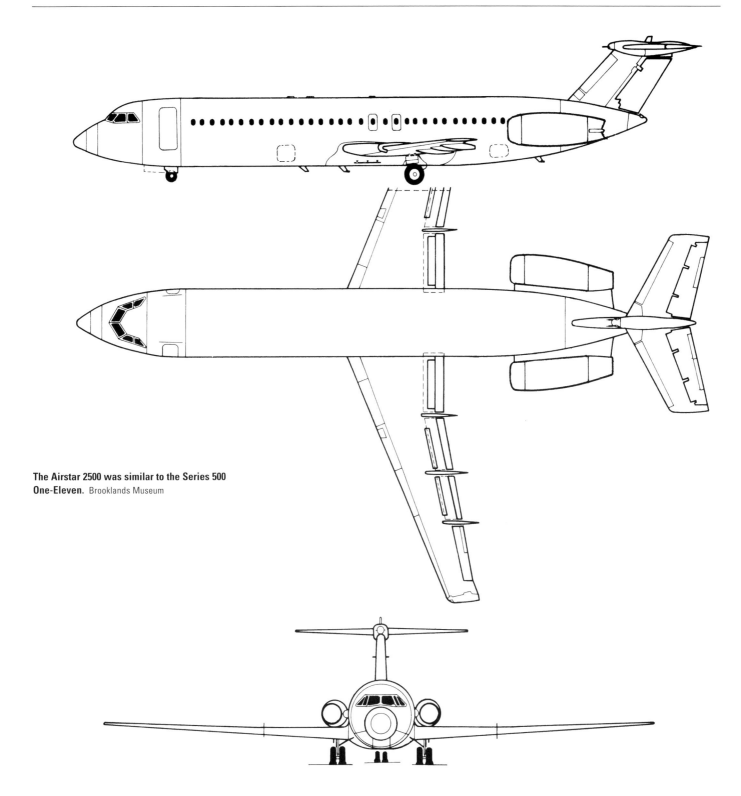

The Airstar 2500 was similar to the Series 500 One-Eleven. Brooklands Museum

national airline's operation, the Series 500 One-Elevens, the Series 400s having been progressively transferred to a charter subsidiary, Liniie Aerienne Romane, LAR, from 1975, continued to form an important element in the airline's complement. Most of the numerous Soviet-built Ilyushin and Tupolev members of

the TAROM fleet were quickly removed from service as it became clear that a new, financially viable, operational regime had to be established.

In April 1990, a new company, Associated Aerospace, announced its intention to order no less than 50 One-Elevens from Romaero, with Associated Aerospace

acting as a marketing outlet for the aircraft. They were to be powered by Rolls-Royce 650 Tay engines and fitted with modern 'glass' cockpits by AIM Aviation at Hurn. Soon after the announcement, however, Associated Aerospace was forced to cease trading and the ambitious plans came to nothing.

A number of new features were incorporated into the Airstar 2500.
Brooklands Museum

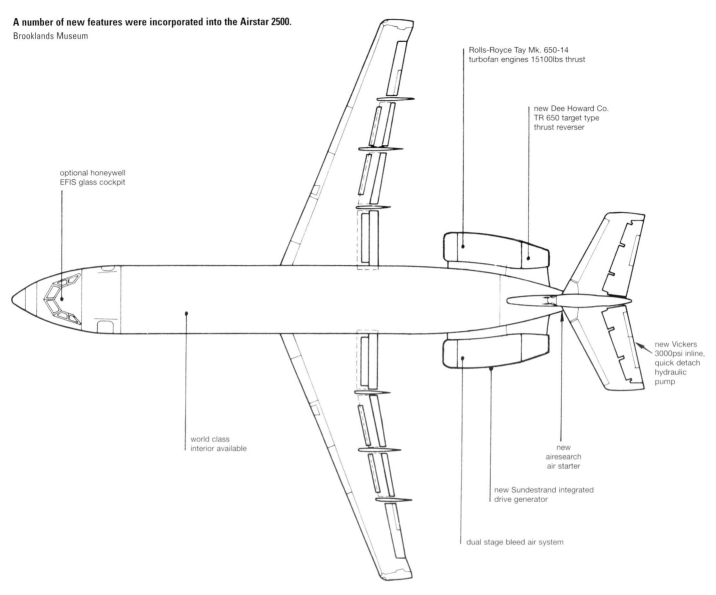

Rolls-Royce Tay Mk. 650-14
turbofan engines 15100lbs thrust

new Dee Howard Co.
TR 650 target type
thrust reverser

optional honeywell
EFIS glass cockpit

new Vickers
3000psi inline,
quick detach
hydraulic
pump

world class
interior available

new
airesearch
air starter

new Sundestrand integrated
drive generator

dual stage bleed air system

The 2400, N650DH, was demonstrated throughout Euurope in 1990. Steve Edmunds

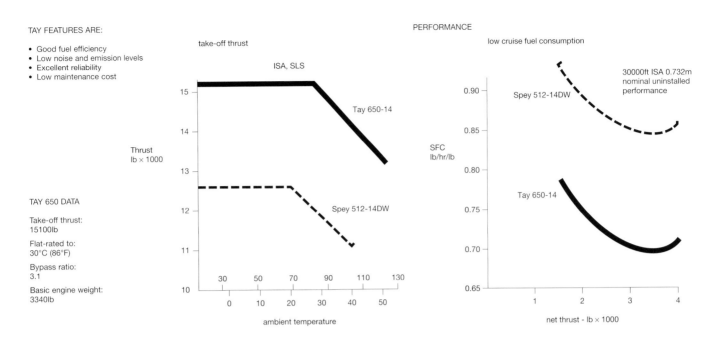

Rolls-Royce Spey and Tay comparisons. Brooklands Museum

On 9 February 1993, Romaero was to be the victim of further raised hopes when Kiwi International Airlines of Newark, New Jersey, announced that they planned to order eleven Series 2500 One-Elevens from them to be powered by Rolls-Royce 650 Tays. Operating low-fare scheduled and charter services from Newark, Kiwi was operating a fleet of Boeing 727s at the time. To be marketed as the 'Airstar 2500', the new One-Elevens were to be delivered from 1995 and an option on a further five aircraft was taken out by Kiwi in June the same year. Kiwi International's cancellation of its interest in the 'Airstar 2500', following financial difficulties, led to the much-delayed programme finally being cancelled on 1997.

The fitting of the Rolls-Royce Tay engine, basically a refanned Spey, had been mooted as far back as the 1970s, but at the time the idea had attracted little interest. This was despite the great improvements in fuel economy, performance, range, and probably the most important as far as the One-Eleven's future was concerned, noise. However, in 1990, the Dee Howard Company, in San Antonio, Texas, flew an ex-American Airlines Series 400 with Tay engines, to be known as the One-Eleven Series 2400. Dee Howard had reached agreements with both Rolls-Royce and British Aerospace to develop and market the proposed conversion of the One-Eleven airframes to

Tay power. The aircraft flew at San Antonio, for the first time in its new configuration, on 21 January 1990.

Dee Howard, founded by Durrell Unger Howard in the late 1940s, was a long-established company that had made its name specializing in developing executive passenger configured conversions of war surplus Lockheed Venturas. Far from being just straightforward cabin conversions, many of the later modifications involved major re-engineering, rebuilding and stretching of the basic aircraft. Even pressurized options were being offered in the 1960s. An ex-Braniff Airways mechanic, Howard had formed the original company, Howard Aero Inc., after his then employer, Slick Airways, moved their operation from San Antonio to California. Starting up as a freelance aircraft mechanic, Howard of Howard Aero Inc. was temporarily based in 'premises comprising the back of Howard's car trunk'.

When the American Airlines fleet of '400 Astrojet' One-Elevens were sold, Dee Howard, by now a much more substantial company, had been contracted by National Aircraft Leasing to convert the sixteen aircraft from the 'Astrojet' fleet that they purchased into corporate configuration. In fact, the aircraft used for the Tay conversion had originally been one of this batch.

The newly re-engined aircraft elicited much comment and interest at that year's Farnborough Air Show in September. This

was especially forthcoming from several operators of executive One-Elevens, as well as the remaining airline operators of the aircraft. Considerable improvement in performance was achieved as well as the much desired reduction in engine noise and the proposed conversion would extend the operating life for many years. Any unmodified Spey-engined aircraft was about to fall foul of the new noise regulations. The new regulations would greatly restrict the use of any One-Eleven aircraft that had not at least been fitted with the hush-kitted engines.

Unfortunately, with 90 per cent of the certification work complete, the Dee Howard Company decided to abandon the One-Eleven project to concentrate on the conversion of the Boeing 727 to Tay power instead. This new work was supported by a sizeable order from the specialist US carrier, United Parcel Services, to convert their large fleet of freighter 727s. There were also reported disagreements between Dee Howard and British Aerospace over the future of Series 2400 and 2500 production.

Other aircraft types were just as affected by the new regulations. The Trident and Caravelle were especially vulnerable and practically vanished from the European airline scene overnight. The last production Caravelle had been delivered in the early 1970s. Greatly increased in size and with much improved performance over its original 1950s concept, the last version of the Caravelle, the Series 12, was capable of carrying up to 140 passengers and was powered by American JT8D-9 turbofans. The Trident managed to continue in production until 1978, mostly courtesy of a large order for Trident 2Es and 3Bs received from the People's Republic of China's state airline, CAAC.

Plans for the proposed development and modernization of the design as the Trident 4 and Trident 5, including twin-engined and Tay-powered versions were eventually dropped. This was partly due to Hawker Siddeley's, and later BAe's, involvement in Airbus Industrie. The Trident development proposals became part of a collabo-

The Fokker F.28 series was extensively redesigned and updated around Tay power, in place of the original Speys and was relaunched as the Fokker F.70 and larger F.100 versions. The Boeing 737 series greatly benefited from the brave decision to proceed with new, re-engined models. The Boeing 737 had very nearly been withdrawn from production altogether, following a year when only four new aircraft had been sold. However, the launch of the Boeing 737-300, powered by more fuel-efficient, and quieter, new-technology engines, in the mid-1980s, rescued the design from possible oblivion. Substantial sales and further developments of the greatly improved aircraft followed.

Dee Howard option for re-engining One-Elevens with Tays seemed to have been ruined by inter-company squabbles as much as the more attractive alternative Boeing 727 on offer, that at least promised Dee Howard a substantial contract and guaranteed earnings.

By the time the world's economy had recovered enough for the airlines to seriously consider replacing their old fleets, the One-Eleven programme had pretty well expired beyond resuscitation. New types such as the Airbus A320 and BAe 146, as well as the relaunched Boeings, McDonnell-Douglas's and Fokkers, had the new aircraft market pretty well to themselves for the foreseeable future. British Aero-

The BAe 146 was eventually stretched to One-Eleven capacity. via Author

rative study that eventually led to the 140–150-seat Airbus-designed aircraft, the A320, in the production of which BAe was to have a large interest.

Originally, the Tridents were to be replaced by 146s on the Hatfield production lines. The delays in the 146 development programme were a definite blow to the old De Havilland factory, but, at the beginning of the new aircraft's production, a healthy number of 146s were rolled out of Hatfield's hangar doors. Sadly for the historic facility at Hatfield, following reorganization, the BAe final assembly work was eventually to be transferred to another British Aerospace factory at Woodford, near Manchester. Woodford had already been producing 146s as a secondary production line. This brought to an end several decades of aircraft design and manufacture at the Hertfordshire airfield.

Even the One-Eleven's old adversary, the DC-9, was stretched by McDonnell-Douglas beyond all recognition. Eventually, the whole range was redesignated The MD80 series and, later, the MD90 types. What had started as a 75-passenger aircraft was now able to carry more than twice that, with greatly increased range and performances.

The initial proposals for improved performance and stretched One-Eleven series had been offered at times of great hardship for many of the world's carriers. Financially beleaguered British governments were unable or unwilling to offer support. This in itself projected, however unintentionally, a lack in confidence in the British aircraft industry as a whole. The political upheaval that had wrecked the Romanian project did little to help the prospects of the type, very much an old design by then, remaining in full-scale production. The

space was now offering stretched versions of the BAe 146, with the aircraft now well able to carry One-Eleven Series 500 loads over similar ranges and operate more efficiently and economically. The airlines still operating One-Elevens were certainly interested in any programme that might extend their operating lives and reduce operating costs, but, by the late 1990s there was no more talk of new versions or reviving any production lines.

However, even if new aircraft were no longer likely to be seen rolling out of any manufacturing facility, the numerous One-Elevens that had already been built by both BAC and ROMBAC had plenty of life left in them. There were few parts of the world that had not seen at least one operator of the type and there were still plenty more stories of their successes, and their failures, waiting to unfold.

CHAPTER SEVEN

Regrouping

Although a handful of One-Elevens had been supplied straight off the production line for corporate and VIP operations, it was not until the airlines started to replace their One-Eleven fleets that such use of the type became more widespread. The idea of a transport aircraft dedicated to the private use of a company's personnel and executives had finally gained popularity after the end of the Second World War. Prior to that time, the availability of second-hand aircraft was limited and the purchase of private brand new aircraft for such exclusive use was limited to exceptionally wealthy citizens, governments or companies. The vast post-war store of low time, surplus military transports on offer to the highest bidder was to lead to a dramatic rise in private and corporate flying, as much as it spawned the independent and charter airline industry.

A number of engineering and refurbishment companies were established specifically to serve this new market. These particularly proliferated in the United States, where nationwide distances of thousands of miles prompted a number of industrial

Executive DC-3 conversions often included panoramic windows. via Author

G-ASYE went on to a private career as N17VK after its BAC test work. MAP

and commercial companies to establish their own air transport operations. Many ex-military transports had their utilitarian troop and cargo-carrying facilities stripped out and replaced by plush lounge-style interiors, with features such as radio-telephones, galleys, bar units and, later, even televisions being installed to their customer specifications.

From early operations with converted Douglas and Lockheed twins, many of the companies graduated to the next generation Convair and Martinliners, many from the second-hand stocks as the airlines replaced them with turbo-props and jets. Increasingly though, the wealthier corporations started to order brand new aircraft in the airliner range, with Convair and Vickers making several important sales in this market. Whether flown in large fleets, or as individual aircraft, the operation of the executive aircraft could vary from daily 'commutes', to exotic world tours, either on private or corporate business. Many were operated on private scheduled networks, flying personnel and equipment between a company's disparate facilities.

As well as the option of owning an aircraft outright, a number of companies elected to lease in their corporate fleets from a third party which actually owned and operated the aircraft, often with crews being provided as well. One such operator was National Aircraft Leasing, of Los Angeles. A member of the Tiger Leasing Group, NAL purchased sixteen of the American Airlines fleet of Series 400s in January 1973. The contract for the work to

convert the aircraft to executive configuration was given to the Dee Howard Company, of San Antonio.

Before delivery to Dee Howard, the NAL aircraft were completely overhauled by American Airlines' Tulsa facility, with new wheels, brakes, tyres and anti-skid systems. Cold Air Units were replaced, all radios, electronics and autopilots, auxiliary power units, generators and engines were totally serviced and the latest modifications were incorporated. After air-testing, the aircraft were delivered to Dee Howard at San Antonio, where de luxe interiors were fitted in place of the standard airliner passenger configuration. The new standard interior design comprised eleven individual seats, one four-seat and two three-seat couches, the latter of which could be converted to beds. There was also a centrally located bar, a separate dressing room, fully equipped galley, conference tables and executive desk. Interior colours, fabrics and the exterior paint scheme were chosen by the customer.

Provision was also made for the installation of updated avionics and inertial navigation systems. National Aircraft Leasing also designed a long-range fuel system for the aircraft. This comprised the fitting of extra fuel cells in the rear of the forward freight hold, which still left 137 cubic feet of hold space even if seven cells were fitted. With the maximum ten cells fitted, range was increased up to 3,950 miles with 45 minutes reserve, carrying up to eight passengers. Three other American Airlines aircraft were sold direct from the

carrier to Jet Travel Inc. for similar conversion work, and two others were sold direct to corporate customers.

While awaiting their turn on the conversion production line, three of the ex-American One-Elevens were leased out by NAL to commercial airline operators. Two went to Austral in Argentina from December 1976 to April 1977. Another was leased, from May to October 1976 to Aeroamerica for use on West Berlin-based inclusive tour charters. Aeroamerica operated a fleet of Boeing 707s and 720s, with the vast majority of its fleet being based at Berlin-Tegel. While in their service, the single One-Eleven wore bright orange and red cheatlines over the basic bare metal finish left over from its time with American.

On its return to NAL from its summer season in Berlin, the Aeroamerica aircraft was leased out again, this time to Pacific American Airlines. Originally founded as Mercer Airlines in 1946, by D.W. Mercer, Pacific American was operating an ageing fleet of Douglas DC-6s, a single DC-3 and a Lockheed Electra turbo-prop, when the One-Eleven arrived in January 1977. Charter flights were operated from Burbank, California, often on behalf of film studios and development companies. Passenger and freight contract charter flights were also operated on behalf of the US Navy from Burbank to various points in California and between Honolulu and the Gilbert Islands in the Pacific.

The converted ex-members of the American Airlines fleet of '400 Astrojets' became popular executive transports, joining the

Five One-Elevens bore the registration N111NA on demo' work. Jennie Gradidge

N5016 flew with Aeroamerica for a summer on charters from Berlin. via Author

already successful ranks of VIP One-Elevens on the airways. Other transfers of One-Elevens from the airline sector to the private and corporate world included the previously mentioned sale of British United Airways' G-ASJA, the first production Series 200. The pair of Series 400s delivered to Brazil's VASP in 1967 were sold in 1974 to Carver Corp. in the USA. They had been replaced in VASP service by increasing numbers of Boeing 727s and 737s.

Initially VASP had transferred the One-Elevens from Rio and Sao Paulo to operate schedules from Brasilia, but eventually they were even to be ousted from there by the growing Boeing fleet. After refurbishment into executive configuration by BAC at Hurn, both aircraft went on to enjoy long new careers as corporate aircraft, still being active over twenty years later.

The original executive One-Eleven, Helmut Horten's long-serving D-ABHH, was

sold in 1975, joining two fellow Series 200s already in service with Tenneco at Houston. The enlarged Tenneco One-Eleven fleet was to continue with its worldwide services for over another decade. Even after Tenneco had decided to dispose of them in favour of a more modern fleet, all three aircraft soon found new executive owners.

Following a summer season lease to Autair International Airways in 1969, BAC converted Series 400 G-AWXJ to executive configuration for possible sale to Aeroleasing SA of Switzerland. Painted in their full colours in 1970, the aircraft was reregistered HB-ITK in preparation for delivery to the company. However, the deal fell through and the aircraft remained under BAC ownership. After a brief period as a demonstration aircraft, during which it was demonstrated to Nigeria Airways in their livery, the aircraft was sold as an executive transport in November 1971 to Robert Loh, of Singapore. A few months later, Loh, a self-made millionaire and ex-taxi driver, leased the aircraft to Air Siam who operated it on their Bangkok–Hong Kong–Fukuoka–Tokyo route between May and December 1972, still with its Singapore registration, 9V-BEF.

(Above) **Executive One-Eleven N114M, 'Lucky Liz', was once VASP's PP-SRT.** MAP

Air Siam leased 416EK, 9V-BEF in 1972. Ron Killick via Jennie Gradidge

401AK, N5032 passed through Heathrow en route to Indonesia. Brooklands Museum

Ford's ex-FAB 420EL joined the Stanstead-based fleet in 1976. MAP

Rolls-Royce/Turbo-Union's G-BGTU, had a freight door fitted. Martyn East

Following its return from Air Siam, who replaced the One-Eleven with a single leased Boeing 707, the aircraft was sold, via BAC, to Indonesia's Pertamina Oil and operated by their air charter division, Pelita Air Service, as PK-PJC and named 'Aron', from May 1973. Pelita operated a huge fleet of rotary and fixed-wing aircraft on contract charters and on private, in-house, schedules throughout the Far East on behalf of Pertamina Oil and numerous other, mostly oil-industry related, corporate clients. Aircraft types operated varied from humble Shorts Skyvans, to Puma helicopters, Grumman Gulfstream executive jets, Fokker F.27 and F.28 airliners and a single executive configured Boeing 707.

As well as its oil industry contracts, between mid-1977 and May 1978, the single Pelita-owned One-Eleven flew a weekly scheduled service from Denpasar to Darwin, in Northern Australia, on behalf of Merpati Nusantara Airlines, an Indonesian independent carrier. Merpati had almost acquired a single ex-American Airlines Series 400 in August 1971, but had been refused an import licence for the aircraft by the Indonesian government. The aircraft had made it as far as being delivered to Jakarta, in full Merpati colours, but had to return to the USA without entering service. The aircraft was then sold on to Out Island Airways and eventually became part of the Bahamasair fleet.

A single ex-airline Series 400 was acquired in 1974 by the Philippine Air Force for VIP work from Manila. The ex-Channel Airways G-AWKJ had been sold to Air Hanson, as G-BIII, for use on their executive charter operations. Air Hanson Helicopters already flew an established VIP charter service. Flown to Newark, in the USA, for executive conversion, on completion of the work the aircraft was delivered directly to Manila. The aircraft had been sold via the Central Bank of the Philippines and was flown on VIP and special missions with 702 Squadron of the Philippines Air Force, registered as RP-C1. This work continued for ten years, until the aircraft was ferried to the UK for storage at Gatwick in 1984.

The British arm of the Ford Motor Company had operated an extensive fleet of executive aircraft over the years, based at Stansted Airport in Essex. Convenient for its main UK manufacturing and design facilities, Stansted was used for many flights, carrying executives, key personnel and even, on occasion, equipment and freight to European production plants and offices. In 1976, the pair of executive VIP One-Elevens were purchased from the Forca Aerea Brasilia and entered service on a private scheduled network to Belgium, Germany and Spain, alongside the established executive fleet of smaller aircraft.

The original pair were joined by an ex-airline One-Eleven Series 400 in 1977, once destined to be the undelivered second aircraft for TAE of Spain, later sold to Bavaria. The new addition was ferried to the USA for fitting out in an executive configuration, before entering service in March, 1978. The three One-Elevens also operated on special services to many parts of the world and were to be active on Ford's behalf for over fifteen years. Eventually, their day-to-day operation was contracted out to Thurston Aviation Ltd, also based at Stansted, although the aircraft remained Ford's property, before two were sold off altogether in August 1993.

A more unusual corporate operation of a One-Eleven was undertaken by Turbo-Union Ltd, an associate of Rolls-Royce, the aero-engine manufacturer. An ex-TACA International Series 400 was converted by BAC at Hurn, being fitted with a large cargo door in the forward fuselage, along with a new load-spreading plywood floor. Thirty-nine seats were fitted in the rear cabin. From August 1979 until early 1994, the aircraft was operated from Filton, near Bristol, carrying personnel, engines and equipment to Germany and Italy in connection with the Panavia Tornado aircraft programme.

The upheavals caused to the operating lives of many of the world's population of commercial airline One-Elevens during the traumatic times of the mid-1970s showed little sign of abating as new commercial operators continued to come and go. The Court Line One-Eleven inventory was soon dispersed to a variety of new owners, as were the smaller fleets of Phoenix and Paninternational. The short-term leasing deals that British Caledonian was able to arrange had helped the Gatwick-based company keep much of their fleet within arm's reach for when financial conditions improved.

British Independent Expansion

One of the new One-Eleven operators was far from a new name on the British independent airline scene. Monarch Airlines had started flying inclusive tour charters from Luton in April 1968, with a pair of ex-Caledonian Airways Bristol Britannias. Monarch was owned by Cosmos, one of the larger holiday companies and much of their early work was undertaken for the parent company with inclusive tour flights from Luton to resorts around Europe and the Mediterranean. The Britannia fleet was steadily expanded over the next couple of years, especially following the failure of British Eagle, several of whose large fleet were taken over. Jets had taken on Monarch's yellow and black colours in late 1971, when the first of a fleet of ex-Northwest Airlines Boeing 720Bs was placed into service.

The Boeing 720Bs were configured for 170 passengers, which was considered rather large for some of the newer holiday markets being developed. The Boeings were also limited if operations from some of the UK's smaller airports were to be considered. With the remaining Britannias all due to be retired by mid-1975, Monarch Airlines started to look for a smaller, more flexible, jet to join the fleet.

Monarch's ex-Court Line One-Elevens entered service in 1975. Steve Bunting

The award of a contract to operate a series of charters for Cosmos from Bristol during the 1975 season saw Monarch negotiating with BAC for the lease of one ex-Court Line Series 500. At the end of February, the aircraft was delivered from Hurn to Luton, following a delay caused by a strike at the BAC plant. As a result of heavy bookings for the Cosmos holidays, a second ex-Court Line aircraft arrived a month later, to provide extra capacity. An intensive programme of training and route familiarization flights followed, which saw both aircraft visiting several British airports over the next few weeks.

Initially the One-Elevens were operated from Luton but on 17 May 1975, the new summer charter programme was opened from Bristol. Throughout the summer the One-Elevens served Alicante, Gerona, Ibiza, Palma, Rimini and Venice from the West Country airport. New services were also operated from both Birmingham and East Midlands, utilizing both the One-Eleven and Boeing 720B fleets. In November, following the initial pair of One-Eleven's successful first season with Monarch, a third Series 500 was acquired from British Caledonian and this aircraft entered service on 11 December with a Luton–Vienna charter. The arrival of Boeing 737-200s in 1982 saw the beginning of the withdrawal of the Boeing 720B fleet. Although these were shortly followed by the larger 737-300s and 757s, the One-Elevens continued to serve Monarch Airlines until the end of

the 1985 season, the last not being withdrawn until October that year.

The beginning of 1975 saw a great increase in the size of the One-Eleven fleet of Dan-Air Services Ltd. Four ex-Court Line Series 500 aircraft were obtained from BAC between January and March. With their 119 inclusive tour passenger configuration conveniently exactly matching that of the Comet 4Bs and 4Cs already in service, the Series 500 One-Elevens were used to replace some of the older members of the fuel-thirsty Comet fleet. As well as the new One-Elevens, a small fleet of Boeing 727s had been acquired for use on the charter network, further displacing the long-established Comets.

The pair of Zambia Airways Series 200s were also obtained by Dan-Air in March, following their replacement in Africa by Boeing 737s. The Series 200s were flown alongside the other Dan-Air One-Elevens on charter flights, but also featured in the company's plans for an expanded scheduled service network. The previous year, 1974, had seen Dan-Air open its scheduled service from Gatwick to Newcastle, its first domestic trunk route. Initially operated by Comets, the route was also promoted by British Caledonian to attract connecting passengers to its scheduled services from Gatwick. In the opposite direction, from early 1975, Dan-Air's scheduled flights from Newcastle to Bergen, operated by the One-Elevens, and Kristiansand, operated by 748 turbo-props, were timed to connect with the London service.

In competition with British Airways/Northeast Airlines Trident flights into Heathrow, Dan-Air's Gatwick flight soon attracted a loyal local following from Newcastle. A particularly popular innovation was the provision of a hot breakfast on the morning flights, comparing very favourably with the rather basic tea and biscuit service offered by BA/Northeast. The original Dan-Air One-Elevens replaced the Comets on the route in late 1974. The arrival of the Series 200s saw the replacement of the Comets on the scheduled services to Montpellier and Perpignan, in southern France, from Gatwick. Now in a high-density 89-passenger configuration, the Series 200s still retained their original Central African Airways cabin wall trim. This featured motifs of stylized native hunters and African wildlife, some of the former in various states of obvious undress, which was to elicit much comment over the years.

As well as the scheduled flights to Gatwick and Bergen, the Newcastle-based One-Elevens would be used for weekend inclusive tour services during the summer. Although the Newcastle base would usually be assigned the shorter-ranged Series 200s for most of the week, the Friday evening Gatwick–Newcastle flight would often be assigned to a Series 300 or 400, specifically with a view to it being better able to operate the longer ranging inclusive tour charters from Newcastle over the weekend. The larger Series 500s also made an appearance at Newcastle, on both the

Dan-Air also took on ex-Court Line aircraft. G-BDAT was once G-AYOR. MAP

scheduled and charter flights, if loads demanded it.

Scheduled Gatwick–Jersey One-Eleven flights were introduced in 1975. Dan-Air had flown schedules from Gatwick to Jersey for some years, although these tended to be strictly seasonal. With the arrival of the One-Eleven, frequencies were increased and the jets were a definite improvement in image over the Ambassadors, the last of which had recently been retired, and the 748s used before. Although the jet speeds on the route were popular with the passengers, the cabin crews were less enthusiastic. They soon discovered what had already been a problem for BUA and BCal cabin crews over the same route for a number of years. With barely 30 minutes, often less, between wheels up and final approach, the cabin crews were hard pressed to complete the full cabin service that they were used to offering on the longer ranging flights. A much reduced refreshment and bar service, with duty-free goods available only on request, became the norm on the shorter jet flights and even that could be a rush on even a

Dan-Air's G-ATVH was christened 'City of Newcastle-Upon-Tyne'. via Author

Dan-Air's One-Elevens began to appear on more scheduled flights. via Author

marginally full flight. However, harassed cabin crews aside, the One-Elevens were a successful addition to the Dan-Air scheduled services to the Channel Islands, operating alongside 748s that continued to fly the lower capacity flights.

Much less successful was the attempt to introduce One-Elevens on the Lydd–Beauvais coach–air service. Dan-Air had inherited the route when it took over Skyways International in 1972. Passengers were transported by coach from London's Victoria Coach Station to Lydd for the cross-

When Dan-Air took over the company, operations were moved to nearby Lydd, which offered a much longer runway and better facilities. Lydd had been used by Silver City Airways car-ferry services, now abandoned by Silver City's successor, British Air Ferries which had decided to concentrate its network on Southend. Dan-Air operated its first Lydd-based coach–air flights on 1 November 1974. The Ostend and Clermont Ferrand routes were soon transferred to Gatwick, leaving the Lydd base with only the Beauvais service year-

uneconomic for jets and the expensive experiment came to an end. The route reverted to an all-748 operation, although higher-capacity Viscounts were leased in to operate it in late years. Dan-Air's One-Elevens did continue to make regular appearances at Beauvais however, on inclusive tour charter services from various points in the UK, carrying groups of Paris-bound holiday-makers. The coach–air service continued in operation for several successful years before being sold off as a package to a newly reconstituted Skyways.

432FD, G-AXOX was one of BIA's first One-Elevens. Brooklands Museum

channel hop to Beauvais, where more coaches took them on into Paris. Skyways Coach-Air, as it was originally titled, had inaugurated the unique service, from Lympne, on the Kent coast, in 1955 using DC-3s. Later, the first production 748s were used from 1962. At the time of the Dan-Air purchase, 748 coach–air services were also operating to Ostend, for onward transport to Brussels, and Clermont Ferrand, for the French Riviera.

round, although a seasonal Jersey flight had been introduced from Lympne in the summer of 1973. The new Dan-Air Gatwick–Montpellier One-Eleven scheduled service was actually a revival of a dormant Skyways licence, originally flown from Lympne by Skyways 748s.

In an effort to boost the service, the One-Elevens made a weekly scheduled appearance at Lydd during 1975, but the thirty-minute hop to Beauvais was soon deemed

Originally outnumbered by the short-bodied One-Eleven fleet, the original Dan-Air Series 500s were to be joined by a pair of aircraft acquired from BCal, one arriving at the end of 1975, the other in early 1976 and an ex-Transbrasil Series 500 was obtained via BAe three years later. The arrival of the extra aircraft allowed the retirement of more Comets, now rapidly reaching the end of their useful lives. Dan-Air was also now operating all the major variants of the One-Eleven at the same time, with Series 200s, 300s, 400s and 500s in service, the only airline to do so.

When British United Airways had been sold to Caledonian in 1970, the owners of the former company had already split off some parts of the operation. British United Island Airways had been retitled British Island Airways and continued to operate their fleet of Dart Heralds and DC-3s on scheduled regional flights, mainly concentrating on services to the Isle of Man and Blackpool, in the north, and the Channel

the scheduled services, contracted with a number of tour companies to operate a programme of inclusive tour charters. To fly the new services a fleet of three One-Eleven Series 400s were acquired from BAe. These had previously been operated by Gulf Air, who had replaced them on the Arabian Gulf regional services with Boeing 737s. Following the short lease of one of their number to British Airways, still in the basic Gulf Air livery, the remainder of the One-Eleven fleet had been returned to the UK in November 1977.

and the Channel Islands. Renamed Air UK, the merged company adopted a bold new livery based on an all-blue fuselage, which was soon painted on the latest One-Eleven to join the fleet, the company's fourth. Appropriately, if belatedly, re-registered G-CBIA, this was the ex-Air Siam/Pertamina aircraft that had been returned to BAe at Hurn in June 1979. G-CBIA was the only one of the One-Elevens to wear the blue livery, the rest just carrying Air UK titles over their basic BIA orange and brown trim.

G-CBIA was the only Air UK One-Eleven to wear the blue livery. Brooklands Museum

Islands, in the south. As BCal found their One-Eleven jets increasingly uneconomic on certain routes, BIA was contracted to operate a number of the scheduled services from Gatwick on their behalf. Flights from Gatwick to Antwerp, Le Touquet, Manchester and Rotterdam were transferred to BIA Dart Herald operation under BCal flight numbers.

In 1978 though, British Island Airways took a new direction and, in addition to

One of the One-Elevens was in BIA service in time for the 1978 summer season, with the two others following in early 1979. One-Eleven operations were based at Gatwick, with contract and *ad hoc* flights being undertaken to many European destinations. In October that year though, British Island Airways was merged with Norwich-based Air Anglia Ltd that operated scheduled services up the British east coast and to the Netherlands, France

This seemed providential as, on 1 January 1982, a brand new British Island Airways was formed and the four One-Eleven aircraft transferred from Air UK. Air UK now wanted to concentrate on building up their regional scheduled services network and leave the jet charter market, as well as withdrawing from most of the scheduled services from Gatwick. Regaining their full BIA colours on their transfer to the new company, a fifth One-Eleven Series

The 'new' BIA introduced several Series 500s, including **G-ALXN**. Martyn East

400 joined the original quartet for the duration of the 1983 season and the first of an eventual fleet of seven Series 500s arrived the following year. With the arrival of the Series 500s, BIA leased out the smaller 400s, with contracts of varying length seeing them in service on behalf of a number of carriers, even including Air UK again, over the next few years.

The Air UK contract involved two aircraft, one leased from May 1985 to April 1988 and another from November 1985 to April 1987. Tentative plans had been made for Air UK to acquire two ex-Braniff Series 200s, and these had even advanced as far as new registrations being reserved. However, the plans were scrapped in favour of the leasing deal with BIA to cover Air UK's scheduled jet operations until newly ordered BAe 146s were delivered. The BIA One-Elevens operated Air UK scheduled flights to Amsterdam from Aberdeen, Edinburgh, Glasgow, Leeds and Newcastle. One of the aircraft also operated for British Airways, still in the Air UK livery with BA titles, from November 1986 to April 1987, mostly on the Irish Sea routes.

Air Florida and Virgin Atlantic leased the BIA Series 400s to operate scheduled feeder services into Gatwick, to link up with their trans-Atlantic flights. Air Florida contracted for four weekly flights from Gatwick to Amsterdam and Frankfurt and two flights a week to Brussels and Dusseldorf. Unfortunately, Air Florida ceased flying on 3 July 1984, bringing the BIA flights to an abrupt end. In 1985, from January to April, Virgin leased a BIA Series 400 to operate their scheduled flight from Gatwick to Maastricht in the Netherlands. Originally operated by leased Viscounts, the Maastricht service was designed to feed passengers from Germany and the Low Countries into the Virgin flights across the Atlantic, However, the flights were not a success and the use of the One-Eleven only added to

G-AXMU in joint BIA/Virgin colours. Aviation Hobby Shop

the increasing losses, causing the withdrawal of Virgin Atlantic from the route altogether.

In addition, the BIA Series 400s found themselves on short-term charter and lease agreements to French scheduled operator, Transport Aérien Transrégional. With TAT, two of the aircraft flew on scheduled domestic routes to Brest, Lille, Marseilles, Mulhouse, Nantes, Nice and Paris-Orly. The lease to TAT lasted from March 1989 to February 1990.

BIA eventually opened their own scheduled services, with flights from Gatwick to Catania, Palermo and Malta. As well as the One-Eleven Series 500s, the company had also leased in a fleet of four McDonnell-Douglas MD-82s, the much enlarged variant of the DC-9, for use on both the charter and scheduled networks.

However, British Island Airways suddenly ceased all operations on 1 February 1990 following financial problems.

The Loss of Laker – and After

Shortly after the reformed British Island Airways took to the skies again, one long-standing One-Eleven operator was forced to fold its wings in a spectacular fashion. On 25 February 1982, Laker Airways was forced into liquidation. In the course of one morning, all operations came to an end and the fleet, including the five One-Elevens, was grounded. By then, in addition to the One-Elevens, Laker was flying a fleet of wide-bodied DC-10s and Airbus A300s. As well as the original charter services, the DC-10s were operating sched-

uled low-fare 'Skytrain' flights to the USA and plans were in hand for similar flights within Europe using the Airbuses.

There was wide speculation that predatory pricing and undue influence on the international banking industry by the established national carriers on both sides of the Atlantic had contributed to the airline's sudden downfall. They had certainly been unhappy about the success of the 'Skytrain' flights and were reluctant to allow Laker any further expansion. A number of subsequent lawsuits gave judgements in previously knighted Sir Freddie Laker's favour, although this was a number of years later and there was to be no rebirth of any UK-based Laker Airways. Instead, Laker eventually set up a new Laker Airways, operating charters and scheduled services based in Florida.

G-AVYZ served Laker Airways until operations ceased in 1982. via Author

---

Freddie Laker

Armed with his £40 gratuity on leaving the Air Transport Auxiliary at the end of World War Two, Freddie Laker, a shopkeeper's son who had trained as an aircraft engineer, went on to become one of the most charismatic, high-profile figures in the British air transport industry. Building up Aviation Traders, originally by buying up surplus RAF and civilian airframes to scrap and provide spares for aircraft engaged on Berlin Airlift operations, Laker eventually established Stansted-based Air Charter Ltd, initially to operate into Berlin on later supply flights. Under Laker's guidance the airline became a leading operator of worldwide charters and scheduled cross-channel air ferry services. Aviation Traders built the Laker-conceived car ferry conversion of the DC-4, the ATEL Carvair, as well as producing the less successful, but technically innovative, Laker-designed, ATEL Accountant executive and feeder airliner project.

After leading the newly-merged BUA through its first years, and seeing the airline's fleets of VC-10 and One-Eleven jets into service, Laker left to form his own airline again. From just two leased Britannia turboprops flying *ad hoc* charters, within fifteen years Laker Airways was operating a large fleet of modern wide-bodied DC-10s on scheduled trans-Atlantic services, as well as several Airbuses and One-Elevens on European charters. Laker's success in bringing air travel within the reach of so many eventually led to official recognition of his achievements with a knighthood. Following the 1982 collapse of the UK airline, Sir Freddie Laker eventually formed a new Laker Airways, based in Fort Lauderdale, Florida, in the USA. The new company, still led by Sir Freddie, originally concentrated on local tourist flights to the Bahamas with Boeing 727s, and later expanded into trans-Atlantic charter services with DC-10s.

Air Manchester Ltd attempted to take the place of Laker's established One-Eleven operation at Manchester. Set up by Sureways Travel to fly their clients, Air Manchester had intended to operate three Series 400 One-Elevens. However, only one aircraft, G-SURE, once Autair, Cambrian and British Airways' G-AVOE, was destined to fly for the company. Delivered from Hurn after refurbishment on 18 May 1982, the aircraft was expected to fly a number of inclusive tour charter services from Manchester, although great difficulties with licensing problems with the Spanish authorities delayed inauguration of the flying programme. The licensing problems delayed operations until 3 June, when a grand total of eight passengers were flown from Manchester to Ibiza. The two other aircraft remained undelivered, although painted

Air Manchester flew for a matter of weeks. D. Goodwin via Jennie Gradidge

BCal took on four of Laker's Series 320AZs in 1982. Aviation Hobby Shop

in full Air Manchester colours, due to further financing difficulties.

In an effort to solve the Spanish licence problems, the aircraft was flown under British Air Ferries' name from September, with the aircraft's operational base being transferred to Liverpool. British Air Ferries also added a great deal of badly needed operational experience to the new airline. Even these drastic moves were unable to save Air Manchester though and all services had ended by November. The sole operating aircraft was returned to BAe and was soon leased out to Dan-Air, still in partial Air Manchester/BAF

livery, pending the delayed arrival of their new BAe 146s.

Four of the Laker fleet found a temporary home with British Caledonian. The last BCal Series 200 flight had taken place on 21 March 1982, between Paris-Charles de Gaulle and Gatwick, and the entire Series 200 fleet had been sold to a new operator, Pacific Express Inc. in California. Extra second-hand Series 500s had been acquired to replace them, but extra capacity was still needed in the short term. The ex-Laker Series 300 aircraft, reregistered G-BKAU, 'AV, 'AW and 'AX, to prevent their being seized against any of

Laker's outstanding debts, entered service in April and continued in BCal service, alongside the Series 500s, until November the following year.

West Germany's charter airlines continued to operate healthy fleets of One-Elevens through the 1970s. Support of the type by two of the country's industry leaders, Bavaria and Germanair, was conspicuous. By 1977, Bavaria had a mixed fleet of two Series 400s and three Series 500s, with another Series 400 out on lease. Germanair was flying five Series 500 One-Elevens, alongside two new wide-body Airbus A300B4s. A small fleet of F.28s had been operated by Germanair from 1972, although they were all phased out and disposed of by 1975. In May 1977, the two airlines merged their operations under the joint name of Bavaria-Germanair Fluggesellschaft. The One-Elevens continued in service through the following summer, although the smaller Series 400s were all disposed of by the end of 1977.

The Bavaria-Germanair name was fated to last only until January 1979, when all operations were merged with yet another large German charter airline, Hapag Lloyd Fluggesellschaft GmbH, of Hanover. At that time Hapag Lloyd was an all Boeing operator, but the ex-Bavaria-Germanair One-Elevens were retained under the new regime, continuing to operate their inclusive tour and general charter services all round Europe and to North Africa and the Canary Islands. Hapag Lloyd, the surviving airline from the merger, started to dispose of some of the seven inherited One-Eleven Series 500s in late 1979. However, the type remained a well-utilized feature of Hapag Lloyd's operations until March 1982, when the last was withdrawn from use in favour of an all Boeing and Airbus fleet. Bavaria, although no longer a commercial charter airline, still survives as a separate company, the owner of a large fleet of leased-out airliners and has given consultancy and operational assistance to a number of carriers.

Following its acquisition of the Mohawk Series 200s, Allegheny Airlines continued to expand the fleet, with the purchase of eight more ex-Braniff Airways aircraft between March and September 1972. The operational sphere of influence of the Allegheny One-Elevens steadily expanded over the years, break-

Bavaria-Germanair retained the merged airline's One-Elevens. via Author

Allegheny flew One-Elevens to Canada as well as within the US. via Author

ing out of their original Mohawk network area. Eventually, they were operating as far south as Tampa, as far west as Chicago and St Louis, and as far north as Montreal and Toronto, as well as flying to most

The inventory of aircraft types in the USAir fleet was an uneconomically varied one and became more so over the years. As well as operating one of the world's largest fleets of the One-Eleven's main rival, the

New Opportunities in the USA

A major factor in the rapid expansion of new operators in the United States in the

USAir continued a high daily utilization for their One-Elevens. Brooklands Museum

major east coast population centres. On 28 October 1979 the company changed its name to USAir Inc., to better reflect its expanded network, as well as promoting its future expansionist ambitions to become a more national and international airline.

During the early 1980s, the ex-Mohawk and Aloha aircraft had their rear ventral airstairs removed as a weight-saving exercise. This brought them into line with the ex-Braniff aircraft that had been originally delivered by BAC with no rear airstairs fitted at all. At the same time, the aircraft's seating capacity was increased to 79, from 74 passengers. The USAir One-Elevens were now almost exclusively based at Pittsburgh and were operated extensively on charters, in addition to their established scheduled services.

DC-9-30, more new and second-hand Boeing 727s and 737s were acquired by the airline from various sources during the 1980s. By 1989, the One-Eleven fleet had been reduced from an all-time peak of 31 to just eight aircraft, as the airline attempted to standardize and reduce the number of different types in service. The last One-Eleven was finally withdrawn by the summer, bringing to an end over twenty years of service to USAir and its predecessors.

The end of the USAir One-Eleven operation was far from the end of the type's utilization on the United States airways though. While the active USAir One-Eleven fleet was being reduced in size, a number of new operators had already decided, right or wrong, that the One-Eleven was the type they wanted for their networks, both scheduled and charter.

early 1980s was the Airline Deregulation Act, passed by Congress in 1978. Previously, any aspiring airline trying to open a new service had to fight any established carriers, who were understandably protective of their networks built up, in some cases, over forty years of hard work. The new act had been introduced in an effort to liberalize the industry, increase competition and substantially reduce fares. The established commuter operators could now look to increase capacity as many of the aircraft size restrictions had been eased. Many also looked to expanding their networks to open trunk services within their catchment area in direct competition with the larger airlines. Perhaps even more importantly, several brand new airlines were quickly established, valiantly trying to carve out their own niche markets. Although the parties

Pacific Express One-Elevens flew on the west coast. Aviation Hobby Shop

concerned still had to obtain FAA approval for their operations, the actual process of opening a scheduled service network was much easier. For both the expanding commuter carriers and the new airlines, the availability of increasing numbers of second-hand, second generation jets, including One-Elevens, available for either lease or purchase at relatively low cost, was a temptation that could not be resisted.

Pacific Express Inc, based at Chico, California, had purchased the surviving BCal fleet of seven Series 200s in late 1981. Operations began on 27 January 1982 on a scheduled network that was eventually to link thirteen points in California, as well as operating to cities in Idaho, Nevada and Oregon. This was the first time that the One-Eleven had been operated on a US

west coast scheduled network. Even American and Braniff's fleets had not operated further west than Texas. Two USAir Series 200s were also leased by Pacific Express from late 1982 to December 1983. Despite a popular following and innovative marketing ploys such as giving away free bottles of liquor to passengers paying higher fares, the fledgling airline was unable to compete against the established carriers in the area. Pacific Express's main rivals, United Airlines and Western Airlines, as well as the more experienced low fares operator Air-Cal, managed to keep their passengers' loyalty and Pacific Express was forced to cease operations on 2 May 1984.

1982 had also seen the One-Eleven enter service with the regional scheduled carrier, Air Illinois. Both acquired from

USAir, a pair of Series 200s were operated from Chicago-O'Hare to Champaign, Evansville, St Louis and Springfield. Air Illinois had opened scheduled services on local routes serving a number of small cities between Chicago and St Louis in 1970. An initial fleet of Twin Otters was later joined in 1973 by a single BAe 748. The turbo-prop distinguished itself by being the largest aircraft certified to fly scheduled services into the small lakeside airport at Meigs Field, close to downtown Chicago. A second 748 was purchased in 1980, followed by the decision to upgrade to pure-jet service with the One-Elevens. Two other small scheduled carriers were taken over, South Central Air Transport, of Natchez, Missouri in 1977 and Decatur Commuter Airlines in 1981, leading to

Air Illinois operated a pair of ex-USAir One-Elevens. Jennie Gradidge

great increases in the Air Illinois network, with scheduled services reaching as far south as Memphis.

Sadly, the crash of one of the 748s, near Pickneyville, Illinois, on 11 October 1983 saw the company being grounded by the Federal Aviation Administration. A National Transportation Safety Board investigation unearthed problems with maintenance and improper record keeping and the FAA was forced to act, following accusations that government cost-cutting had led to it not being as vigilant as it should have been on inspecting Air Illinois operations.

Air Illinois was allowed to restart operations in March 1984 but was never able to recover from the previous bad publicity. The two Series 200 One-Elevens were not to be part of the reconstituted scheduled operation. One was returned to USAir, the other sub-leased to Wright Airlines, of Cleveland. This aircraft only flew in Wright service for three months, from July to September 1984. In November that year, Air Illinois leased the One-Eleven out again to Atlantic Gulf Airlines, of Tallahassee, Florida. With Atlantic Gulf, the One-Eleven operated twice daily schedules from Tallahassee to Miami. Later, the One-Eleven scheduled network was extended to include three weekly flights from Miami to Puerto Plata in the Dominican Republic and five flights a week from Miami to Providenciales, via Grand Turk.

As well as the single Series 200, two Series 400s were acquired by Atlantic Gulf to operate the extended network, one actually on sub-lease from Air Illinois that had obtained the aircraft specifically to lease on to Atlantic Gulf. The other Series 400 was also operated by the company on behalf of Grenada Airways on a twice weekly Miami–Grenada scheduled flight.

Atlantic Gulf Airlines suspended their scheduled operations in September 1986. However, the services from Miami to the Caribbean were kept open for a while, with the operation of the One-Elevens being taken over by Challenge International Airlines and APA International Air. The services were not a financial success though and had ceased by early 1987. The company later reopened their scheduled network under the new name of Challenge Air International using a small fleet of leased Boeing 737s, but once again the operations came to an end following mounting losses. A separate cargo division, Challenge Air Cargo, continued to operate throughout the Caribbean and to Central and South America.

An early customer for the enlarged version of the BAe 146 was Air Wisconsin, of Appleton, Wisconsin. The airline's president, Preston H. Wildbourne, had already caused a stir in the industry by replacing its fleet of nineteen-seat Sweringen Metros with fifty-seat De Havilland Canada DHC-7s. The order for 100-seat BAe 146s was seen as an even braver, possibly foolhardy, move. Pending the delayed delivery of their new aircraft, British Aerospace leased four Series 200s from the idle ex-Pacific Express One-Eleven fleet to the company from January 1985. Flying from Chicago-O'Hare, the One-Elevens were used on scheduled flights to cities such as Appleton, Cedar Rapids, Green Bay, Kalamazoo, Mosinee, Rhinelander and Toledo, among others.

The One-Elevens continued in Air Wisconsin service for a time after the 146s were finally delivered, eventually bowing out to their four-engined successors in 1986. In the meantime, Air Wisconsin had also taken over another large successful commuter airline, Mississippi Valley Airlines, acquiring their fleet of Fokker F.27s and Shorts 330 and 360s in the process. Air Wisconsin was now poised to become a fully fledged United Express carrier, affiliated to the huge United Airlines, feeding traffic into their main domestic and international hub at Chicago-O'Hare.

Two Series 400s were obtained from British Aerospace by another Illinois-based commuter carrier, Britt Airways Inc., being delivered in June 1984 and March 1985. Both were ex-Autair/Cambrian/BA aircraft that had been part of Air Manchester's thwarted plans. Ex-G-AVOE/G-SURE had operated briefly for Air Manchester, and ex-G-AVOF/G-BMAN had been painted in Air Manchester colours but had remained stored at Hurn with BAe.

Once they were delivered to Britt Airways and placed on the US register, the One-Elevens were operated on scheduled services from Chicago to Cedar Rapids, Champaign, Evansville, Indianapolis and Terre Haute. Britt had been one of the pioneering local service carriers, beginning operations as Vercoa Air Service in 1956. In 1968 Vercoa had become one of the first of many Allegheny Commuter carriers, flying its scheduled network for the benefit of feeding passengers into Allegheny's main network from smaller cities. In 1975, Vercoa was purchased by William Britt and renamed Britt Airlines. A year later, in 1976, Britt Airways was formed to operate under its own name, separate from the Allegheny Commuter contract, utilizing Fokker and Fairchild F.27s and FH-227s.

As well as their scheduled services alongside the Fokkers and Fairchilds, the One-Elevens flew leisure passengers on charter contracts from Chicago and other local points to Atlantic City, on behalf of Sterling Transportation. In 1985 up to three charter trips a day were also being flown from Columbus, Ohio, to Orlando, Florida.

In February 1986, Britt was purchased by People Express Inc., of Newark. Although it continued flying under its own name, Britt's operations became more and more associated with the new parent company. The One-Elevens were finally sold off in August 1987 and Britt eventually became a unit of Continental Express, following the absorption of People Express by Continental Airlines.

Three of the ex-BCal and Pacific Express aircraft were leased to Cascade Airways, of Spokane, Washington, in September 1984. Cascade had been operating regional scheduled services, based on the Seattle, Spokane and Portland areas, since its founding by Mark Chesnutt in 1970. Phenomenal growth had seen the company establish itself as a major regional carrier, with a large fleet of turbo-prop commuter aircraft, including new BAe 748s. The upgrade of equipment to the One-Elevens was seen as a natural progression, especially as Cascade's main rival in the area, Horizon Air, founded by Milton G. Kuolt in 1981, had already experimented with a short-lived DC-9 operation and had recently introduced Fokker F.28 jets into service alongside their own turbo-prop commuter aircraft. Horizon Air had benefited from the demise of Pacific Express, taking over many of the Pacific Northwest regional routes abandoned by the bankrupt carrier.

Cascade Airways had also purchased two Series 400 One-Elevens by February 1985 and the quintet of jets were operating over the airline's busier routes. Twice daily Seattle–Portland–Boise–Idaho Falls–Pocatello and two daily Seattle–Spokane, one of which continued to Calgary in Canada, One-Eleven services were flown. Three daily Seattle–Pasco flights, two of which continued to Walla Walla and the other to Lewiston were also operated by the jets.

Competition with Horizon Air over the similar route networks was intense and financially damaging to both airlines. The companies had merger talks as early as 1983 but it was not until July 1985 that a formal agreement was reached for Horizon Air to acquire Cascade Airways, the initial plan being that Cascade would continue to operate separately as a subsidiary. Whilst awaiting the finalization of the talks, Cascade wet-leased the capacity of both its One-Elevens and Beech 1900 turbo-props to Horizon Air for use on its services. Legal formalities and Department of Transportation approval for the merger were not com-

Yet another low-fare start-up carrier on the other side of the United States, Florida Express Inc., had begun operations with no less than nine ex-USAir Series 200s in January 1984. Based at Orlando, the Florida Express fleet operated scheduled services to numerous US domestic points as far north as Milwaukee and south to the Bahamas, as well as a comprehensive network within Florida. In early 1986 the first of the seven ex-BCal/Pacific Express

Braniff – Again!

The saviour came from a rather surprising direction, with Braniff taking over the airline on 1 March 1988. A few weeks before, Florida Express had already reached an agreement to operate as an associate company, as a Braniff Express carrier, but the full merger was initiated instead. The original Braniff Airways had ceased flying following a dramatic finan-

Florida Express based their fleet at Orlando. D. Goodwin via Jennie Gradidge

The 'new' Braniff Inc. took over Florida Express in 1988. MAP

pleted until January 1986. Even this contained restrictions and the management of Horizon decided these were unacceptable. Kuolt cancelled the merger and Cascade was forced, by mounting losses and its inability to find a new partner to bail it out, to cease operations on 7 March 1986. Cascade attempted to sue Horizon for breach of contract, but the legal case was dismissed.

Series 200s migrated southeast across the USA to Orlando and six Series 400s, acquired from various sources, were also in Florida Express service by 1986. The rapid expansion of Florida Express resulted in the company swiftly over-stretching itself and by 1988 it was facing increasing losses and looking for a new injection of cash to save it.

cial collapse in May 1982, bringing to an end, literally overnight, nearly sixty years of scheduled airline operations. The company managed to remain dormant until new backers were found and a reconstituted Braniff Inc. restarted limited Boeing 727 operations from Dallas/Fort Worth, albeit over a much reduced route system, on 1 March 1984.

The Orlando-based services of Florida Express added a valuable network of services to the new company. Ironically, a number of the ex-Florida One-Elevens had been delivered to the original company in the mid-1960s and were taking up Braniff titles again after a gap of up to twelve years.

In late 1985, Braniff Inc. had opened a new hub operation at Kansas City and soon ran down their operations from Dallas in favour of the new Midwest facilities. By late 1988, Dallas was no longer a base for the company and all operations were conducted from either Kansas City or Orlando.

Group for charter services from Las Vegas. However, all four were returned to the lessor later that year and there is doubt as to whether any commercial operations were ever undertaken.

What will almost certainly turn out to be the last attempt at a One-Eleven service in the USA died with the cancellation of the Kiwi International Airlines contract for Tay-powered ROMBAC One-Elevens. Had this abortive project come to fruition, no less than sixteen aircraft would have been based at Newark, New Jersey, operating scheduled services throughout the

The 1980s also saw the end of several long-established One-Eleven operations around the world. May 1982 saw the last Series 500 being withdrawn by LACSA of Costa Rica. A One-Eleven operator since 1967, LACSA had finally replaced their British twin-jets with Boeing 727-200s. LACSA had also operated their One-Eleven fleet closely with Cayman Airways, having operated on the island airway's behalf from Grand Cayman to Kingston, Jamaica, for the first time in 1970. Cayman had gone on to operate their own aircraft from 1978, when two second-hand

Classic Air flew few, if any, commercial operations. via Author

Several of the One-Elevens were moved to operate from Kansas City, alongside newly acquired Boeing 737s. New, leased Airbus A320s were on order to update the fleet. However, shortly after the first of the new aircraft had entered service, Braniff Inc. filed for bankruptcy and all flying ceased on 29 September 1989.

In an effort to stave off the increasing losses, Braniff Inc. had attempted to raise funds by selling much of the fleet and leasing them back from the new owners. As a result of this, twelve of the fleet of eighteen One-Elevens were actually owned by Guinness Peat Aviation at the time of the company's second collapse.

Classic Air Inc. was established in March 1990, a passenger-carrying offshoot of the cargo airline, Buffalo Airways. Four ex-USAir Series 200s were taken on charge from the International Leasing

northeast United States, and down south to Florida and the Caribbean. Kiwi was, itself, a company set up to take advantage of the deregulation act, and turned out to be one of its many victims.

The Airline Deregulation Act had certainly achieved its goal of stimulating competition and reducing fares for the travelling public. Unfortunately, it also led to a series of short-lived airline operations, the frequent demises of which led to a lack of confidence in the industry as a whole. The new competition also led to considerable losses among the major carriers. In the case of the once great pioneering airlines, Eastern Airlines, Pan American World Airways and the original Braniff Airways, these financial losses, to a certain extent brought about by the inability of the carriers to adapt to the ways of the new order, were to lead to their bankruptcy.

aircraft were delivered. One was ex-British Midland and Transbrasil, the rapidly expanding Brazilian airline having disposed of the last of their One-Elevens, in favour of an all Boeing 727 fleet, the same year. The other new Cayman aircraft was ex-Court Line and LACSA.

A daily Grand Cayman–Houston scheduled flight was opened by Cayman Airways and the established Grand Cayman–Miami flight was now operated up to three times a day. Once again, higher-capacity Boeings, initially leased Boeing 727-200s, later replaced by 737s, deposed the One-Elevens which were both to find new homes with British Island Airways at Gatwick. However, owners and operators of a number of executive and corporate One-Elevens, and other aircraft, eager to take advantage of the island's favourable tax laws, already had a great many aircraft

Cayman Airways began One-Eleven operations with leased aircraft. MAP

(Below) **Mediterranean Express was based at Luton.** Ian MacFarlane via Jennie Gradidge

registered in Grand Cayman, a situation which continues to this day.

Peru's Compania de Aviacion Faucett, one of the few Series 475 operators, had also adopted the Boeing 727, although the smaller Series 100 was their choice. Airport improvements and restructuring of the domestic scheduled network had made the One-Eleven 475's special performance redundant and both the 475s and a single second-hand Series 500, initially leased and later purchased from BAC, were withdrawn in late 1982.

Both ex-Faucett Series 475s then spent prolonged periods in storage until they were finally purchased in 1987 by a new UK-based airline, Mediterranean Express, of Luton. Although both aircraft were painted in the company's colours, only one, G-AZUK was placed into revenue service. Charter flights from Luton, mostly to Italy, although many European points were served, were only operated until January 1988 when the company ceased flying. The

other aircraft, G-AYUW, had its pre-service overhaul halted in November 1987 and the hulk was eventually sold off for use in water-misting fire-retardant trials at Hurn. Although commercial operations had ended, Mediterranean Express continued to exist as a company and eventually its licences and operating authority were sold to Trans European Airways of Belgium which used them to establish a new UK-based subsidiary, TEA-UK, operating Boeing 737s from East Midlands Airport.

The other launch customer for the Series 475, Air Pacific, of Fiji, disposed of their small fleet in late 1982, replacing them with larger Boeing 737s. One Series 400, acquired second-hand, had already been scrapped in 1978, following the discovery of serious corrosion. The surviving two Series 475s were ferried to the UK and both ended up with British military registrations. One was used by the Empire Test Pilots School, the other joined an ex-BUA/BCal Series 200 and an ex-

Philippine Airlines Series 400, with the Royal Aircraft Establishment, for research work on a variety of projects.

Central American Sunset

An even longer-established One-Eleven airline than LACSA and Cayman Airways was TACA International Airlines SA, of Honduras. Their original Series 400s, joined briefly by a leased LACSA Series 500 in 1981–82, had been operating scheduled regional services around Central America and flying further afield across the Gulf of Mexico and the Caribbean since 1966. Later in their 22-year-long career with TACA, the aircraft were used increasingly for numerous and varied charter flights throughout Central America, especially to Mexico, alongside their scheduled operation commitments. The last of the faithful TACA One-Elevens were finally retired, replaced by Boeing 737s in 1988.

Air Pacific's 479FU, DQ-FBV became ZE432 with the ETPS. Martyn East

A last flurry of new Central American One-Eleven activity took place in 1991 when Servicios Aereos Rutas Oriente, trading as SARO Airlines, leased a single Series 200 in 1991. Operating from its Monterrey, Mexico, base, the aircraft flew scheduled services to Acapulco, Cancun, Leon-Guanajua, Mazatlan and Torreon, as well as charter flights throughout the region. Introduced in March 1991, the aircraft was withdrawn from use after less than a year's service and stored at Monterrey in February 1992.

Although far from an outstanding success, the SARO Airlines' experience at least showed that, even 25 years after its introduction, there were airlines around the world willing to consider the One-Eleven. Whether on the local jet airline services it had originally been designed for, or the very different rôles that its new operators constantly devised for it, the One-Eleven still seemed to have a part to play.

TACA International operated One-Elevens from 1966 to 1988. Brooklands Museum

CHAPTER EIGHT

New Faces, Old Problems

North of the United States' border, Canada's sole One-Eleven operator, Quebecair, continued to operate their fleet on both scheduled and charter services. The original pair of ex-British Eagle Series 300 aircraft had been joined by a second-hand Series 400 in 1973, with two more arriving in late 1982. A Series 200 was also leased from USAir from May 1982 to January 1983.

Quebecair's jet operations had also been further expanded with the introduction of

disposed of by 1980. However, leased Boeing 737s entered service in 1979 and the gradual acquisition of more of the American twin jets had seen the One-Elevens displaced by the end of 1986. BAe 748s and Convair CV-580s took over from the ageing F-27s on the local routes and a pair of McDonnell-Douglas DC-8-60s were introduced for use on a revived long-range charter programme. Unfortunately, the completion of the fleet modernization

following that November. Airways International had been formed by a Cardiff-based travel agency, Red Dragon Travel Ltd, specifically to operate their inclusive tour services from Cardiff, the new airline's base, and Bristol.

For the benefit of those not versed in the Welsh language, 'Cymru', pronounced 'Cumry', is the Welsh name for the principality, with the grammar of the Welsh language turning 'Airways International

Quebecair's ex-PAL and Bavaria 402AP, CF-QBK. Peter Vine via Jennie Gradidge

Boeing types, second-hand 707s and 727s during the 1970s and 1980s. The Fairchild F-27 turbo-props continued to operate over local scheduled services within Quebec. As well as flying on the higher-density scheduled services, all the jets, One-Elevens included, were utilized on a growing charter network, mostly on behalf of the airline's own travel company, Vacances-Quebec.

Financial problems, with both the scheduled and charter networks losing money, led to drastic rationalization, which saw the Boeing 707s and 727s being

plan only provided a temporary respite. Mounting losses forced government intervention in order to protect the socially vital scheduled network and, eventually, Quebecair's operation was absorbed into the newly formed Canadian Airlines International, along with several other independent Canadian airlines.

Quebecair's two ex-British Eagle Series 300s had found themselves returning 'home' to the UK in 1984. The first of the pair was delivered to Airways International Cymru Ltd in April 1984, the second

Cymru' into 'Wales International Airways'. Rather than take up their old British Eagle registrations, the aircraft were given new ones, with a Welsh language theme. C-FOBN, ex-G-ATPH became G-YMRU and C-FQBO, the ex-G-ATPI became G-WLAD (Gwlad being Welsh for 'Country'). In common use within the airline and the industry as a whole the airline was soon known more simply as 'Welshair'. The aircraft were leased by Airways International from Havelet Leasing, who had purchased them from Quebecair.

To help cover the 1984 summer season's flights until G-WLAD was ready to be delivered to Cardiff, an extra One-Eleven, British Island Airways Series 400 G-AXMU, was leased in and operated in a leased out to British Midland Airways from late 1985. British Midland, flying the One-Eleven in their full livery alongside their DC-9 fleet, used the aircraft to replace Viscounts on the Leeds/Brad- and the leased G-AXMU soon acquired reputations of some unpredictability and the on-time arrival back in the UK was no guarantee that the aircraft would be declared serviceable for the next charter.

G-YMRU entered service in a modified Quebecair all-blue livery. Aviation Hobby Shop

New Airways Cymru colours were adopted in 1986. Mary Kerby

mixed Airways Cymru/BIA livery. The first aircraft, G-YMRU entered service in basic bright blue Quebecair colours, with Airways Cymru titles in red. A new red, white and blue Airways International livery was finally adopted by G-YMRU in 1985.

G-WLAD actually spent little time flying for its new Welsh operator, being ford–Heathrow route. It also made occasional appearances on other scheduled routes from Heathrow to Teesside.

The, by now, rather vintage One-Elevens were starting to show their age somewhat and their time with Airways Cymru was beset with technical problems. Both the airline's own G-YMRU If anything, G-AXMU was the worse of the two and there was little regret at seeing the aircraft returned to BIA at the end of the lease. Particularly spectacular was the frequent need for a 'wet-start', due to the common unserviceability of the Auxiliary Power Unit. When successful, the wet-start resulted in impressive flames shooting out of the engines as they finally started up.

The situation reached the stage that an on-time arrival was a cause for comment and after one such memorable occurrence an anonymous wit released a spoof press release within the company:

PLANE ARRIVES ON TIME! Drama at Cardiff Airport, by our insight team, Wally Jumbojet.

There were shock scenes at Cardiff Airport last night when CYM flight 592 from Malaga landed on runway 30.

Said an official, 'We have no idea how this happened. A group called Airways Cymru is claiming responsibility'.

This is the timetable of events in what is being called the Welshair drama. 09.30 Flight CYM 592 takes off from Malaga. 11.50 Flight CYM 592 lands safely at Cardiff.

As passengers, looking relaxed and smiling after their two hour ordeal, filed quietly through the arrivals lounge, I spoke to former Whiskey salesman Monty Prattwinkle about his nightmare experience. Wearing a blue blazer and old cakeian tie Mr Prattwinkle told me, 'There was no panic. Everyone remained calm. Half way through the flight a young stewardess served a meal. It was all very civilised.'

Last night worried Airways Directors were still asking the question 'How did it happen? And what can be done to prevent similar airline arrivals taking place in the future?'

That meal in full:

1 Bread Roll,
1 Ryvita Biscuit,
1 Portion 'Swiss Mountain' ACS Butter,
1 Airways Cymru 'Ham'n Coleslaw Experience',
1 French-style Mousse,
1 Salt and Pepper,
1 Plastic knife, fork, spoon,
1 Scented Towelette.

A single Boeing 737-200, G-BAZI, was acquired from Britannia Airways in early 1985, but it sadly did not herald the end of the airline's technical delay problems. Within Britannia, G-BAZI had always been regarded as something of a maverick aircraft and it continued its reputation for delays and ongoing technical faults with Airways Cymru. Nonetheless, the company had been successful in gaining several important charter contracts and the One-Eleven and 737 were kept busy, albeit usually at least an hour or two late, throughout the year. Cosmos was one of the major travel companies that entrusted their clients to

Airways Cymru replacing their own Monarch Airlines subsidiary on flights from Bristol and Cardiff.

Despite the problems, the airline had a reputation as a friendly carrier with a close-knit staff. Perversely, their technical reputations engendered the aircraft with a 'personality' and they were soon held in a certain amount of personal affection by all who worked with them.

Mary Kerby joined the company as a flight attendant in early 1985:

The One-Eleven size was a gripe at times for the cabin crew as the small galley area was confined to the front, there was only one toilet on board which proved to be a nuisance if it became blocked and being close to a storage area some passengers often mistook the storage cupboard

passenger seated in the last aisle seat port side being temporarily moved for take-off and landing to a crew seat on the flight-deck so that the crew member could have the rear seat for safety reasons. No-one seemed too bothered about this arrangement though, despite it being embarrassing for the crew having to approach the passenger and apologise for the inconvenience. The only time it proved really troublesome was if the passenger concerned was nervous and needed to remain with their travelling companion, then a real juggling of passengers had to be performed. However, whoever got moved usually got a tour of the flight-deck during the flight, which most people loved.

The aircraft's talent for technical problems was not confined to turnround times on the ground and could sometimes cause

(Left to right), **Mary Wong, Mary Kerby and Claire Thomas on G-YMRU**. Mary Kerby

for the toilet despite the signs. The toilet was also near the rear exit and some passengers even mistook this for the toilet and depressed the exit handle which the flight deck crew were alerted to by warning lights. Fortunately no-one could actually open the door in flight.

The aircraft had 89 seats but the three cabin crew had a problem as only two forward crew seats were fitted. This usually resulted in the

problems for Mary and the other cabin crew in flight too:

On one occasion I was on an inbound flight close to Cardiff when an engine failed, resulting in the oxygen masks being deployed. Most passengers had the sense to don them properly, but some had no idea and one woman put more value on her lost earring (as a result of the mask strap snagging it), than her life! The embarrassing thing was that the crew portable oxygen masks registered as full but two out of the three failed to work! However, on landing safely the whole aircraft cheered. After the event my cabin staff manageress was more concerned about my untidy neck bow which had been loosened as per emergency instruction!

As G-YMRU had passed through several different operators by the time it reached the company, the cabin was starting to look a bit tatty. Several different designs of seat cover were in use at the same time, dotted irregularly around the passenger cabin. With Dan-Air performing all major maintenance on the aircraft at Lasham, the distinctive orange-striped Dan-Air seat cover started to make appearances in odd seat blocks throughout the cabin, standing out among the late 1960s/70s 'flower power' look acquired from their time with Quebecair. A very visible left-over from the Quebecair years was a large multi-toned, carpet-material wall covering on the forward bulkhead. As the very front row of seats had no window, the luckless passengers assigned to them were forced to stare at this throughout the flight.

A single Boeing 737-300, leased from Sunworld International Airways of Las Vegas entered service in early 1986. Airways International Cymru was now flying one One-Eleven, one 737-200 and the 737-300. The diversity of the small fleet led to many problems, not least of which was the inability for one to usually step in to cover the delays of another, even if they were

available. Both operationally and economically this diversity was a nightmare as many positioning flights had to be made between the two main operating centres of Cardiff and Bristol. Even if the aircraft did not need to move from one airport to the other, the crews usually did, having to be transported back home to Cardiff or over to Bristol to begin their duties. A number of chartered light aircraft were often used for crew transport if time was of the essence, otherwise company transport, a well utilized mini-bus, spent its days shuttling backwards and forwards over the Severn Bridge.

The Boeing 737s, especially the Series 300, were a definite improvement over the One-Elevens as far as being able to offer a proper cabin service to the passengers was concerned.

Mary Kerby recalls:

They were much more appreciated than the One-Elevens and had a modern interior, more room in the cabin and the galley, plus there were 2 or 3 toilets and adequate seats forward and aft for the crew! The 737-300s had front and rear galleys and the later aircraft had ovens! No more Ham'n Coleslaw Experience!

The original 737-300 was returned to its owners at the end of the 1986 summer season. However, another 737-300 took its place for 1987. The 737-200 , had spent the winters of 1985 and 1986 away on lease, first to Air New Zealand and then to Aer Lingus the following year. For 1987 a lease was planned to a new US charter operator and the aircraft was despatched to Miami

to start work on the contract. However, the airline failed to start operations and the Airways Cymru Boeing was impounded against the other airline's debts. A long legal wrangle ensued, including a gallant, if probably foolhardy, attempt by the Welsh carrier's crew to 'rescue' the aircraft and fly it away without official permission. As a result of this action, Airways International Cymru was dragged into the mire of US litigation and, in January 1988, the airline's owners wound the company up to try and avoid any further losses.

The long-absent One-Eleven, G-WLAD, had ended its lease with British Midland in 1987, but was immediately transferred to BMA's associate company, Manx Airlines. With Manx, G-WLAD was used for the important Isle of Man–London Heathrow service while the airline was awaiting the delivery of a BAe 146 originally planned to take over from Viscounts on the route. It was returned to Airways Cymru shortly before the company ceased operations and had the airline's titles repainted over the Manx livery in preparation for its re-entering service alongside G-YMRU on that winter season's remaining charters.

Both One-Elevens were repossessed and stored at Lasham, G-YMRU later being leased to Dan-Air for the summer of 1988, with a new registration, G-BPNX. A new airline company, Amberair, was formed at Cardiff to take over the outstanding Airways Cymru charter contracts and flew two 737-200s, including the ex-G-BAZI, now safely returned from the USA and

Manx leased G-WLAD after its BMA contract ended. Aviation Hobby Shop

reregistered G-BOSA. At the end of 1988 though, Amberair was acquired by Bristol-based Paramount Airways, itself destined to cease operations at the end of 1989.

BCal Departure

A few months after Airways International Cymru ceased to exist, another, much longer established, One-Eleven operator was to be lost to the industry. On 14 April 1988, British Caledonian Airways was merged into British Airways, losing its identity in the process.

BCal's main national rival, on both short and long-haul services, British Airways had been privatized in 1987 and was no longer a government-owned corporation. Although, publicly, BCal had welcomed the privatization, it was rather concerned with the large injections of cash into British Airways by the government, in order to improve its financial situation prior to launching share sales on the stockmarket. BCal itself had suffered badly from the adverse commercial effects on its South American routes, following the Falklands' War with Argentina. Political and economic problems in the West African states

man, Sir Adam Thomson, the founder of the original Caledonian Airways in 1961, and British Airways' Sir Colin Marshall and Lord King shortly after the British Airways privatization in 1987.

Finally, on 16 July 1987, it was announced that BCal had been purchased by British Airways for £237 million. The news came as a complete surprise to all but a handful of British Airways and BCal executives. The thought that the bitter enemies could come to an amicable, harmonious, merger was seen as an impossibility.

Initially, Lord King announced that he intended to 'cherish the best of BCal' and

BCal's One-Elevens operated over the European network. Steve Bunting

Financially, BCal had never really recovered from the turbulent years of the cost-cutting 1970s and the worldwide recession that started to make itself felt in the mid-1980s did little to help the situation. Despite this, the company had been expanding its network, with new long-range routes to the Far East as well as a much expanded trans-Atlantic service. Wide-bodied McDonnell-Douglas DC-10s, Boeing 747s and Airbus A310s had replaced the Boeing 707s on the long-haul work and Airbus A320s were on order to start to replace the One-Eleven fleet from 1988. On the European network, more important cities were added and frequencies increased, mostly at the expense of charter services which became less and less important as a source of regular revenue to the airline.

served by the airline severely reduced revenues from the once profitable region.

The growing financial problems within BCal placed the airline's management in an almost impossible situation. It began increasingly to look as if a merger was the only likely alternative to probable bankruptcy. There were few alternatives as far as possible UK airline buyers were concerned. There was simply no company big enough to consider the take-over of BCal, other than British Airways itself. Negotiations with Scandinavian Airlines System and KLM, the Dutch national carrier, were frustrated by limits on the amount of foreign investment allowed in UK companies at that time and soon the alternative options to liquidation came down to one. Private talks began between BCal's chair-

that the company would retain its own identity. Ex-employees of Northeast Airlines and Cambrian Airways must have smiled ruefully at this, having been 'victims' of previous such absorptions into British Airways and been given similar promises. Sure enough, shortly after BCal finally ceased to exist the following April, Gatwick-based ex-BCal aircraft were soon appearing in full British Airways livery. The new Airbus A320 fleet was delivered to Gatwick on schedule, but also in full British Airways colours.

Following the merger, the routes and equipment of BCal were split into their long and short-haul elements. Previously there had been no division, other than by aircraft type and licences held, between the two styles of service in BCal. Cabin crews were checked out on both the long-haul wide-bodied aircraft and the One-Elevens for the European routes. They would usually be assigned to short-haul work for one to two weeks and then to long haul for two to three weeks. After the merger, the ex-BCal cabin crews were asked to permanently choose between long and short-haul assignments. The long-haul aircraft continued their services as before. The short-haul element, consisting of thirteen One-Eleven 500s and the newly arriving A320s, joined forces with British Airways' small fleet of Boeing 737s already based at Gatwick for a handful of European routes. As far as the scheduled services were concerned, BCal no longer existed.

new owners some years later. British Airtours, then flying Lockheed Tristars and Boeing 737s, was drastically reformed and took on the Caledonian Airways name and Scottish-themed image, tartan uniforms and all, keeping the Caledonian golden lion logo flying. Initially operating as a wholly owned British Airways company, the new Caledonian Airways was later sold on to a tour operator and became independent again.

The thirteen ex-BCal Series 500 One-Elevens were gradually moved on from Gatwick, as the Airbus A320s, themselves fated to be transferred over to Heathrow within a few months, were delivered and more Boeing 737s were assigned to British

first of its own 737s in service in 1982. The first of a fleet of Boeing 757s followed a year later; both American aircraft were obtained with a view to replacing the British-built Trident and One-Eleven fleets on European and domestic routes.

Initially, the noisy and fuel-thirsty Tridents were first to be targeted and were gradually withdrawn from service as the Boeing fleets grew in size, the vast majority of them being scrapped. The 737s did make inroads into One-Eleven country though, as they entered service on the Berlin services, finally displacing the last German-based One-Eleven aircraft in 1986. There had already been major changes in the Internal German Service, with flights moving to Tegel from

G-AWYR was among the BCal fleet swiftly repainted in BA colours. Martyn East

The Caledonian name did manage to live on, though hardly in the spirit that the BCal employees might have deduced from Lord King's merger statement. British Airways' Gatwick-based charter subsidiary, British Airtours, was officially merged with Caledonian Airways (Prestwick) Ltd, which had continued to exist as a paper company. BCal's own independently operated charter subsidiary, Cal-Air International had been formed jointly with the Rank Organisation, after the collapse of Laker Airways using two of their high-density, charter-configured, DC-10-10s. Cal-Air was sold off to the Rank Organisation, and was eventually renamed Novair, before being closed down by its

Airways' short-haul network at Gatwick. All the One-Elevens were transferred to the Birmingham and Manchester bases by the end of the 1988 summer season. The arrival of the ex-BCal aircraft helped to replace the last of British Airways Series 400s, which were sold off.

Since its BEA days, British Airways had long cherished a dream of operating Boeing aircraft on their short-haul network. Finally, the airline gained government approval to place an order with Boeing, with fuel efficiency and lower noise claims justifying the import of the American types. Following the wet-lease of a handful of Boeing 737s from Dutch charter operator, Transavia, British Airways placed the

Templehof following an upgrading of facilities at the latter. With the reunification of Germany, British Airways eventually withdrew from the domestic network, passing the German-based services and crews over to Deutsche BA, a new carrier part-owned by BA and local German interests. Old West German service rival, Pan American World Airways, ceased operations due to bankruptcy at the end of 1992.

Drama at 23,000ft

Back in the UK, the continuing heavy daily utilization of BA's One-Elevens was not without incident. On 10 June 1990, a

BA also took delivery of three new 539GLs, including G-BGKG. Steve Bunting

BA's One-Eleven Fleet remained very active through the 1980s. Steve Edmunds

Series 500 was operating a scheduled Birmingham–Malaga flight, with 81 Spanish-bound passengers and a crew of five. The day before, the left front windscreen had been replaced during normal maintenance. Unfortunately, the wrong-sized fastenings had been used and shortly after the aircraft reached 23,000ft over Oxfordshire, the windscreen gave way, causing an explosive decompression. Everything not held down was sucked out through the now gaping window, including the aircraft's Captain, Tim Lancaster. Fortunately for Captain Lancaster, the First Officer and one of the Stewards, managed to grab his legs before he vanished into oblivion. Another Stew-

ard helped the first keep hold of the Captain as the First Officer took control of the One-Eleven. Unable to drag the injured Captain Lancaster completely back into the aircraft against the slip-stream, the two Stewards held on for eighteen minutes as the aircraft made an emergency landing at Southampton, their Stewardess colleague having to calm and prepare the alarmed passengers on her own back in the cabin.

The British Airways One-Elevens, their numbers temporarily boosted by the arrival of the ex-BCal fleet, were increasingly used on the regional international and domestic services. They also appeared on the trunk domestic Shuttle routes into Heathrow, as

back-up aircraft following the retirement of the last Tridents. A major withdrawal of the type started in 1991, with four being disposed of that year, closely followed by six more in 1992. On 30 October 1992, the type had been totally replaced by Boeing 737s at Manchester, with G-AVMO operating the last scheduled BA One-Eleven flight into Manchester from Brussels. Birmingham finally followed suit in July 1993.

In recognition of the type's contribution to the airline over twenty-five years, two of the original ex-BEA One-Elevens were earmarked for preservation, rather than follow their colleagues onto the second-hand market. In March 1993, the pair of aircraft were

G-AVMO is preserved for display at the Cosford Aerospace Museum. M.L. Hill

released from the ignominy of storage at Hurn and flown to new museum homes. G-AVMU arrived at Duxford, for the Duxford Aviation Society Museum, on the 4th, and G-AVMO arrived at Cosford, home of the Aerospace Museum, on the 22nd. Both locations already displayed preserved examples of airliners previously flown by British Airways and its predecessors.

Although the mainline British Airways was no longer to operate the One-Eleven in its own right, the withdrawal of the airline's last aircraft did not see the end of operation of the type in British Airways colours.

Maersk Air Ltd had initially been formed as Birmingham Executive Airways in 1983, operating a fleet of 19-passenger Jetstream turbo-props on scheduled services from Birmingham to Copenhagen, Geneva, Milan, Stockholm, Stuttgart and Zurich. Slightly larger Grumman Gulfstream 1s and a short-lived SAAB 340 operation later supplemented the Jetstreams. Services also operated on behalf of British Airways from Birmingham to Aberdeen, Edinburgh and Glasgow. The company name was also changed to Birmingham European Airways, in an effort to

dispel a local myth that had arisen that the airline was an executive charter operation, not a publicly accessible airline service.

In 1988, the airline became a part of Maersk Air A/S, the Danish scheduled and charter airline, itself owned by the well-known shipping group. A pair of 50-passenger Maersk Air Fokker F.50s were leased for a short while and operated over the Birmingham-based network with Birmingham European titles. In 1990, five ex-British Airways Series 400 One-Elevens were purchased. Previously, British Airways had operated a One-Eleven Series 500 for

Birmingham European's One-Elevens all came from BA. Steve Edmunds

Birmingham European on the routes to Copenhagen and Milan during the winter of 1989/1990. As the Birmingham European Series 400s were delivered, they entered service on scheduled routes from Birmingham to Amsterdam, Belfast, Copenhagen, Cork, Dublin, Geneva, Milan, Paris, Stockholm and Stuttgart. Inclusive tour flights were operated, especially at weekends. The company also operated on behalf of British Airways on flights from Birmingham to Brussels and Frankfurt, and a Frankfurt–Newcastle service. One of the One-Elevens was sold in August 1991, but the capacity short-fall was made up by leasing in British Airways Series 500s for some services, as before.

On 25 October 1993, Birmingham European was merged with Brymon Airways, headquartered in Plymouth. As a result, the One-Elevens took on a new Brymon European Airways livery, otherwise continuing their scheduled operations from Birmingham as before. One aircraft was despatched to the Brymon base at Bristol, from Monday to Friday, where it was used for two return flights a day to Paris, in place of turbo-prop DHC-8-200s. Back at Birmingham, a newly delivered ex-British Airways Series 500 took up the Brymon European livery and joined the Series 400s on their European network.

Back to BA – Kind Of!

Barely nine months after the merger, Brymon European was split again into its two previous components. The merger had not been a success, either operationally or financially. There was little if any integration of the two operations, the use of the One-Eleven on the Bristol–Paris route and the use of the DHC-8s on some of the less busy flights from Birmingham being the only visible sign of co-operation. Brymon was sold to British Airways and was to go on to operate as a wholly owned subsidiary under the British Airways Express banner. The Birmingham base became Maersk Air

G-AWYS wore the short-lived Brymon European titles in 1993. MAP

G-AWBL took up BA colours yet again, after a five-year break. MAP

Ltd, independent of British Airways, but contracted to operate as a franchised British Airways carrier. Under this agreement, Maersk Air operated its scheduled services in full British Airways livery, its staff wore BA uniform and with the in-flight service was redesigned to BA standard. The flights were now operated under BA flight numbers and sold as such on BA's reservations system. Charter flights continued to operate in Maersk Air's own name though, using the company's original 'VB' flight prefix.

The Maersk Air One-Eleven fleet shared a wealth of the type's operational history between them. Two of the Series 400s were ex-Autair and Cambrian Airways aircraft and had originally worn BA colours nearly twenty years earlier, following the original creation of British Airways

The four Maersk Air Series 400 One-Elevens were displaced by the arrival of the later Series 500s and the addition of Boeing 737-500s that finally ousted them by 1996. The Series 500s continued to operate on the Maersk Air/British Airways schedules from Birmingham, especially to Amsterdam, Belfast and Paris. However, the arrival of new 50-passenger Canadair Regional Jets in 1998 soon saw the type relegated to back-up duties, followed by their total withdrawal from service.

Shortly before the UK-based One-Elevens started undergoing their great upheavals and changes, across the Irish Sea, Aer Lingus's quartet of Series 200s finally and quietly ended their operational lives with the airline. For over 25 years, the four aircraft had performed efficiently on the European scheduled and charter

leased out to LANICA in 1967. EI-ANE, 'St Mel' was next to be withdrawn on 4 January 1991, following its operation of flight EI525, a Paris–Manchester–Dublin service. 'St Mel' had been the first of Aer Lingus's One-Elevens and had operated their first scheduled service with the type over the Dublin–Cork–Paris route on 6 June 1965. Within weeks, the remaining two aircraft, EI-ANG, 'St Declan' and EI-ANH, 'St Ronan' followed. 'St Ronan' on 22 February 1991, with a Dusseldorf–Dublin service and 'St Declan' on 3 March after a Liverpool–Dublin flight. All four were flown to Shannon Airport for storage and to await their eventual fates.

By the retirement of their One-Eleven fleet, Aer Lingus no longer had the scheduled Irish airline scene to themselves. In July 1985, a single, 18-seat, turbo-prop

Small Maersk Air titles were the only sign of the true operator. MAP

in 1974. One of these was the much bought, sold, leased out and generally well-travelled G-AVGP, the first Channel Airways aircraft. Another, by then re-registered G-BBMG, the second Channel Airways aircraft, originally G-AWEJ. The fourth was the ex-American Airlines aircraft once painted up for the once hopeful, but never operational, Orientair, of Berlin.

Under the new style of service, a second Series 500 was acquired in May 1994, joined in 1996 by a third. All three Series 500s were originally supplied to British United and had come to Maersk via British Caledonian and British Airways. The last two delivered had also spent time leased out to other operators after their BA service.

services of Aer Lingus. Originally expected to be quickly replaced by the Boeing 737, the One-Elevens ended up finding their own niche on the thinner scheduled jet routes to the UK and Europe, as well as being chartered for substantial programmes of inclusive tour flights.

Inevitably, even larger, new generation Boeing 737s were about to roll off the Seattle production lines and were on order by Aer Lingus to replace not only the One-Elevens, but also the early series 737s that had been meant to replace them decades earlier. The first Aer Lingus One-Eleven to be withdrawn was, EI-ANF, 'St Malachy', after operating flight EI993 from Frankfurt to Dublin on 30 November 1990. 'St Malachy' had been the aircraft

Bandierante airliner had formed the initial fleet of Ryanair Ltd. Operated over a service from Waterford, in the east of Ireland, to London, the Bandierante was soon proved to be too small and was joined by a pair of BAe 748s. Heartened by their initial success, the Ryan family, owners of the airline, looked to areas where they could expand their operation and were soon being moved by new ambitions to challenge Aer Lingus as a major scheduled service operator.

New low-fare scheduled services were quickly opened from regional Irish points, Waterford and Knock, as well as the capital, Dublin, to Luton Airport, just north of London. As more licence applications were filed, Ryanair looked around for more capacity and found it in the One-Eleven.

EI-ANG was the last of Aer Lingus's long-serving fleet. Steve Edmunds

Ryanair's first One-Eleven was a Romanian-built 561RC. Martyn East

In fact it was a ROMBAC One-Eleven Series 500, leased from TAROM that entered service on the Dublin–Luton route on 1 December 1986. Two more One-Elevens arrived from the same source in March and April 1987 and the fleet was doubled to six with the arrival of three more leased aircraft from Romania in 1988.

There then followed several years of comings and goings as extra aircraft were leased in, usually from Romania, to cover busy periods. The One-Elevens were also increasingly used for inclusive tour charters as well as the expanding scheduled network. From Dublin, the One-Elevens were used on routes to Glasgow, Liverpool, Luton, Munich, Paris, Prestwick and Stansted. Most of the less profitable region-al services were gradually run down as the flights from Dublin took precedence.

In 1986, Ryanair acquired control of Luton-based London European Airways. London European had started operations in 1985, flying a single leased Vickers Viscount on a Luton–Amsterdam route. Within weeks, another Luton-based carrier, Euroflite, was acquired, adding the Luton–Brussels route, and a Shorts 330, to the company's services. Financially though, the exercise was not a success and London European ceased flying completely later that year. Extensively reorganized by Ryanair, London European restarted scheduled operations over both the Luton–Amsterdam and Luton–Brussels routes in May 1987. To operate the flights, a ROMBAC One-Eleven was transferred from Ryanair and flown in London European's full colours.

The following year, London European started trading as Ryanair Europe and turned its attention to operating inclusive tour and *ad hoc* charters from Luton, dropping its own scheduled flights altogether. Not surprisingly though, the aircraft were also extensively used on Ryanair's own schedules from Luton, especially to Knock and Cork. 1989 saw the arrival of the single ex-Mediterranean Express Series 475 that spent much of its time leased out. First of all it was leased for three months to Swedish airline, Baltic Airways for operation on a short-lived scheduled service from Malmo to Southend. On its return, the aircraft was leased out again, this time to Loganair, replacing an earlier Series 500 also leased from Ryanair Europe, for use on their Manchester–Edinburgh scheduled route.

In 1990, the Luton-based fleet consisted of three leased Series 500s and the Luton aircraft reverted to operating under the London European name on charter flights from various points around the UK. 1990's attempt at newly independent charter operations were not a financial success though and the company went into receivership in May 1991, the aircraft reverting to Ryanair in Dublin.

Four ex-British Airways Series 500s were leased by Ryanair in May 1993, the last of the Romanian aircraft being returned to Eastern Europe that October. In November, the One-Elevens opened a twice daily Dublin–Birmingham scheduled service, the last route to be inaugurated for Ryanair by the type. Second-hand Boeing 737s started to be delivered in the spring of 1994, leading to the eventual return of the remaining One-Eleven aircraft to their owners.

Lauda Lease

Another small carrier to benefit from the availability of TAROM's mixed British and Romanian-built fleet of One-Elevens was Austria's Lauda Air. Formed in early 1979 by Austrian racing driver Niki Lauda, the company initially operated a small fleet of Fokker F.27 turbo-props from Vienna. The arrival of the leased One-Eleven Series 500s saw the airline begin a phenomenal period of growth. From the beginning of commercial operations, Lauda had stated his intention to challenge the state-supported Austrian Air-

London European's 561RC operated from Luton. via Author

lines that until his arrival on the scene, had enjoyed a virtual monopoly of the scheduled Austrian airline market.

Delivered to Vienna in early 1985, following refurbishment and modification work by BAe at Hurn, the pair of One-Elevens were used on inclusive tour and *ad hoc* charter work. One aircraft was returned to Romania at the end of its lease in November and a single Boeing 737-200 joined the remaining One-Eleven in December. The single One-Eleven continued to operate until it was replaced by another Boeing 737, a larger Series 300, in July 1986. Lauda Air went on to continue to expand, opening its first scheduled services shortly afterwards.

The first ex-Lauda operated One-Eleven went on to be leased out again following its return to TAROM, joining two others on

lease to Turkish independent, Istanbul Hava Yollari, already operating a small fleet of Caravelles. For 1986, Istanbul's fleet operated inclusive tour charters to Turkish resorts from many countries in Western Europe, as well as local and regional charter work and scheduled domestic flights. Interestingly, the leased One-Elevens were eventually replaced, by 1988, by more Caravelles, the One-Eleven's early arch rival.

Other TAROM One-Elevens also found themselves leased out on contracts of varying success. One Romanian-built, ex-TAROM, One-Eleven was delivered to Dimex, the government transport organization, in 1990. In February 1991 the organization was renamed Romavia, short for Romanian Aviation Company. In April, it began operating commercially under newly issued licences in direct

London European became Ryanair Europe in 1988. Steve Edmunds

competition with TAROM. Two more ROMBAC One-Elevens were delivered in 1992 and the trio operated charters and scheduled services alongside a single Boeing 707, a pair of Ilyushin IL-18 turboprops and an assortment of Soviet and Western-built helicopters. Jaro International, a fellow Romanian charter company, established in 1990, eventually replaced their leased TAROM One-Elevens with a pair bought from British Airways in late 1993. Jaro also sub-leased one of their aircraft to another Turkish charter operator, Air Alfa in 1994.

Adria Airways of the former Yugoslavia, operated Romanian aircraft on summer leases in 1985, 1986 and 1987. Adria's inclusive tour charter network to Yugoslav resorts, as well as carrying Yugoslavs abroad to their own holidays, encompassed most of Europe and North Africa. In addition to the leased One-Elevens, Adria already operated its own fleet of DC-9s and MD-80s of various marks, and newly delivered A320 Airbuses. The violent political changes in the former Yugoslavia saw the tourist market in the newly independent republics collapse, with the result that Adria cut back considerably its operations and returned all the leased aircraft. Eventually, as peace was restored throughout most of the region, Adria emerged as the new national carrier of Slovenia.

The unique all-cargo Series 475 was also to become part of the leasing exodus from Romania. Anglo Cargo Airlines had begun operations in 1983, initially utilizing a Boeing 707 on worldwide freight charter flights from Gatwick. On 17 March 1986, the freighter One-Eleven was delivered on lease to Anglo Cargo at Manston Airport in Kent. From Manston, the One-Eleven operated a wide variety of cargo charter services, mostly confined to European operations, while the 707, now joined by a second example, continued worldwide flights from Gatwick. The One-Eleven was especially popular for livestock charters and, at other times, was kept busy with *ad hoc* general freight work.

Lauda Air's One-Elevens were leased from TAROM but were UK-built. via Author

Adria's leased One-Elevens operated ITs. Ian MacFarlane via Jennie Gradidge

The unique 487GK/F flew from Manston with Anglo Cargo Airlines. via Author

As delivered to the UK, the One-Eleven at first carried the basic TAROM livery, still with its Romanian registration, YR-BCR, with Anglo Cargo titles. After eighteen months, the aircraft was re-registered in the UK as G-TOMO and painted in the company's full white, red and blue colours.

A single, leased Boeing 757 freighter, the first of its type designed for cargo operations, entered service with Anglo Cargo in August 1991, the One-Eleven continuing its busy charter programme around Europe. More 757s were planned and the possibility of moving into passenger charter operations, using Boeing 737-400s was being investigated. Unfortunately, the move into the new generation of jets was short-lived for Anglo Cargo, as all operations ceased on 13 January 1992. G-TOMO was finally returned to TAROM in July, after lying idle for over six months. The sole 757 ended up with once One-Eleven operator, Challenge Air, at Miami.

In the early 1990s, the fashion for deregulation of the airline industry was spreading away from the American and European markets that had spawned it. In India and Pakistan, two more carriers were formed to take advantage of the new spirit for freer enterprise that was challenging the longer-established airlines that had been used to having the field to themselves up until then. In both cases, the ever available Romanian pool of One-Elevens played its part.

In India, Citylink Airways was one of several new airlines that sprang up to compete against the entrenched Indian Airlines Corporation. Two ROMBAC-built Series

500s were leased from Romavia and delivered to Delhi in late 1992. The aircraft were placed into service on routes to Bombay and Calcutta, in a two-class configuration. Unfortunately Citylink was simply unable to compete against the might of Indian Airlines, as well as the flood of rival newly formed independent airlines, and ceased trading in October 1993.

Across the border, in Pakistan, Aero Asia inaugurated scheduled services over routes from Karachi to Islamabad and Lahore in May 1993. Competing directly against Pakistan International Airways, Aero Asia had been founded by the Tabani family. Initially, two ROMBAC One-Elevens were used, joined by others as the network was expanded to include Faisalabad, Multan, Pasni and Peshawar. Unlike Citylink in India, Aero Asia managed to thrive and, by 1998, was operating 26 flights a day to seven points within Pakistan. The cities of Bishek and Sukkur were also served, and the growing One-Eleven fleet was joined by a single Boeing 707.

Philippine Leaseback

As Aero Asia was laying plans to introduce its first One-Eleven, one long-term eastern hemisphere operator of the type was withdrawing its last aircraft. Since Philippine Airlines took delivery of their first Series 400 in April 1966, the One-Eleven had been a part of the daily life of the airline. The initial Series 400s had finally been replaced by the larger Series

500 in 1972. Twelve of the Series 500s were to be operated; they started to be replaced by Boeing 737-300s from 1989. The whole PAL One-Eleven fleet was actually sold to Guinness Peat for $26 million, and then leased back until they were retired as the 737s were delivered. The One-Elevens' replacement was slow, however and it was not until 31 May 1992, that Series 500 RP-C1185 flew the last Philippine Airlines One-Eleven service, flight PR278, from Legaspi to Manila, ending twenty-six years of uninterrupted One-Eleven service to the airline.

Barely had the first Boeing 737 been delivered, than a Philippine One-Eleven incident attested the ruggedness of the aircraft. On 21 July 1989, on landing at Manila in the rain, a PAL Series 500 overshot the runway, crossing a super-highway, striking four vehicles en route, and came to rest on a railway track. Although, tragically, eight innocent people were killed in the highway collisions, none of the aircraft's occupants were seriously injured.

One of the Philippine Series 500 fleet had actually been unfortunate enough to suffer no less than two in-flight bomb explosions. RP-C1184, acquired second-hand in 1974 from Germanair, was first subjected to this abuse in 1975, when one passenger was killed and several others injured. After six months of repairs at Hurn, the aircraft was delivered back to Manila. However, two and a half years later the same aircraft suffered another bomb explosion, coincidentally in the same rear toilet area and also in-flight, blowing a hole in the roof. Fortunately, once again the fuselage withstood the extensive structural damage and a safe landing was made. Following initial repairs on site, the aircraft was ferried to Hurn for extensive work and eventually returned to daily use with Philippine Airlines, finally being retired in January 1992.

Following the end of the 1982 inclusive tour contracts it had taken over from Air Manchester, British Air Ferries had returned the Series 400 to BAe. Reverting to an all turbo-prop operation, with Viscounts and Dart Heralds, BAF continued its Southend-based contract, *ad hoc* and inclusive tour flights. As cheaper, and more convenient, sea ferry services had taken most of their original cross-Channel

a Jersey-based associate, Jersey Air Ferries being formed to take particular advantage of the island markets. East Midlands-based Inter City Airways, and their subsidiary, Guernsey Airlines were bought by BAF's owners, the Jadepoint Group, the latter initially becoming a separate operational division of the airline, re-equipping with BAF-owned Viscounts. After operating an early production aircraft on short-term lease, an order was placed for ten BAe 146s, to take over from the Heralds and Viscounts. However, events overtook these ambitious plans and none of the original 146 order were to be delivered.

Unfortunately, despite early indications of success, the rapid expansion of the

cial position of the parent company, not the airline itself, but also served to give BAF a valuable breathing space.

The Virgin contract, short-term leases and a healthy succession of *ad hoc* charters helped keep the airline afloat and, by May 1989, the company was healthy enough to be sold on to new owners, Mostjet, as a viable operation. Another British Viscount charter airline, Baltic Airlines that also operated as Hot Air, was merged into BAF during the administration period. The reorganized and revitalized British Air Ferries started looking at options for expansion again.

In the spring of 1990, BAF took delivery of three ex-Braniff Series 200s, on lease

BAF's 201AC, G-BDAF had originally been BUA's G-ASJG. Steve Edmunds

traffic, BAF's car ferry network had been progressively run down. Over the years, the scheduled routes were transformed into more conventional passenger-based flights, replacing the venerable Bristol Freighters and ATEL Carvairs with the second-hand Dart Heralds and ex-British Airways Viscounts. To further increase utilization of their new aircraft, BAF also developed a thriving short and long-term leasing operation.

A major expansion of the scheduled services was attempted in the mid-1980s, with a number of BCal's short-haul flights from Gatwick, those previously operated by Air UK to Guernsey and Rotterdam, being flown in co-operation as 'BCal Commuter' services. A much enlarged programme of schedules and contract charter flights to the Channel Islands was undertaken, with

scheduled network was followed by a period of major maintenance problems with the Viscount fleet. Marketing problems with new routes, in particular Dutch carrier KLM's refusal to promote the Rotterdam service on its computerized reservations system, saw more potential revenue slipping from BAF's fingers. The airline's own scheduled network was closed down altogether at the end of 1987, although contract scheduled flights continued on Gatwick–Maastricht, Luton–Maastricht and Luton–Dublin routes operated on behalf of Virgin Atlantic Airways.

On 8 January 1988, the company was placed into Administration, under the 1986 Insolvency Act, the equivalent of the Chapter 11 bankruptcy protection facility in the United States. This situation had actually been brought about by the precarious finan-

from Guinness Peat Aviation. One of the aircraft was to be used only as a source of spares and did not enter commercial service with British Air Ferries. All three aircraft had originally been among the first delivered to British United in 1965; the first, once G-ASJG, now re-registered G-DBAF, entered service with BAF with a Stansted–Mahon charter on 3 August 1990. The second, originally BUA's G-ASJH, now registered G-OCNW, operated its first BAF revenue flight, a Luton–Malta IT charter on 24 November. After its delivery flight from Kansas City on 18 April 1990, the spares aircraft retained its Irish registration, EI-BWI, and had originally been British United's G-ASJC. The two operational aircraft were both kept busy in inclusive tour flights, configured for 78 passengers and in early 1991 the ex-Ryanair

EI-BWI was ferried from Kansas to Southend for spares use. MAP

Europe Series 475 joined the fleet. Although first painted in BAF colours in April, G-AZUK did not enter service until 30 June, with a Vienna–Ankara charter.

British Air Ferries turbo-prop fleet was gradually run down in size after the delivery of the One-Elevens. The Dart Heralds were the first to go, followed by Viscounts that were retired as the aircraft became due for expensive major maintenance checks. The withdrawn aircraft tended to languish at Southend, their hulks providing a valuable source of spares for the survivors. The Viscounts that remained in service were increasingly used for a Parcel Force contract operated for the Post Office, with several sectors being operated carrying first-class mail and urgent parcels every night. Viscount passenger charter flights were still operated, particularly on

lucrative oil industry-related contracts carrying rig workers from Aberdeen to Sumburgh in the Shetland Islands.

The company renewed its acquaintance with the BAe 146 in 1991, when a convertible passenger/freight aircraft joined the One-Elevens for charter work. With its convertible capabilities, the 146 tended to be utilized for more *ad hoc* work, while the One-Elevens continued on their regular IT contracts from many different airports around the UK. The jet operations were now being based at Stansted in preference to the original BAF facility at Southend. After suffering for many years from a reputation for bad access and poor facilities, Stansted had recently opened a new ultra-modern terminal complex, including a direct high-speed rail link to central London. Both commercially and

operationally it made more sense for BAF to make the move from Southend Airport. The airline's administration and the maintenance division, now operating as separate subsidiary, World Aviation Support, remained at Southend.

The inclusive tour work was increasing to the point that British Air Ferries leased in extra capacity in 1992, initially in the form of Jugoslovenski Aerotransport Boeing 727-200s. Political unrest in the former Yugoslavia led to the aircraft being returned to Belgrade within a couple of months, as BAF was unwittingly breaking UN sanctions against Serbia. Their replacements took the form of two Adria Airways MD-82s, registered in yet another former Yugoslav state, Slovenia.

A more permanent solution to BAF's capacity problem was found later that year. On 8 November 1992, the almost unthinkable finally happened when Dan-Air Services, one of the longest-operating and most fiercely independent British airlines, was bought out by British Airways. This released no less than eleven One-Eleven Series 500s onto the market, the leases for which were snapped up by British Air Ferries.

Although the early 1990s' loss of the British Airways and Dan-Air fleets certainly heralded the end of one era for the One-Eleven, another was about to begin. Once again, the basic operational soundness and continuing commercial usefulness of the aircraft saw its reputation rise above mere corporate history.

G-OCNW entered BAF service with a Luton–Malta charter. via Author

CHAPTER NINE

Sunset, Sunrise!

Throughout the 1970s and 80s, Dan-Air had continued to increase the size of their One-Eleven fleet. The last of the declining complement of Comets were finally withdrawn from use in November 1980, as more Boeing 727s and One-Elevens arrived, later augmented by Boeing 737s and a short-lived, wide-body, Airbus A300 operation. The One-Eleven fleet's main source of revenue over the years, inclusive tour charters, gradually took second place to an expanded scheduled service operation. The switch from charters was gradually forced on Dan-Air as the tour operators developed a preference for using airlines in which they also held a financial interest. Dan-Air had no travel company shareholders and was soon up against new rivals in the charter market such as Air Europe, Airtours International and Orion Airways, all owned by former Dan-Air travel company customers.

Short and long-term leases had seen Dan-Air's fleet of all aircraft types increase and shrink with the seasonal demands over the years. The Arkia, LACSA and Hapag Lloyd fleets all provided new permanent One-Eleven fleet members, with ROMBAC One-Elevens also being leased in from TAROM for the busy summer months. TAROM also

Dan-Air's first One-Eleven, G-AXCK, stayed with the airline until 1983. MAP

525FT, G-TARO was leased by Dan-Air for 1984–85 operations. Steve Edmunds

A revised red/black livery survived only for a few months. MAP

came to similar seasonal leasing arrangements with Adria Airways and Jugoslovenski Aerotransport, both of Yugoslavia, the UK's British Island Airways and Ireland's Ryanair. However, industry unease in Western Europe over the use of Romanian pilots, and the validity of their licences, used to crew the aircraft during the UK leases, led to most of these contracts either being discontinued, or at least not renewed.

The addition to the fleet of an ex-Arkia aircraft, in 1979, had a distinctly profound effect on the rest of Dan-Air. As usual, the One-Eleven was placed into service in a hurry, with no time for it to be repainted in Dan-Air's full livery. In the end, Dan-Air titles and the famous 'Compass Rose' tail logo were applied, but the aircraft remained in Arkia's red white and blue colours. Dan-Air had only recently modified their own

livery, with the traditional black and red colours redesigned into a more modern style. However, the Arkia arrangement had found favour with Dan-Air's Chairman and founder, Fred Newman, and instructions were issued to change the company colours again. The Arkia red and blue bands were reversed, slightly repositioned, a brighter blue used, and a brand new Dan-Air image was born.

There was even the odd occasion where Dan-Air was in a position to lease out its own excess capacity. Series 500, G-AXYD was leased to British Caledonian for two separate periods, in 1984 and 1987. Although the aircraft had been delivered new to the original Caledonian, in 1970, before being sold by BCal to Dan-Air in 1976, its return to its original home was not welcomed by all the BCal crews, especially

the cabin staff. The Dan-Air galley layout was totally different from BCal's, with once familiar, easily found items and equipment in totally different places. It soon acquired the unbeloved nickname of 'Yankee Doodle', instead of the proper suffix, 'Yankee Delta'. Lyn Moreton was a BCal cabin attendant at the time of the second lease:

The lease of the Dan-Air aircraft totally horrified the BCal cabin crew as the amenities were so basic in comparison to our own aircraft. The galley was not compatible with the BCal equipment. You could not place coffee pots under the taps and they had to be filled from jugs, which was so slow. Also, a collapsible trolley was installed. This had to be assembled in the galley and then loaded with glasses, minerals, spirits, wines, beers, etc. On short flights this was rarely achieved before the aircraft had started its descent!

509EX was leased to BCal in the new Dan-Air colours. MAP

G-BJYM, a 531FS, came to Dan-Air from LACSA. MAP

With the aircraft assigned to many of the shorter domestic flights on BCal's scheduled network, particularly from Gatwick to Manchester or Jersey, its appearance was soon dreaded by many of the legendary 'Caledonian Girls'. Crewing and operations staff soon learnt to be cagey about giving away too much information as to aircraft allocation in response to a Cabin Attendant's 'casual' enquiry.

According to Lyn, a flight assignment to 'YD could be:

A real nightmare, many cabin crew members would rather call in sick if they managed to find out in advance that they had been assigned to a 'Yankee Doodle' flight.

Obviously, being used to it, Dan-Air's own crews coped admirably with the galley layout and the One-Elevens were flown throughout the 1980s on both charter and scheduled services. With larger Boeing 727s and 737s steadily taking over more of the dwindling inclusive tour charter contracts, the spare One-Eleven capacity was used to expand the scheduled routes. New schedules from Gatwick to Aberdeen, Belfast, Cork and Dublin, and regional European schedules such as Manchester–Zurich and Berlin–Amsterdam were opened. The Aberdeen base had grown out of the company's involvement in the mid-1970's 'Oil Boom' when newly discovered North Sea oil was first being brought ashore in Scotland. A large fleet of BAe 748s had originally been based at Aberdeen to serve a number of very profitable contracts, carrying oil company

personnel and cargo. The scheduled services to Gatwick, and later Manchester, were opened by the One-Elevens to take advantage of the increasing traffic through the city's airport at Dyce. Even when the initial oil-related work began to die down the scheduled One-Eleven flights remained.

Surviving flight programmes show the variety of services the type operated on for Dan-Air. For instance, for the week of 14–20 August 1981, representative aircraft of each of the four main types of One-Eleven flown by the company operated the following itineraries:

Series 200
Friday:
Gatwick–Dublin–Gatwick–Cork–Aberdeen–Gatwick.
Saturday:
Gatwick–Jersey–Gatwick–Newcastle–Bergen–Newcastle–Gatwick–Newcastle–Aberdeen.
Sunday: Aberdeen–Newcastle–Gatwick–Montpelier–Gatwick–Jersey–Cardiff–Jersey–Cardiff–Gatwick.
Monday:
Gatwick–Dublin–Gatwick–Cork–Gatwick–Beauvais–Gatwick.
Tuesday:
Gatwick–Dublin–Gatwick–Toulouse–Montpelier–Toulouse–Gatwick.
Wednesday:
Gatwick–Dublin–Gatwick–Cork–Gatwick.
Thursday:
Gatwick–Dublin–Gatwick–Toulouse–Montpelier–Toulouse–Gatwick.

Series 300
Friday:
Gatwick–Mahon–Gatwick–Malta–Gatwick.
Saturday:
Gatwick–Malta–Gatwick–Vienna–Gatwick–Athens.
Sunday:
Athens–Gatwick–Faro–Gatwick–Rome–Gatwick.
Monday:
Gatwick–Manchester (for maintenance, for the rest of the week).

Series 400
Friday:
Gatwick–Bergen–Gatwick–Beauvais–Gatwick–Dusseldorf–Gatwick.
Saturday:
Gatwick–Genoa–Gatwick–Jersey–Cork–Jersey–Gatwick–Alicante.
Sunday:
Alicante–Gatwick–Ibiza–Palma–Gatwick–Toulouse–Gatwick.
Monday:
Gatwick–Aberdeen–Gatwick–Nice–Gatwick.
Tuesday: Gatwick–Gibraltar–Gatwick.
Wednesday:
Gatwick–Bergen–Gatwick–Ibiza–Gatwick.
Thursday:
Gatwick–Milan–Gatwick–Aberdeen–Gatwick.

Series 500
Friday:
Venice–Gatwick–Naples–Gatwick–Hanover–Gatwick.

Saturday:
    Gatwick–Palma–Gatwick–Malaga–
    Gatwick–Ibiza.
Sunday:
    Ibiza–Gatwick–Tangier–Gatwick–
    Valencia–Gatwick.
Monday:
    Gatwick–Corfu–Gatwick–Ibiza.
Tuesday:
    Ibiza–Gatwick–Barcelona–Gatwick–
    Milan–Gatwick.
Wednesday:
    Gatwick–Madrid–Gatwick–Rimini–
    Gatwick.
Thursday:
    Gatwick–Dijon–Gatwick.

The Berlin-Tegel based One-Eleven, for most of that week Series 400, G-AZED, operated IT charters to Faro, Gatwick, Gerona, Heraklion, Lisbon, Mahon, Naples, Palma, Salzburg and Shannon, as well as twice daily scheduled services on the Tegel–Amsterdam route. Tegel was also responsible for the operation of a pair of Boeing 727-100s that had been especially converted, with extra fuel tankage and accommodation for less passengers, to allow longer-ranging charter work than the UK-based aircraft. The extra fuel capacity also came in useful as the low-level flying through the Berlin 'Air Corridors' over East Germany, restricted to 10,000ft, or even lower, resulted in a greatly increased fuel consumption for jet engines designed for use at much higher altitudes. Another important market for the Tegel-based fleet was transport of foreign workers, particularly from Turkey, into Berlin and other West German cities, in addition to the more usual holiday resort work.

Regional Movement

Aircraft continued to be based on rotation at Manchester, Newcastle and Berlin, as well as the majority of the One-Eleven fleet shuffling back and forth from Gatwick. The original One-Eleven base at Luton had been closed in 1974, although a ground services unit continued to handle visiting aircraft of Dan-Air and other airlines for a number of years. Operational bases had also been located at Birmingham, Bristol, Edinburgh, Glasgow and other UK cities for varying periods through the 1970s and 80s, but most were closed down after their contracts were awarded to the new charter carriers by their travel company owners.

Manchester was now a major maintenance base for Dan-Air, with most of the work on the One-Eleven and BAe 748 fleets, in particular, being transferred to the new facility from Lasham. With the expansion of the maintenance work at Manchester from 1976, Dan-Air had become the second biggest employer at the airport after the Airport Authority itself. Operationally, at least two Series 500s were usually based there at any one time, as well as two 727s, with 737s arriving in later years.

A major success for Dan-Air in the early 1980s followed the take-over of the Inverness–London route after it was dropped by British Airways. Operating into Heathrow from March 1983, Dan-Air's first scheduled service to London's premier airport, the route was one of the longest domestic flights in the UK. The airline made a point of recruiting locals to provide cabin crew on the Inverness-based service, under the energetic leadership of Base Stewardess Maureen Perera, transferred from the

closed Glasgow base. The enthusiasm of her team towards 'their' route was almost entirely responsible for turning what had been an uneconomic thorn in British Airway's side into a profitable operation, very popular with its regular passengers. A feature was made of promoting local Highland delicacies in the in-flight service, including a Grouse breakfast when the game-bird was in season. A warming 'tot' of the local whisky was also popular on the early morning departures during the cold, dark Highland winters. The original short-bodied One-Elevens allocated to the route soon gave way to Series 500s as load factors rose. As well as increasing frequencies on the London route, an Inverness–Manchester service was opened in April 1985.

Also in April 1985, a scheduled Manchester–Heathrow One-Eleven route was opened, in direct competition with British Airways 'Super Shuttle'. Unfortunately, this new route turned out not to be financially viable and operations on it ceased in September. However, a Manchester–Gatwick service opened in 1988 and was much more successful.

One-Elevens featured in most of the scheduled route expansion by Dan-Air throughout the 1980s. In fact, once again, as had happened so often with other operators, the One-Elevens soon became victims of their own success, being replaced by larger Boeing 737s as soon as booked loads justified it.

Despite the increasing emphasis on the scheduled network, Dan-Air still managed to find some time for the charter work that had been the company's bread and butter for so many years. April 1985 saw Series 500, G-AWWX, carrying the BBC Symphony

The pair of 207AJs continued in use, mainly on schedules. Martyn East

G-ATPJ at Manchester, a major Dan-Air base for many years. Steve Bunting

G-BDAT was in service with Dan-Air from 1975 until 1992. Steve Bunting

Orchestra on a tour of Spain, visiting Alicante, Madrid, Valencia and Barcelona. Captain Bryn Wayt, First Officer Bernie Stillgoe and the cabin crew of Carole McCarthy, Hazel Lloyd, Jean Whales and Wendy Everest accompanied the orchestra throughout the tour and attended every concert, a welcome change from the increasingly predictable scheduled services.

Other changes to the 'routine' included the holding of the Highest Ever Haggis Auction, on 5 February 1988. In support of that year's Comic Relief Day, a charity auction was held among the passengers on board a scheduled service, DA085, from Aberdeen to Gatwick. Captain Wayt provided the haggis, alleged as having been 'shot earlier the same morning on the Scottish Haggis Moors'. The sale of the haggis, at 33,000ft over Carlisle, raised £120 and over £360 in total was raised for the charity on the one flight. Elsewhere, similar

fund-raising antics all over the airline's system, both on flights and at airports, saw Dan-Air's staff and passengers contribution to Comic Relief passing £3,000. A year later, on 27 Mary 1989, Captain Wayt was in command on another One-Eleven charity event. Listeners of Moray Firth Radio bought tickets for a Charity Auction Pleasure Flight and were treated to a 40-minute flight from Inverness, taking in the sights of the Scottish Highlands.

One Captain's Eye View

Captain Wayt had been transferred from the dwindling Comet fleet in 1979 and was eventually to fly 6,660 hours on the One-Elevens. In answer to the inevitable question, Captain Wayt responded:

Which was best? The Comet. Because it had more power and it was a smoother ride for the passengers. Losing an engine on a Comet was not a problem it was on the One-Eleven. The Comet was nicer to handle than the One-Eleven and with 80 degrees of flap when landing, the cushion of air that was trapped between you and the ground ensured the smoothest of landings. I do not want to blow any self propelled trumpets, but I could land a Comet 4C smoother than any other machine I have flown. That is not to say I could not land a One-Eleven smoothly, but it was a far more difficult task that escaped me on quite a few occasions.

My time on the Comet was enjoyed and enhanced by the presence of a Flight Engineer. These fellows had an impressive grasp of the complicated technical side of the aircraft, especially the electrics. They were a very valuable resource, but sadly the accountants put an end to them. As an example, the One-Eleven would fly the same amount of passengers, 119, from Gatwick to Athens in roughly the same time, but burning half the fuel and saving the annual salary of a Flight Engineer!

As the Comets made money for Dan-Air, so did the One-Elevens. They could do everything the Comet could do, but cheaper. Changing from one to the other was going from the comfortable 'Rolls-Royce' feel of the Comet to the 'Ford' ambience of the One-Eleven series. Don't get me wrong, I loved the One-Eleven during all the 6,660 hours I flew them. I loved their sturdy build which gave me enormous confidence during all phases of flight. I also appreciated their built-in airstairs and the APU, things the Comet never had. Air conditioning on a Comet, stuck on the ground due to an ATC delay sometimes meant reverting to opening the over-wing exits and all the available doors!

Some other memories prompted by Captain Wayt's logbook include:

5th–10th March 1981. A British Leyland charter to Vienna. Five days in the Vienna Hilton no less! Not the sort of hotel Dan-Air put its crews in normally. The aircraft, G-AXCK (Series 400), stayed over with us.

22nd March 1981. Amsterdam–Berlin Tegel, G-AZED (Series 400), with hyenas and tropical birds for Berlin Zoo.

Captain Wayt and crew, with decorated G-AWWX, during the tour. Bryn Wayt

4th August 1981. Whilst off-duty, I just happened to be passing through the Gatwick Operations Office, having seen my wife off to Canada, when they urgently needed a Captain. Special authorization had to be obtained for me to fly in civvies, fortunately it was only a positioning flight. Authorization was also needed for me to take my son, Callum, too, otherwise he would be left at Gatwick whilst we got a taxi to Bristol and flew the aircraft back. A nice adventure for him. The First Officer was M, (Mitch), Miller, now a very rich training Captain with Cathay Pacific.

2nd August 1982. On G-BJYL (Series 500), 'Raffle at Venice'! The log book shows us five hours late back to Gatwick. To keep the passengers happy whilst Air Traffic played silly bug-

deliberate policy by Dan-Air as more and more tour companies were continuing to take a financial stake in their own airline operations. In an apparent contradiction to the new policy, however, a new all-charter base, utilizing one of the Boeing 727s, was opened at London-Stansted in 1991. By then, only two of the One-Elevens were still operated in 119 inclusive tour passenger configuration. The rest were now operated in a refurbished, 109-passenger, scheduled service layout.

Unfortunately, the erosion of its charter revenue coincided with the expense incurred in trying to establish itself as a viable competitor to the major European scheduled operators. Dan-Air's high

even higher losses as the months went by. Also, there was little if any profit yet in the expanding scheduled network, further draining resources. Early cost-cutting measures included the sale of Dan-Air's maintenance operations and the sale of its shares in the ground-handling associate, Manchester Handling.

Despite the sale of the engineering facilities bringing in £27.5 million, Dan-Air came very close to financial disaster in early 1991. The company was saved by the collapse of the International Leisure Group that owned rival Gatwick-based carrier, Air Europe. Initially operating ILG's inclusive tour charters, once a Dan-Air contract, Air Europe had expanded

The short-bodied One-Elevens had left the fleet by the end of 1991. MAP

gers with slot allocations I used to think up 'projects' such as guess the time we will take-off! The prize was usually a bottle of whisky.

The short-bodied Series 200, 300 and 400 One-Elevens were sold or returned to their lessors by Dan-Air by the end of 1991, having been replaced by BAe 146s, leaving eleven Series 500s in the fleet. The One-Eleven scheduled services now included major European destinations from Gatwick such as Amsterdam, Barcelona, Berlin, Madrid, Nice, Oslo, Paris, Rome, Stockholm and Vienna, among others. On many of the new European routes, Dan-Air had replaced British Caledonian as a competitor to British Airways. On the busier flights, Boeing 737s were also being used more often alongside the One-Elevens.

The move away from charters was a

standard of customer service on the scheduled routes was gaining favour with the travelling public and the company even won awards for the best airborne cup of tea! However, actual passenger revenues on routes where the airline was in competition with national carriers were still disappointing. Despite successfully introducing a much praised 'Elite' executive class service, with the handicap of having no marketing link to a larger carrier offering code-share and frequent flyer style incentives, as well as only limited interlining opportunities available through Gatwick, Dan-Air was having difficulty attracting the more profitable, high-yield business traffic.

The higher operating costs of the Boeing 727s and the remaining charter configured One-Elevens, only contributed to

rapidly and entered into scheduled European services, often in direct competition with Dan-Air. On the day the over-extended ILG suddenly ceased operations, 2 March 1991, Dan-Air only had enough funds available in its coffers for barely a couple of days' more flying. The sudden transfer of Air Europe's stranded scheduled passengers, as well as rescue flights for the inclusive tour holiday customers, brought a welcome influx of cash to Dan-Air and saved it from going the same way as Air Europe.

Even with the cost-cutting regime in full swing, new scheduled routes were still being opened in 1991 and 1992. Services opened from Gatwick to Athens, Barcelona, Oslo, Rome and Stockholm during this period in an attempt to strengthen the scheduled network and return the company to

BAe 146s took over many of the One-Eleven scheduled services. via Author

profitability. However, discreet moves were already being made by the directors to find a buyer for the airline.

It was already clear that any surviving Dan-Air Services would almost certainly be reduced in size. Options such as changing the name, to get away from the company's previous all-charter carrier reputation, and concentrating solely on the scheduled network were studied. When, by 1992, the sale of the airline as a going concern was still a likely outcome, Richard Branson's Virgin Atlantic Airways entered into negotiations, with a view to relaunching the European schedules under a new 'Virgin European' banner. Unfortunately, these talks came to nothing and, on 23 October 1992, it was announced that British Airways had purchased the assets of the airline. The 'token' price for the entire airline was a paltry £1.00! However, in the deal, British Airways assumed responsibility for all Dan-Air's, not inconsiderable, outstanding debts and the legal rights regarding redundancy of any staff forced to leave were better protected than if the company had been allowed to go into liquidation.

Although the loss of the historic airline's identity was to be regretted, it was at least saved from the ignominy of a sudden public bankruptcy and a few, albeit very few, jobs were saved.

Dan-Air's Last Days

British Airways had made it clear that it was only interested in the Gatwick-based scheduled services and had no need for the Aberdeen, Berlin, Inverness, London-Stansted, Manchester or Newcastle-based operations. Where flights operated from these bases into London, they would be taken over by BA, or its associates, from London and the local Dan-Air staff were made redundant. In the end, over 1,600 of the airline's 2,000-plus staff were to lose their jobs. British Airways chose only to retain the Boeing 737-300 and -400 fleets, and their crews. The One-Eleven, BAe 146, Boeing 727 and Boeing 737-200 fleets would be disposed of. The surviving operations were merged with British Airways existing Gatwick-based European services as 'British Airways European Operations at Gatwick', a new wholly owned subsidiary company. In later years the company name was thankfully modified to the less jargon-orientated, 'EuroGatwick' in daily use, although all licences, contracts and operating certificates continued to be held under the original title.

Unlike the more dramatic overnight demises of Air Europe, British Eagle International Airlines, Court Line Aviation and Laker Airways, the staff and crews of Dan-Air had to work on for several weeks after their fate was decided and try to maintain their hard-won reputation for service in the face of their impending redundancy. Apart from the lucky few who were offered positions with the new BA operation at Gatwick, most of the staff were looking at very uncertain futures. To their credit, a great many passengers and industry commentators were moved to publicly congrat-

ulate them on the professionalism shown by the Dan-Air staff right up to the end.

When the merger was completed at midnight on 8 November, the last of the One-Elevens had already been flown into storage at Bournemouth or Southend Airports between the 2nd and the 6th. One of the most poignant closing services was the last scheduled departure on the Newcastle–Gatwick route. One-Eleven, G-BDAT, operated the last flight, DA107, on the morning of 2 November, closing down over thirty years of Dan-Air's presence at the airport. A great many past and present Newcastle-based staff gathered to say goodbye to their regular passengers and be present at the sad historic occasion. The crew made a point of turning the aircraft towards the emotional crowd gathered in and around the terminal and flashed the landing lights in farewell before taking off for Gatwick.

The very last revenue-earning service by a Dan-Air One-Eleven took place on the morning of 6 November 1992. G-BCWA arrived at Gatwick at 09.37, from Toulouse, as DA910. Under the command of Captain Threlfall, the aircraft carried 34 passengers on its last commercial Dan-Air flight. Within the hour, after disembarking its last Dan-Air passengers, the aircraft left Gatwick in the hands of Captain Noble, bound for its birthplace at Bournemouth-Hurn, landing at 11.05. Twenty-two years before, 'WA, then G-AXMK, had first been rolled out of the BAC paint-shop, resplendent in turquoise Court Line colours as 'Halcyon Star'.

Two of the Dan-Air One-Elevens, G-BDAS and G-BDAT, were delivered direct from Gatwick to BAF at Southend Airport, the rest being gradually ferried to Hurn. G-BDAS and G-BDAT were repainted with British Air Ferries titles over their former Dan-Air colours and entered service on charters from Stansted, replacing the remaining short-bodied BAF One-Elevens. Re-registered as G-OBWA (ex-'AT) and G-OBWB, (ex -'AS), the aircraft heralded a significant change on the way for British Air Ferries. G-OBWA entered BAF service first,

flying a charter from Stansted to Istanbul on 7 December 1992, with G-OBWB operating a Stansted–Amsterdam flight on the 9th. Two other ex-Dan-Air One-Elevens, G-BCWA and G-BCXR had also been ferried from Hurn to Southend, but did not enter service, being scrapped for spares.

On 6 April 1993, British Air Ferries was renamed British World Airlines and the aircraft adopted a completely new white and maroon livery. The name change was brought about by a concerted effort to update the company's image. Even though

the car-ferry service had ceased over twenty years before, the British Air Ferries name was still heavily identified with it and the new name and styling were designed to finally put this to rest. A renewed marketing emphasis was also to be placed on passenger flights, particularly inclusive tour and *ad hoc* charter work, with the jet aircraft, as the convertible Viscount fleet was being run down and gradually disposed of. In markets where turbo-prop operations were to continue, such as the oil industry charters from Aberdeen, new aircraft,

Ex-Paninternational and LACSA G-BJYL was with Dan-Air from 1982. MAP

G-BDAE at Amsterdam a few weeks before the end of operations. M.L. Hill

167

BAF had become British World in April 1993. MAP

initially ATR-72s, were ordered to replace the long-serving Viscounts.

As the name change took effect, the remaining Dan-Air Series 500 One-Elevens were being moved to Southend for maintenance and refurbishment in preparation for either re-entering service with British World or passing on to new operators. Two of the aircraft, G-AXYD and G-BJMV, remained in storage, despite having new registrations reserved in the 'G-OBW' series. Eventually, though, five of the ex-Dan-Air aircraft were all busy with charter flights for British World, alongside the BAe 146s, from crew bases at Stansted, Gatwick and Manchester, by the summer of 1993.

Flushed with the momentum of the successful relaunch of the company, British World Airlines even opened a new scheduled route in June 1993. The opening of the route had been planned for 24 May, but licensing problems held up the inaugural flight for a month. However, on 28 June, G-OBWD finally opened the thrice weekly Stansted–Bucharest scheduled service. The aircraft was christened 'City of Bucharest' in honour of the flight. A 'World Class' business class standard of cabin service was promoted on the flight that was increased in frequency to four a week in December.

Within three months of the Bucharest launch, studies were undertaken for a second new scheduled flight from Stansted to Lourdes, a destination already regularly served by British World on charters. Unfortunately, despite extensive discussions and negotiations, no scheduled Lourdes flight was opened. The Bucharest schedule was closed down, after mounting losses, in the spring of 1994 and British

World returned to an all-charter operation. The loss of the scheduled service did little to reduce the One-Eleven fleet's utilization, as new, much more profitable, charter contracts were soon signed to fill the gap.

British World's Bucharest flight had suffered from public perception problems with the Stansted-based flight. Despite the new terminal facilities and fast rail link to London, public acceptance of Stansted as a viable airport for scheduled flights was slow in building up. The rival TAROM flight from Heathrow still managed to attract most of the traffic between the two cities, the anti-Stansted prejudice playing a great part. The high-yield World Class traffic was also very light, with most of the paying customers who were lured to Stansted preferring to go for the cheapest option, mirroring Dan-Air's problems with their Gatwick-based scheduled network. The increase in scheduled traffic from Stansted did come about eventually, mostly thanks to the efforts of long-established operator, Air UK, later renamed KLM.uk after the Dutch carrier increased its shareholding in the British independent airline. Ireland's Ryanair and new British Airways low-fare subsidiary, GO, as well as a number of other visiting European airlines, also made major contributions to the rise of new scheduled traffic from Stansted.

As well as its growing presence in the inclusive tour market, British World Airlines continued to offer its spare capacity for work on other carriers' services. As with the original British Air Ferries leasing operations, if the contract called for it and was of long enough duration, the customer airline's identity would be adopted by the

aircraft. Both the BAe146s and One-Elevens were involved in such a charter for Belgian airline, Sabena. Painted in Sabena's livery, the aircraft were flown on scheduled services from Scotland to Brussels, covering the late delivery of Sabena's BAe146/Avroliner RJ aircraft.

The sudden appearance on the second-hand market of the large One-Eleven fleets of both British Airways and Dan-Air Services, none of them particularly new examples, would normally have preceded an airframe scrapping frenzy. However, with British Airways only retaining the Dan-Air pilots qualified on the newer Boeing 737s, there was also a large pool of type-rated crews available ready to operate the aircraft for any enterprising new owner.

Exodus to Africa

One proposed deal came as no great surprise, as it involved continuing what had become a steady flow of surviving One-Elevens of all types in the previous few years. With substantial fossil fuel and mineral reserves being exploited, the West African country of Nigeria had experienced a great increase in national wealth. Unfortunately, local corporate corruption and political unrest led to much of this wealth being squandered, but as always in such a volatile atmosphere, certain individuals and companies benefited from the flow of cash. One result of this was the discovery that there was room for the establishment of several new local airlines to offer competition to the beleaguered Nigeria Airways, itself suffering great financial difficulties.

British World's One-Eleven 500s serve on charter and leasing services. MAP

Several new airline operators came and went in Nigeria, most of extremely dubious financial standing and with very doubtful safety records. However, the mid-1980s saw the appearance of a number of carriers that managed to survive and actually managed to build sizeable reputations for efficiency and whose operations have been commercial successes, under less than ideal conditions. Whether by coincidence or design, no less than six of the most successful have become substantial operators of the One-Eleven.

One of these, Okada Air with a main operations centre at Benin, was earmarked as a possible buyer for the remaining British Airways Series 500s, also stored at Hurn. Seven of the aircraft were painted in Okada's colours, complete with gold Benin Bronze mask logo. Unfortunately, the deal was never finalized and the aircraft were eventually moved to Filton for further storage, still in basic Okada livery.

Okada Air had started flying One-Elevens in late 1983, following the purchase of the ex-Laker Series 300s previously used by BCal. The three aircraft retained most of their BCal livery, with the lower gold line painted over in blue and the Benin Bronze emblem replacing BCal's rampant heraldic lion. The aircraft joined a mixed fleet of aircraft, including Caravelles and Boeings of various marks, operating regional charters and domestic scheduled services.

Between November 1985 and July 1992 no less than three more Series 300s, thirteen Series 400s, three Series 500s and even two elderly Series 200s were acquired from various sources. The airline appeared to be scouring the world for its fleet, with examples gathered in from the cast-aside fleets of the Royal Australian Air Force, British Airways, British Island Airways, Britt Airways, Dan-Air, Quebecair, USAir and even executive operators. The last Air Malawi One-Eleven was one of the Series 500s joining the fleet, having been replaced by Boeing 737s in mid-1992. Not surprisingly, considering the difficulties posed to airline operations in that part of the world, both operational and climatic, there were accidents and the scrapping of ageing airframes to provide a source of spares led to further losses in the world's One-Eleven population. However, in 1998 Okada Air could still muster fifteen flyable One-Elevens of various marks for revenue service.

July 1987 saw the arrival on the Nigerian scheduled airline scene of General and Aviation Services Ltd, operating its new airline division as GAS Airlines, later renamed GAS Air Nigeria. Administered from

5N-AOK was seized by the UK authorities and later scrapped. Steve Bunting

Ilorin, the new fleet was based at Lagos, GAS's first aircraft being a Series 400 leased from TAROM. This was eventually replaced, in 1989, by two more Series 400s bought from TAROM's charter subsidiary LAR. Plans to acquire a Series 200 were abandoned in 1991, but a further Series 400, an ex-Air Malawi aircraft, arrived in 1993, although this was later placed into storage. The two ex-LAR One-Elevens fly a domestic scheduled network encompassing Ilorin, Kaduna, Kano, Lagos, Maiduguri and Yola. An international service to Accra was flown in 1990, but abandoned after only three months as uneconomic.

Three of the ex-Braniff fleet, two Series 200s and a single Series 400 were obtained, via Guinness Peat Aviation, by the Aviation Development Company Ltd, of Lagos, Nigeria in late 1990 and early 1991. Operating as ADC Airlines, the One-Elevens entered service on domestic scheduled services, and to Conakry in neighbouring Guinea. The first Nigerian airline to issue public shares in 1994, ADC Airlines by 1998 also flew a Boeing 707 and small fleets of Boeing 727s, McDonnell-Douglas DC-9s and a single ATR-42 turbo-prop.

Late 1990 saw the start of the arrival of yet more One-Elevens, in the form of no less than eleven Series 200s from USAir, for another carrier, Kabo Air Ltd. With its administrative headquarters at Kano and its maintenance base at Jos, Kabo Air operate the One-Elevens on scheduled services from Lagos. Points served from the capital include Abuja, Enugu, Jos, Kaduna, Kano and Port Harcourt, with Abuja–Minna and Kano–Maiduguri scheduled flights also operated. A contract is also held for transport of Nigerian troops in support of ECO-

MOG, the West African Military Force, in operations in Liberia. Two of the Series 200s were to only be used as a source of spares, however five Series 400s were added to the fleet between 1991 and 1993. In 1998, nine of the One-Elevens remained in service on the scheduled network and domestic charters, alongside six Boeing 727-200s.

The quartet of faithful Series 200s retired by Aer Lingus found their way to Lagos in late 1991 and early 1992. Hold-Trade Air Services Ltd placed them into service from a base at Kaduna on yet another domestic scheduled network, as well as regional and international charters. One of the aircraft, 5N-HTA, once EI-ANG 'St Declan', skidded off the runway on landing at Kaduna on 29 August 1992 and was severely damaged, so severe as to be deemed irreparable and the aircraft was scrapped. The surviving three aircraft, however, continue in daily service to the present day.

The last Nigerian airline, to date, to place the One-Eleven into revenue service was Oriental Airlines, also of Lagos. Two ex-BCal/BA Series 500s entered service in 1993 and 1994. One of the aircraft crashed on approach to Tamanrasset in September 1994, but the small airline managed to recover, acquiring a replacement Series 500 from the UK in 1995.

Although the majority of the original North, South and Central American operators had put their One-Elevens to one side by the mid-1980s, one loyal airline maintained its fleet, mostly purchased new, for several more years. Austral Lineas Aereas, of Buenos Aires had been flying the type since 1967. Although the last of their Series 400s were disposed of by the beginning of 1982, following the delivery

of the first of Austral's fleet of McDonnell-Douglas MD-81s, leased from the manufacturer, the fleet of Series 500 One-Elevens still continued to flourish. As well as the aircraft acquired new from BAC, no less than seven second-hand Series 500s had been obtained over the years, either leased or purchased. Despite the Falklands War with the UK threatening to disrupt spares supplies, Austral's British-built One-Eleven fleet managed to continue their successful operations, even gaining patriotic 'Las Malvinas son Argentinas' stickers at the height of the conflict.

Austral's extensive Argentinian scheduled network was augmented by both domestic and international charter flights throughout the region, work on which the One-Eleven fleet was especially busy. Carriage of passengers to Argentina's mountain lake resort areas, both from within the country and from neighbouring nations, was an established market since the original Austral/ALA days and was a valuable source of revenue for the company. In the early 1970s, Austral had acquired Lagos del Sur SA, which operated a number of hotel and resort complexes. In addition, Sol Jet SRL was established to operate holiday and tourist services similar to the European style of inclusive tour, providing even more utilization for the aircraft fleet. From the original staid colours, the One-Elevens had later been decorated in a variety of highly visual schemes, from various multicoloured hues of the 1970s, to a more businesslike red, white and blue livery, with a large 'AU' logo on the forward fuselage.

In an effort to force the government-owned Aerolineas Argentinas to improve efficiency, Austral had been officially

521FH, LV-JNS was to serve Austral for over 22 years. MAP

DC-9s and MD-80s eventually replaced the Austral One-Elevens. via Author

encouraged by the authorities to compete as the country's second-force carrier. The company started to make healthy profits in 1973, although this was followed by several years of nationwide inflation and political revolution. Regardless of some of the earlier government decisions regarding route awards and increased subsidies later being reversed in Aerolineas Argentinas' favour, Austral continued to grow commercially and its position as strong, independent competition to Aerolineas Argentinas was definitely good for the local airline industry as a whole.

As the Argentine economy slowly recovered from the turbulent 1980s and early 1990s, Austral gradually replaced the One-Eleven fleet with more MD-80s of various marks. By early 1994 only two One-Elevens remained in regular service, although new services were still being inaugurated by the type to Rio Cuarto, Santa Rosa and Viedma. In spite of this last rush of new activity, even these last examples were eventually disposed of.

Although Austral's One-Eleven days were finally over, the aircraft had found a new South American champion, this time in Chile. Linea Aerea del Cobre SA, more familiarly known as LADECO, had taken delivery of some of Dan-Air's short-bodied One-Eleven fleet, on lease from International Lease Finance Corporation from November 1990. Two Series 300s were initially delivered, followed by two Series 200s a year later.

Originally founded to exploit air transport services for the Chilean copper indus-

try, LADECO had enjoyed steady expansion since its late 1950's inauguration of scheduled services. Serving both popular holiday areas in the south and the prosperous industrial centres of north Chile, LADECO was already operating a modern jet fleet of Boeing 727s and 737s when the One-Elevens arrived. Although possibly a bit antiquated next to the Boeings, the One-Elevens provided LADECO with a useful, economic, aircraft for less busy routes or to supplement the larger aircraft on extra services. Regional international operations had been expanded to include a scheduled route to Miami. The One-Elevens operated domestic scheduled flights from Santiago to Antofagusta, Arica, Balmaceda, Concepcion, Iquique, La Serena, Puerto Montt, Temuco, Valdivia and Vina del Mar, and internationally to Mendoza in Argentina.

The One-Eleven continued to make its presence increasingly felt under other African states' skies, as well as Nigeria. Shabair, of Lubumbashi, Zaire, placed two One-Elevens, a Series 400, followed by a Series 200, both obtained from Guinness Peat, in service in September 1990 and March 1991. The aircraft operated on scheduled service from Lubumbashi to Kalemie, Kananga, Kinshasa and Mbuji-Mayi, as well as regional charter flights. Shabair was eventually merged with another Zairian carrier, Zaire Airlines, in 1997. Even with political and economic disruption rife within Zaire, later reverting to its original name of Congo, Zaire Airlines continued to operate the One-Elevens, alongside a fleet of assorted Boeings. Eventually,

however, the continuingly volatile political situation led to the company suspending operations, hopefully only temporarily, in 1998.

Another Zairian operator, Cargostar, acquired two ex-BA Series 500 in 1994, later changing its name to Express City. Details of their actual One-Eleven operations, if any, are few and far between and, in 1998, the airline was listed as operating a single Boeing 727-200.

Further south on the African continent at Lansaria, South Africa-based Nationwide Air acquired the ex-Rolls Royce/Turbo-Union Series 400 freighter in late April 1994. Since 1991, Nationwide had operated a fleet of Beechcraft King Air light twin turbo-props on contract charters for the United Nations, the South African Post Office and a domestic express parcel courier operator. In 1995, another operator, Cape Airlines, was purchased, along with the authority to operate Johannesburg–Cape Town scheduled services. Further One-Elevens, all Series 500s, started arriving in late 1994 and, by August, 1995, no less than six Series 500s were operating on Nationwide Air's scheduled routes. Within months, Nationwide Air had expanded beyond all recognition and was providing viable competition to the incumbent, South African Airways, on domestic routes.

The first three Series 500s were all ex-Ryanair/London European aircraft, owned by Tollhold Ltd and acquired via British World Airlines, who also overhauled the aircraft at Southend before the long delivery flight to South Africa. The next trio of

Nationwide began One-Eleven operations with 409AY, ZS-NNM. MAP

aircraft all came from Cyprus Airways, the airline having replaced them in Eastern Mediterranean service with Airbus A320s. The Nationwide Air network soon expanded to include Durban and George. Increasingly unusual among the surviving One-Eleven operators, the Nationwide aircraft operate in a mixed-class configuration, seating 12 business class, and 82 economy passengers.

As traffic grew, Boeing 727-100s joined the fleet, but the One-Eleven complement had still grown to a total of ten in 1998. An important code-share agreement had been signed with the Belgian national airline, Sabena, with Nationwide Air providing feeder services into Sabena's flights from South Africa to Europe. As part of the code-share operation, Sabena titles were painted on the Nationwide Air One-Elevens, alongside their own. This was yet another occasion that Sabena's name had appeared on One-Elevens, despite the Belgian airline never having actually acquired any of their own and, indeed, being an early customer for the One-Eleven's first rival, the Caravelle twin jet.

As the turn of the century approached, the One-Eleven continued to prove itself to be a viable commercial aircraft, surviving the financial ups and downs of the ever changeable aviation industry. Major operators had once again disposed of their One-Elevens, or been forced from the commercial scene themselves, only for their aircraft to be found new homes with willing new owners and operators. This was all the more remarkable considering that the original basic aircraft had been subjected to only limited development, unlike its more numerous American rivals that had continued in production with larger, modernized and more powerful versions. That there always seemed to be a customer waiting in the wings for any available airframes was an ongoing tribute both to the One-Elevens and the personnel that had designed and built it.

Sabena titles were also applied to Nationwide's fleet. MAP

CHAPTER TEN

Partying On

Even if the commercial United States airlines had finally withdrawn the last of their One-Elevens, the aircraft remained popular as an executive transport, many aircraft having their avionics and other systems updated and replaced as often as their interiors were re-upholstered in the latest fashion. Keeping them equipped with the most modern computerized navigation aids belied their twenty-plus airframe years. Whether flying individuals, corporate staff members or sports teams, over the years, the One-Eleven has managed to retain its standing as a leading executive jet. As late as the end of 1997, of the 143 jet airliners of 19 different types used worldwide for private and executive services, One-Elevens accounted for 31 of them.

The vast majority of the executive One-Elevens are of the 400 Series. The very first of the version, G-ASYD, itself continued in use with its manufacturer as a corporate aircraft with British Aerospace, as well as providing a flying platform for much research and development work. The aircraft was converted back to its Series 475 configuration, following the scrapping of the proposed Series 670 for the Japanese markets. This was to be the last of its metamorphism,

Corporate One-Elevens boast some very plush interiors. Brooklands Museum

At the end of a busy life, G-ASYD was retired to Brooklands. Martyn East

from Series 400, to 500, to 475, to 670 and back to 475. Finally retired from BAe service in October 1993, with 6,787 hours of flying and 6,325 landings under its belt, the historic aircraft was presented to the Brooklands Museum in July 1994, for display at the former Vickers/BAC/BAe Weybridge site at Brooklands.

Non-commercial use of the One-Eleven in the UK continued with the research work originally carried out by the fleet operated by Royal Aircraft Establishment. Based originally at the RAE airfields at Bedford and Farnborough, the unit was later moved to Thurleigh, in Bedfordshire. In April 1991, the RAE was merged into a new body, the Defence Research Agency and the three One-Elevens on charge at

the time, a Series 200 and a pair of Series 400s, were transferred to the new organization. Research work undertaken by the aircraft included the original Blind Landing programme, research into steep angles of approach in order to reduce noise nuisance, as well as flight control, communications and navigation systems research. One Series 400 was fitted with external video cameras for monitoring control surfaces and engines not visible from within the cabin. The ventral stairs area was later modified on this aircraft to accept a chute for launching sonobuoys.

The other RAE Series 400, an ex-Air Pacific Series 475 aircraft, was extensively modified to accept an experimental Blue Vixen radar installation to be used on the

Sea Harrier aircraft. This aircraft was later exchanged with a late production Series 500 originally acquired by GEC Ferranti Defence Systems Ltd from British Airways. The Series 500 had been bought by GEC Ferranti to test ECR90 Radar equipment intended for the new European Fighter Aircraft. The Blue Vixen programme had ended and the Series 400 was able to accept the ECR90, with its previous modifications, rather than set about a lengthy conversion of the Series 500. An agreement was reached for a swap and the Series 400 and 500 were exchanged in March 1994. The DRA Series 500 was earmarked for radar research work, replacing a Vickers Viscount and English Electric Canberra. In 1994, the three DRA One-

XX919 began research work in 1974, after five years as an airliner. MAP

Elevens, and a single Series 400, also an ex-Air Pacific Series 475, operated by the Empire Test Pilots School, moved to Boscombe Down. At the time of writing, the DRA Series 200, originally British United Airways' G-ASJD, was the oldest One-Eleven flying.

European and Air Bristol at Filton

Back in the commercial world of scheduled and charter airlines, the type was also still managing to make a valuable contribution. Whilst the British World One-Elevens were building the revamped company's new reputation, the faithful type was still making an appearance with yet more new United Kingdom operators, despite its increasing age. Although the deal with Nigeria's Okada Air had fallen through, the remaining ex-British Airways fleet of Series 500s did not remain homeless for long.

The European Aviation Group had been established in 1989 by Paul Stoddard, an Australian-born entrepreneur. The company had originally purchased the Royal Australian Air Force VIP fleet, consisting of their two One-Eleven Series 200s and three Dassault Falcon 20 executive twin-jets. The Falcons were soon sold on to new owners and the pair of One-Elevens eventually followed suit in December 1991, when the aircraft were disposed of to Okada Air.

Later, the surviving sixteen ex-British Airways were purchased, originally to be resold as the previous aircraft had been. However, as no serious buyers had come forward after the Okada Air contract failed to materialize, a new subsidiary, European Aviation Air Charter was established in 1994 to operate the fleet commercially. The new company's first revenue flight took place on 16 February 1994, from Bristol to Lyons.

Initially, European had intended basing itself at Cardiff, but operating restrictions saw the airline move over the Severn Estuary to Bristol's Filton Airport, home of the original Bristol Aeroplane Company

G-BGKE joined the DRA in 1994, later re-registered as ZH763. via Author

G-AVMH operated European's first charter, from Bristol to Lyons. MAP

factory, now a major British Aerospace facility. As the British Aerospace-owned airfield was not licensed for full commercial operations, Filton proved even more restrictive for European Aviation, with the vast majority of revenue flights requiring expensive positioning flights at the beginning and end of any contract. In an attempt to rectify this fund-draining problem, the entire operation was eventually moved south to Bournemouth-Hurn and an engineering base was set up at the old

and consumables. The stock could be accessed through a computerized worldwide Inventory Locating System, (ILS), and is held in a 120,000 square foot warehouse complex, located at Ledbury, in Herefordshire. One-Eleven technical libraries are also available, covering publications, drawings, structural repair manuals and component repair manuals.

The European One-Eleven fleet quickly settled into its 'new' home at Hurn and it was not long before the airline was involv-

Belfast International, at Aldergrove, for the One-Eleven route. The other aircraft still flying charters for European Aviation Air charter were involved in a great deal of inclusive tour work from Bournemouth-Hurn, Gatwick and Manchester, as well as several other UK airports being regularly visited on *ad hoc* and contract flights. The aircraft are usually operated by EAAC in a standard 104-passenger configuration, with 50- and 70-seat executive class arrangements available if required.

European's G-AVML has flown a variety of charter contracts MAP

BAC site. Rather appropriate for a One-Eleven-equipped airline. With more suitable passenger handling facilities and room for expansion, Hurn gave European Aviation Air Charter scope for a financially viable base for the airline.

As well as their aircraft, a large inventory of spares and equipment was acquired from the RAAF and British Airways. The Dan-Air and FLS Aerospace supplies were also obtained at a later date. In addition, a great deal of Airbus, Boeing, British Aerospace, McDonnel-Douglas and Lockheed material was eventually purchased from British Airways and added to the company's stock, available to airlines and other operators throughout the world.

A sister company, European Aviation Maintenance Ltd, took charge of this large spares stock, with an inventory of in excess of 350,000 items for the One-Eleven alone. This ranges from engines, thrust reversers, APUs, airframe, systems and avionic components, to ground equipment

ing itself in a number of important charter and leasing contracts, of both short and long-term duration. The number of UK airports not visited by European's fleet was soon a dwindling one. Leasing deals saw the aircraft operating on behalf of Air UK, Jersey European and Ryanair. Once again, Sabena leased in One-Eleven capacity, this time from European Aviation, for the Scotland–Brussels scheduled services. Once the remaining ex-BA aircraft had been refurbished and placed into service, even more aircraft were gradually acquired to help out with the increasing workload and, by then, ten operational-Series 500 One-Elevens were in the fleet.

The Jersey European Airways contract saw European operating the London/Stansted–Belfast route for JEA, the aircraft being painted in full Jersey European colours. Although JEA utilized the 'downtown' Belfast City Airport for all other services, operating restrictions dictated the use of the much longer runways at

A regular European Aviation Air Charter customer for *ad hoc* work is the Tyrrell Racing Team, for the high-speed world of Formula One car racing. Both personnel and spares were frequently carried to and from world championship events by EAAC. From the 1998 season, European became involved in the sponsorship of Tyrrell. Part of the Hurn hangar facilities was also being converted to allow the installation of a wind tunnel, to assist in the aerodynamic design of the Tyrrell cars. June 1998 also saw the opening of a new training department at Hurn. Consisting of flight-deck simulators for the One-Eleven, Boeing 727 and the Lockheed L1011 Tristar, a complete One-Eleven fuselage is also available for cabin crew training. As well as training the airline's own crews, European Aviation is actively promoting the availability of the new facility among other carriers.

The problems created by Filton's lack of a full commercial licence were being addressed by British Aerospace, the airfield's owner following the BAC and BAe mergers, and applications had been made for permission to build a proper passenger terminal and other associated facilities. In the 1950s, when the authorities had been looking around for a site to replace Bristol's original airport, the pre-war Whitchurch, Filton had been among the candidates. However, at the time, the Bristol Aeroplane Company was making very good use of the airfield, being busy with the production of a number of aircraft

when Lulsgate was closed by bad weather. However, the lack of substantial terminal facilities meant that the diversions were restricted to smaller aircraft on scheduled commuter services, and on the few flights that were allowed in, passengers were usually required to remain on board the diverted aircraft until coach transport over to Lulsgate arrived. Passengers on international flights also had to wait until arriving at Lulsgate before being allowed to clear through the customs and immigration for-

runway, capable of accommodating long-haul aircraft, became a major argument used by British Aerospace in its attempts to gain government approval for the proposed project.

Another airline had also been attracted to Filton by the prospect of British Aerospace's lengthy runway becoming available for commercial operations. Air Bristol was established by Bryan Beal and Tony Auld, who had both originally been executives with Brymon Airways, of Plymouth. Bry-

Air Bristol commenced Filton–Toulouse services with G-AVMT. MAP

types and the company was reluctant to allow commercial traffic to interfere with their development and test flying. Eventually the local council selected an ex-RAF airfield at Lulsgate Bottom, south of the city, to become the new Bristol Airport.

The fact that Lulsgate had mainly been used by the RAF for bad-weather training should really have given the burghers of Bristol a hint of possible problems ahead, but the plans went through and Lulsgate was opened in 1957. Throughout its commercial history, the hilltop location of Lulsgate has led to numerous weather-related difficulties, especially in the winter months, from fog and low cloud. Technical innovations in instrument landing systems made for some improvement over the years, but even in the 1990s weather diversions and delays plagued the airlines that operated to and from Lulsgate.

In the early 1990s, British Aerospace eventually agreed to make Filton available to take a limited number of diversions

malities. Any larger aircraft, mostly those on the holiday charter services, were forced to divert to airports further afield, such as Birmingham or Cardiff.

With the increasing use of the Filton factory for Airbus component production, rather than aircraft assembly, British Aerospace was using the site less and less for its own flying and began looking for new uses for its expensive airfield facility. A limited amount of executive and private flights had been handled at the airport for a number of years, however, the handful of daily movements was hardly putting much strain on the mostly dormant giant runway. Close to the junction of two major motorways, the M4 and M5, and enjoying direct nationwide train links via nearby Bristol Parkway Station, the potential of the site as a public airport facility was finally recognized and British Aerospace made the first moves towards gaining permission to open it up to commercial airline services. Filton's much better weather record and longer

mon had opened a base at Lulsgate in 1990 and had been one of the first scheduled carriers to obtain permission to use Filton as a diversion airport. With the prospect of full commercial airline operations beginning at Filton, Air Bristol was founded in early 1993 with a view to opening a scheduled network to be based at the new facility. A fleet of BAe 146s was proposed, with their quiet operation being regarded as a major advantage in trying to win local support.

Unfortunately, British Aerospace's plans were to come to nothing. Resistance of local residents, mostly on housing developments built close to the airfield in the years when flying had decreased, was vociferous. The management of Lulsgate, viewing the Filton plans as a direct challenge to their own operations, also made very loud objections to the various government committees and hearings held to review the project.

In the meantime, Air Bristol did begin operations from Filton in October 1993.

However, with the company's plans for BAe 146 scheduled operations in abeyance, subject to the Filton licensing hearings, only charter flights were to be operated. The most important charter contract was for a once daily, Monday to Friday, Filton–Toulouse–Filton, 'Air Bridge', flight, carrying British Aerospace employees to and from the Airbus factory. Instead of the BAe 146s, two ex-British Airways Series 500 One-Elevens, later joined by a third, were leased from European Aviation, then still based at Filton as well. Apart from the British Aerospace Air Bridge contract, *ad hoc* charter services were also operated from other UK airports, including Lulsgate.

Initially the aircraft were crewed by a mixture of British Aerospace and Air Bristol pilots with Air Bristol's own cabin crews. The twelve Filton-based cabin staff were employed on a 'freelance' basis, being paid on a flat-rate-payment basis per flight. They mostly consisted of experienced cabin staff, with previous flying experience on a variety of types with many different carriers.

Typical of these was Vikki Chatham, who had originally flown for British Airways on Boeing 747s, before leaving to raise her family. Other crew members included ex-Dan-Air and British Caledonian One-Eleven cabin staff. Welcoming the chance to return to flying, after working in ground-based passenger handling for Dan-Air at Lulsgate for several years, Vikki found the One-Eleven a little different from the wide-bodied aircraft she had been used to:

> Being 'petite', everything was a lot more accessible to me on the One-Eleven than it had been on the 747. Originally the cabin was laid out in standard five abreast seating, two one side of the aisle, three the other. However, this was later changed to a much more spacious and comfortable 2-2 club class style arrangement.

One of the aircraft would be assigned to the BAe service and the others were made available for *ad hoc* charters. The new configuration was popular with the British Aerospace passengers on the Toulouse run and contracts for numerous corporate charters were soon forthcoming as a result of the new luxury available. New customers for this work included several orchestras, sports teams and their supporters and entertainment stars. Rock star Phil Collins and his entourage were among the famous names carried on tours around the UK and Europe.

(Above) **An early 119-seat layout for the 'Airbridge' to Toulouse.** AB Airlines

The new style interior was popular with corporate clients. AB Airlines

Vikki and the other crews welcome the break away from the daily BAe routine that the *ad hoc* charters brought:

I went to many interesting places on corporate work. In particular, a soccer team charter to Slovakia was an eye opener, being the first time I had visited the former eastern bloc. Amusing, in a black humour way, was the fact that a square of toilet paper, that had to be bought from a rather insistent attendant, cost more than a beer in the bar had!

The orchestra charters took us all over Europe, although the stowage of their precious instruments always caused problems. We also flew a party of golf supporters up to St Andrews. As the local hotels were all full because of the

ing in the sun or, more often than not, just sleeping off the early start.

I was with the company for four years and can honestly say, hand on heart, that I have never worked with such wonderful people and had such a memorable time in all my flying career.

Air Bristol to AB Airlines

One of the One-Elevens was repainted with large 'Shannon' titles and transferred to a new base at Shannon Airport in Eire. From December 1993, a daily Shannon–Stansted scheduled service was opened under the name of 'AB Shannon'.

at Aldergrove, under the marketing name of Air Belfast.

In 1997, the Air Bridge contract was awarded to Jersey European Airways, using a Toulouse-based BAe 146, and the Filton base was closed down altogether. The company was reorganized as AB Airlines, with the original Bristol connection now being non-existent. In May of 1998, the company was floated on the UK stock exchange, only the second British airline to do so. One One-Eleven aircraft had been returned to European, but replaced by another, maintaining the fleet strength at three. Although the Belfast schedule was closed in May 1996, the Shannon service thrived and a Shannon–Birmingham

G-AVMT was repainted in a distinctive 'Shannon' livery. AB Airlines

tournament, we had to spend the day-stop, waiting for the passengers to get back later that afternoon, at the RAF Leuchars Officers Quarters. Very different and interesting.

The Toulouse service called for a very early start to the day, as the flight departed from Filton at 07.00. It was a unique service in that the passengers were very frequent passengers and we got to know them personally. It made for a very informal, friendly, atmosphere on a flight that was rarely full. While waiting for the afternoon return trip back to Filton, we would while away the time in Toulouse by shopping, usually for wine, going for lunch at a nearby village, relax-

As the Filton licensing applications dragged on, Air Bristol began to look for more regular sources of income. Except for the Toulouse service that continued its unique operation from Filton, the company's administration and operations were eventually moved to London-Stansted in an effort to encourage more charter work. The Filton-based complement of cabin staff was reduced to only five, solely for operation of the Air Bridge flight to Toulouse. In March 1995, the company also opened a new Belfast–London schedule, based at Belfast's international airport

service was inaugurated in April 1998, with both routes being promoted as a code-share service with Aer Lingus. Once again the One-Eleven was featured in the Aer Lingus timetable, a place the type had earlier enjoyed for a quarter of a century.

New scheduled services were also opened from London-Gatwick to Lisbon, from April 1997, and to Nice and Berlin in 1998. The Berlin route is operated to Schonefeld, the original East Berlin airport now being developed by the reunited Germany as an eventual replacement for Templehof and Tegel as Berlin's main airline gateway. The

AB Airline's Bryan Beal and Tony Auld with a One-Eleven crew. AB Airlines

scheduled services from Heathrow to the eastern Mediterranean, British Mediterranean went on to become a British Airways franchise carrier, with a much expanded fleet and new scheduled services to Egypt, Georgia, Jordan and Syria. While remaining a major shareholder in British Mediterranean, Romero recognized another gap in the UK scheduled service network and set up Euroscot Express to exploit it.

Euroscot Express wet-leased Series 500 One-Eleven, G-AVMT, from European, to open scheduled services from Bournemouth-Hurn to Glasgow and Edinburgh. Operations began in September 1997 with weekday flights to Glasgow, supplemented by weekend flights to Edinburgh. The new service was primarily aimed at leisure travellers, with fares starting as low as £39 plus tax. However, the routes were soon also attracting business customers as Bournemouth-Hurn offered an attractive alternative to local businessmen and women who welcomed not having to face the northbound trek to Gatwick or Heathrow. When required to be taken out of service for maintenance, the Euroscot aircraft was replaced by a European Aviation Air Charter One-Eleven. European already supplied the crews for the aircraft, allowing Euroscot Express to operate while actually only employing ten of their own staff.

Following the cessation of several long-running services, Bournemouth-Hurn had

services to Nice were operated by AB Airlines under a code-share agreement with Luton-based Debonair. In the summer of 1998, a pair of leased Boeing 737-300s entered service on AB Airlines' scheduled routes from Gatwick, heralding the arrival of six 'new generation' Boeing 737-700s on order for January 2001 delivery. However, with the availability of new hushkits being developed by European Aviation, the One-Eleven is still expected to remain a useful member of the fleet thereafter.

The ex-AB Airlines One-Eleven which had already returned to European was soon leased out for another new scheduled operation. Euroscot Express was established at European's base at Bournemouth-Hurn by Jack Romero, the original founder of British Mediterranean Airlines. Originally operating a single Airbus A320 on

G-AVMW operated with AB Airlines in a hybrid European livery. MAP

experienced a steady decline in scheduled passenger traffic. This was a far cry from the days when Bournemouth-Hurn had seen constant comings and goings of scheduled flights to the Channel Islands and northern France, the varied services of fledgling inclusive tour carriers, not to mention the numerous movements associated with Vickers, and later BAC's, building of Viscounts and One-Elevens at their factory based at the airport.

The new Euroscot venture was a welcome addition to the services offered by

Finally a Quieter One-Eleven?

An ex-Philippine Airline Series 500 was due to begin testing of a new muffling system in early 1999. Developed jointly by European Aviation and the Quiet Technologies Corporation of Miami, the $10 million programme is designed to see the surviving One-Elevens through Stage 3 noise regulations and prolong their operational lives as long as possible into the twenty-first century. In co-operation with Aravco Ltd, the corporate management

A number of ex-United Airlines Boeing 737-200s and early production Airbus A300s were purchased by European Aviation and delivered to Hurn during 1998. Being of a similar late 1960s/early 1970s vintage to many of the company's One-Elevens, wholesale replacement of the established aircraft by the 737s is unlikely, especially in view of the investment already undertaken in the hushkitting programmes. Both types joined the One-Elevens on European's charter and leasing services later in the year. However, present

Euroscot Express wet-leased their One-Eleven from European. MAP

Bournemouth-Hurn and 55,000 passengers were carried on the Scottish routes in their first year. In 1998, minor changes were made to the Euroscot Express operations, with a leased ATR72 turbo-prop joining the One-Eleven on lower-capacity flights and allowing the serious consideration of possible expansion of the route structure from Hurn to new destinations, with an Amsterdam route due to be inaugurated in November 1998.

A single Boeing 727-100 had been acquired by European in 1995. However, the Boeing never entered commercial service with the airline and was eventually disposed of. Although European's One-Elevens escaped being replaced by the 727, their future with the carrier was increasingly dependent on the success of the new hushkitting programme.

organization, a Series 400 aircraft is also expected to join the original aircraft. This is with a particular view to possible conversions of the numerous executive One-Elevens of the short-bodied versions in service worldwide, for which Aravco will assume responsibility.

As well as the further hushkitting of the One-Eleven's noisy Speys, a similar programme is also being studied by European Aviation for the auxiliary power unit. Efforts are also being made to modernize and standardize the EAAC One-Eleven's flight-deck avionic systems as much as possible. With the European's One-Elevens being obtained from a variety of sources and built for different initial customers, a mixture of Smith and Rockwell-Collins systems are scattered among the different aircraft.

plans certainly see the One-Eleven as an active, hopefully soon a little quieter, member of the European Aviation family for some time to come.

Right up until the 1960s, one feature of commercial airliner operation was the rapid turnover of airframes through the airline's fleets. Technical advances were so swift that what was once at the cutting-edge was soon outdated. Investment in new fleets, in order to keep them on a par with the competition, involved the airlines making enormous economic investments at very regular intervals. The flagship type of any fleet seemed to change almost with the seasons or as often as the stewardess's hemlines. At the end of the 1950s and early 1960s, large numbers of comparatively young piston and turbo-prop-engined aircraft were, literally, put

TAROM-operated One-Elevens from the mid-1960s through to the 1990s. Brooklands Museum/Steve Edmunds

out to grass, to await the breaker's torch. Luckier aircraft went on to supply capacity to the rapidly blossoming charter markets, providing their new owners with relatively modern aircraft at a comparatively low cash outlay. The modern tourism and leisure industry practically owes its existence to the mass replacement of late model propeller-driven aircraft by jets on the world's mainline scheduled routes.

However, once the jet airliner became established, this established pattern suddenly changed beyond all recognition. With less vibration to increase engine and airframe wear and tear in daily use and generally more reliable powerplants and systems than had been experienced in the piston and turbo-prop eras, airlines had less incentive to replace the aircraft as frequently. Most of the early jets found themselves in service with their original owners for up to twenty-five years, or even longer.

Except in the rather limited field of supersonic travel, airliner speeds were pretty well as fast as they were going to get and increasing years of experience were making airframes, engines and systems as

safe as they could be. The first widebodies saw the displacement of many narrow-bodied jets to the less dense routes or new owners, but things soon settled down again. The OPEC fuel crisis sent the engine manufacturers scurrying off to make their products as fuel-efficient as possible and environmental pressures were soon making noise reduction just as important an issue. When the new engines were available, they were soon linked up to airframes, old and new, and the status quo was re-established, with progress becoming slower again as physical limits were being reached.

When the arrival of the new technologies saw another generation of early jets displaced, some were certainly fated to be broken up, but this was now more usually to provide spares for their contemporaries so that they could continue operating with new owners and operators. That many early jets still grace the airport ramps of the world, giving little indication of their actual age and managing not to look out of place alongside their younger, high tech 'replacements' is a tribute to their initial modern design.

One-Eleven versus The Rest

That the One-Eleven had less commercial success, in terms of airframes sold, than its rivals is an undeniable fact. The phrase, 'What if?' is one that haunts the history of British aircraft manufacturing. 'What if' the US authorities had not managed to stall the initial sales of the aircraft to airlines such as Bonanza, Frontier and Ozark? 'What if' BAC had offered a larger version of the One-Eleven earlier? 'What if' more powerful engines had been made available to the One-Eleven designers? 'What if' the whole programme had not been sold, lock stock and barrel, to what turned out to be a politically corrupt and commercially inept regime? After all, hindsight always enjoys 20-20 vision.

Comparatively low sales figures aside, it cannot be denied that the One-Eleven was certainly a successful design operationally. Once the cause of the stalling problems was swiftly recognized and rectified, the type soon settled down into reliable day-to-day operation. The passengers certainly liked, and continue to like, the aircraft. Crews who spend their working hours in

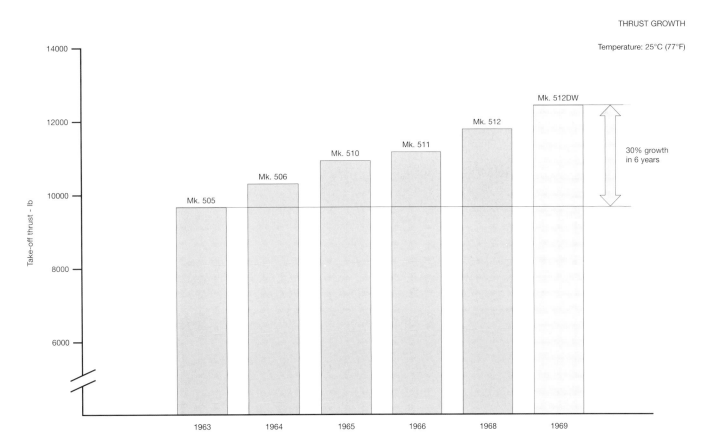

The Spey was developed to its full potential in the 1960s. Brooklands Museum

them also continue to like them, allowing for those annoying technical hiccups that an ageing aircraft design can develop at the most inconvenient moments.

Even so, many years after the first aircraft was rolled out at Hurn, the classic lines give a modern appearance. The aircraft arrived at just the right time to exploit the new niche market of European inclusive tours in the late 1960s. The passengers, more used to being bounced around in ageing Vickers Vikings or having their hearing

much noisier the cabins of even the 'new technology' versions are.

The operators, for the most part, profited from the aircraft's use. Where the airline did fail, it was unlikely to be directly due to the use of the One-Eleven. Fuel crises, economic downturns and political ructions have all played their part.

Where the One-Eleven, originally a basically sound concept and with a lot of potential, was probably most let down, was the usual bugbear of the British aircraft

production and, possibly even more important, led to customers returning to order the newer aircraft once their initial versions had been outgrown by the traffic.

It was a policy that cost money though, and therefore one not likely to prove popular with any British Government, of any political persuasion, being asked for support. In the end, it cost McDonnell-Douglas a lot more than mere money and their take-over by arch-rival Boeing in 1997 caused shock-waves throughout the industry worldwide. However, both the DC-9, in its developed MD-90 incarnation, and the Boeing 737 continue in volume production to the present day. The MD-90 has now been rechristened the Boeing 717, regarded by many purists as a sacrilege of the first order. Nonetheless, both types continue to dominate the airline order books, despite the growing threat of a spirited and increasingly successful European bid from the Airbus.

When faced with the choice of the One-Eleven or the DC-9, the latter tended to have an edge from the point of view of extra freight capacity, thanks to a larger hold. This was more important to scheduled operators as a source of extra revenue, than to the charter airlines, which tended to only need sufficient space for their passengers' baggage. The passenger cabin of the DC-9 was also slightly wider, with its 'double-bubble' fuselage, compared to the One-Eleven's more circular design, giving a fraction more elbow room.

The arrival of the Boeing 737 on the scene changed the goalposts beyond recognition. The increased revenue-earning potential of the larger aircraft, with its small aircraft handling characteristics, flexibility and economy of operation soon had it overtaking both the One-Eleven and the DC-9 in popularity with airline managements. Although it suffered several periods of slow sales, with shrewd management the Boeing managed to recover enough to measure its production in thousands, and still counting. Even with the success of the smaller Airbus products, designed to rival the 737, development and production continue apace. Ironically, the larger versions of the 737 and DC-9/MD80-90 are now capable of carrying passenger loads in the range of their once 'giant' ancestors, the pioneering Boeing 707 and DC-8.

The Fokker contribution to the short-haul jet race, the F.28, sold in respectable numbers, once their programme got off the

The One-Eleven cabin was an improvement over its predecessors. Brooklands Museum

impaired by noisy Airspeed Ambassadors or Canadair Argonauts for hours on end, thought they were entering a space ship straight from the pages of science fiction. Only two hours to Spain and not much more to Greek or North African resorts helped open the floodgates of mass tourism. On scheduled services the One-Eleven, and the other short-haul jets, proved the need for reliable, fast, comfortable air transport up to the standards of longer-reaching flights. The classic advantage of rear-engined aircraft's quiet passenger cabin continues to be a plus. Cabin crews transferring to Boeing 737s, with their wing-mounted engines, noticed how

industry, boardroom dithering and a lethal conflicting mixture of governmental indifference and interference.

So, who did win the, undeclared, second generation short-haul jet airliner race? The Sud/Aérospatiale Caravelle was developed on successfully from its first generation roots, but was effectively out of the running by the time the One-Eleven and its contemporaries appeared. The direct rival DC-9 and late-coming Boeing 737 certainly overtook the One-Eleven as far as sales are concerned. The gamble of offering several versions from the start, and upgrading and uprating them as fast as the technology would allow, definitely led to increased

The Caravelle enjoyed a long production run, but slow sales. via Author

Improved Boeing 737s outsold the competition. US Airways via Author

ground. The developed versions, the Fokker F.70 and F.100 seemed poised to take over the local airliner jet market abandoned when the One-Eleven ceased production. The sudden cessation of trading by Fokker, in 1996, left several potential customers with the loss of at least one option. The Fokker type's main European rival, the BAe 146, had been suffering from political interference with its makers. The resulting reorganization, merging, renaming, demerging and relaunching of the company and its products did little to help the BAe 146 and/or Avro Regional Jet's sales. The loss of Fokker came as the relaunched 'Avroliner' was finally being recognized as a viable and, perhaps more importantly, permanent feature of the airliner scene, its existence perhaps a little less influenced by government whim. So, perhaps, a British successor to the One-Eleven, at least in the short-haul markets, has managed to emerge from the gunsmoke after all.

G-ASJI, 1965 to 9Q-CSJ in 1998. A long journey. via Author/MAP

Epilogue

A postscript or two; The Shabair Series 200, originally delivered to BUA as G-ASJI in 1965, was badly damaged on landing at Mbugji-Mayi in July 1994. Despite originally being declared to be damaged beyond repair, the aircraft later reappeared, flying regularly, with ITAB titles. In July 1998, the aircraft, still with its Zairian/Congo registration of 9Q-CSJ, emerged from hangars at Southend wearing new 'Air Katanga' titles.

Also, October 1998 saw the departure of the last pair of Series 500s operated by Maersk Air, finally ousted from Birmingham by the new fleet of 'new technology' Boeing and Canadair Regional Jets. G-AWYR and G-AWYS, both also originally delivered to British United Airways as their first Series 500s, in 1969, were destined for more tropical climes than the British West Midlands. Following repainting at Coventry, the aircraft set off on delivery to their new owners, Executive Airline Services of, where else, Nigeria. After the delivery from the UK, via

Malta, Algeria, and a long trans-Saharan sector to Kano and Lagos, the aircraft are destined for a new lease of life on EAS's scheduled services from Lagos to Abuja, Kaduna and Port Harcourt.

Shall we just say you obviously cannot keep a good One-Eleven down, even if it is thirty-odd years old. With luck, a few visionary airline and corporate operators, and a successful Stage 3 hushkitting programme, at least some of the old girls should be around for a good few more years to come.

Customer Codes

Each individual One-Eleven customer's aircraft was identified by the model number and a unique letter coding. These remain with the aircraft throughout its life. For the sake of brevity and simplicity, throughout the text, aircraft have only been identified by their basic series number, eg, 200, 300, 400, 475 or 500. Where it can be identified, aircraft have had their customer number mentioned in photograph captions. Customer identification codes were as follows, for either actual or proposed, ie not built (*), models of the One-Eleven;

Mohawk's N1125J was a 204AF and BEA's G-AVMH was a 510ED. Brooklands Museum

200AB BAC	301AG Kuwait Airways	400AM BAC	500EN BAC
201AC BUA	303 BMA*	401AK American	501EX BUA
202AD Western Airways*	304AX British Eagle	402AP PAL	509EW Caledonian
203AE Braniff	320L-AZ Laker	403 Page*	510ED BEA
204AF Mohawk		405 Aviaco*	511EY BKS*
205AG Kuwait Airways*		406 British Eagle*	515FB Panair
206AH Bonanza Airlines*		407AW TACA	516FP Aviateca
207AJ Central African		408EF Channel	517FE Bahamas
208AL Aer Lingus		409AY LACSA	518FG Court Line
209 Hawaiian*		410AQ Victor Comptometer	520FN Sadia
211AH Helmut Horten		412EB LANICA	521FH Austral/ALA
212AR Tenneco		413FA Bavaria	523FJ BMA
214 Page*		416EK Autair	524FF Germanair
215AU Aloha		417EJ USAF*	525FT TAROM
217EA RAAF		419EP Englehard Ind.	527FK PAL
		420EL Austral/ALA	528FL Bavaria
		422EQ VASP	529FR Phoenix
		424EU TAROM	530FX BCal
		432FD Gulf Aviation	531FS LACSA
		475EZ BAC	534FY LANICA*
		476FM Faucett	537GF Cyprus
		479FU Air Pacific	538GG Faucett*
		480GB RAF*	539GL BA
		481FW Air Malawi	561RC TAROM
		485GD SOAF	562RC Rombac
		487GK TAROM	
		488GH Mouaffak al Midani	
		492GM McAlpine Aviation	
		496RD TAROM*	

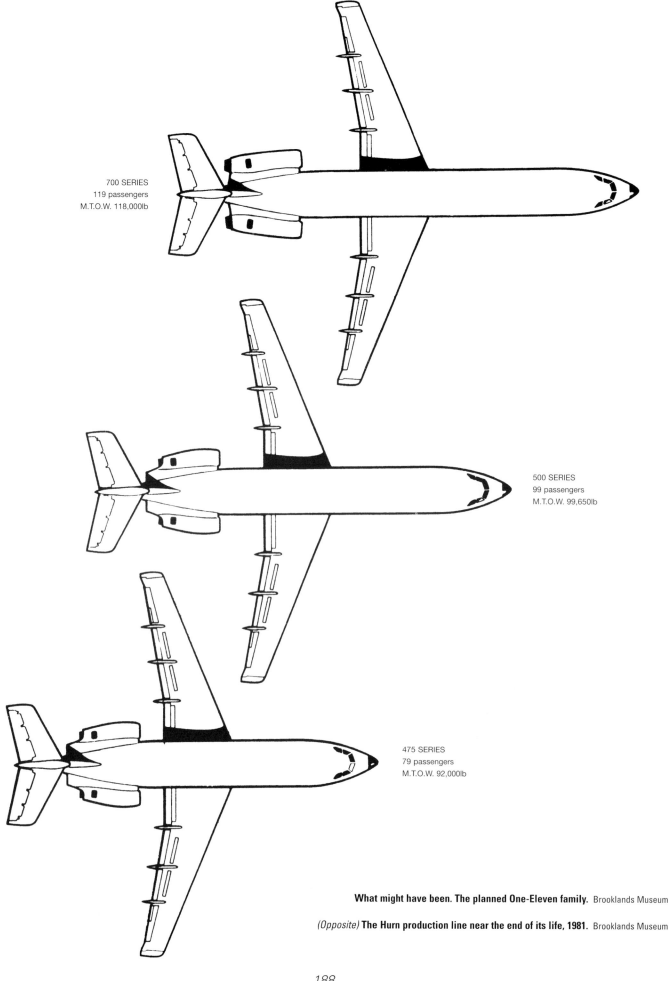

700 SERIES
119 passengers
M.T.O.W. 118,000lb

500 SERIES
99 passengers
M.T.O.W. 99,650lb

475 SERIES
79 passengers
M.T.O.W. 92,000lb

What might have been. The planned One-Eleven family. Brooklands Museum

(Opposite) **The Hurn production line near the end of its life, 1981.** Brooklands Museum

Technical Comparisons

Technical Comparisons of the One-Eleven with its Rivals and Contemporaries;

	WING SPAN	FUSELAGE LENGTH	MAX PAYLOAD		TYPICAL RANGE	
			lb	Kg	Miles	Km
One-Eleven Series 200	88ft 6in	83ft 10in	17,595	7,981	875	1,408
Series 300	88ft 6in	83ft 10in	20,025	9,083	1,430	2,301
Series 400	88ft 6in	83ft 10in	20,025	9,083	1,430	2,301
Series 475	93ft 6in	83ft 10in	21,269	9,647	1,865	3,001
Series 500	93ft 6in	97ft 4in	26,418	16,359	1,705	2,744
Caravelle 6	112ft 6in	105ft	18,395	8,344	1,430	2,301
DC-9-10	89ft 5in	104ft 4in	18,050	8,187	1,311	2,110
DC-9-30	93ft 4in	119ft 4in	29,860	13,544	1,100	1,770
Boeing 737–200	93ft	100ft	34,000	15,422	1,850	2,977

Index